Praise for

Dancing Under the Red Star

"Very few stories rise to the level of stirring the deepest parts of my soul. But this is one. Some would call this a tragedy. That is not my sentiment. This amazing chronicle represents the power of the human soul and illustrates the unique potential in each of us. Margaret Werner's suffering has become a light encouraging us all that there are greater possibilities within each one of us."

—DON MILAM, author of *The Ancient Language of Eden*

"This is the heart-stirring story of a young woman who lost everything and endured unspeakable horrors, yet lived to tell about it. Margaret's voice speaks for those who did not survive and tells how they were abandoned by American business interests. Her hope, courage, and faith will inspire you to triumph over hardship and injustice."

—MELODY GREEN, international speaker and author of *No Compromise*

"I loved this book! *Dancing Under the Red Star* grips your heart and forever changes your perspective of humanity, God, and the world. This book is destined to be a classic that will inspire generations to come to believe in one's dreams and have faith in the preserving power of God. A must-read for the progressive mind."

—DR. MYLES MUNROE, founder and president, Bahamas Faith Ministries International, author of *Rediscovering the Kingdom*

"Every once in a while a book grips one's heart because it seems more than humans are capable of imagining. This true story is remarkably compelling. Part heartrending biography, part epic documentary, *Dancing Under the Red Star* reads more like a spy novel and adventure film blended into an action movie script. Margaret Werner's life offers a valuable peek behind a part of the Iron Curtain that many Americans have never seen before. Read it, weep, and thank God you live in America today!"

—TOMMY BARNETT, pastor of Phoenix First Assembly
and author of *Hidden Power*

"A must-read! A book that engulfs the reader and forces one to live through the terror that Margaret felt."

—RON WEINBENDER, presidential envoy, Full Gospel
Business Men's Fellowship International

"Karl Tobien shares with us a powerfully griping narrative of God's grace, power, and direction. Be sure to allow yourself plenty of time, because you won't be able to put this book down. It's definitely a once-in-a-lifetime reading experience!"

—PAT WILLIAMS, senior vice president, Orlando Magic, and
author of *American Scandal*

"I am forever changed by the hope Margaret Werner displayed. Her story is truly inspiring for people in all walks of life; I am forever in love with this woman and her life!"

—DONNA JOHNSON, film producer

DANCING
UNDER THE ЯED STAR

DANCING

UNDER THE RED STAR

The Extraordinary Story of
Margaret Werner,
the Only American Woman
to Survive Stalin's Gulag

KARL TOBIEN

WATERBROOK
PRESS

DANCING UNDER THE RED STAR
PUBLISHED BY WATERBROOK PRESS
12265 Oracle Boulevard, Suite 200
Colorado Springs, Colorado 80921
A division of Random House, Inc.

Details in some anecdotes and stories have been changed to protect the identities of the persons involved.

ISBN 1-4000-7078-3

Library of Congress Cataloging-in-Publication Data
Tobien, Karl 1956-
   Dancing under the red star : the extraordinary story of Margaret Werner, the only American woman to survive Stalin's gulag / Karl Tobien.— 1st ed.
      p. cm.
   Includes bibliographical references.
   ISBN 1-4000-7078-3
   1. Werner, Margaret. 2. Americans—Soviet Union—Biography. 3. Women prisoners—Soviet Union—Biography. 4. Political prisoners—Soviet Union—Biography. 5. Political persecution—Soviet Union. I. Title.
   DK34.A45W478 2006
   947'.004130092—dc22

                              2005036179

Printed in the United States of America
2006—First Edition

10 9 8 7 6 5 4 3 2 1

☆

I solemnly dedicate this writing to three mothers—
three women I have loved,
three who sheltered the storm,
three whom I now solely credit for my very existence:
Margaret Tobien, my mother;
Elisabeth Werner, her mother;
and Tina Tobien, my wife and eternal soul mate,
without whose tremendous love and kindness,
patience, unwavering support, and abounding faith
this book would never have seen the light of day.
I thank you for things I will never adequately repay,
and I thank God for you in ways I will never adequately express.
I love you, Toonces!

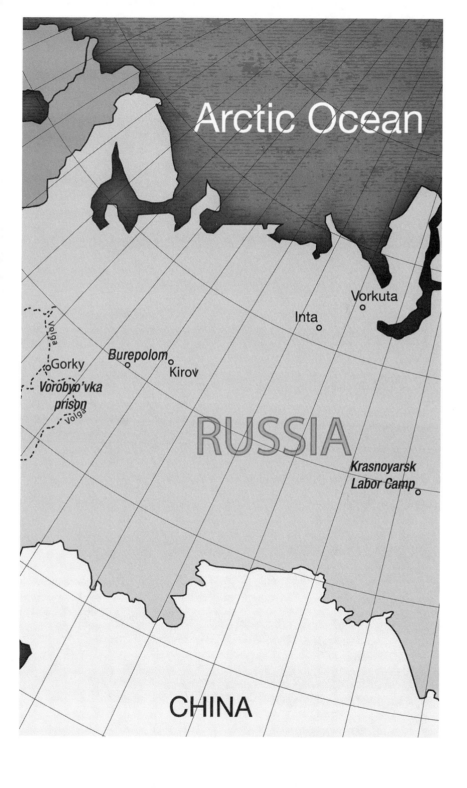

CONTENTS

THE GULAG

The Gulag (an acronym in the Russian language for the Main Directorate for Corrective Labor Camps) began in 1918 as a penal system of forced-labor camps established by the Soviet regime after the Bolshevik Revolution.

Joseph Stalin expanded the system, beginning in 1929, to accelerate industry and to exploit the Soviet Union's natural resources (like the mining of coal, copper, and gold) in its barely habitable northern regions, particularly the Siberian tundra. Over the next ten years, the Gulag spread through all twelve of the Soviet Union's time zones, sending more than 18 million innocent people through its system—4.5 million of whom were never heard from again.

By 1953, the year Joseph Stalin died, more than 30 million people had passed through the Gulag: prisoners of the Russian Civil War; former aristocrats, businessmen, and large landowners incarcerated alongside murderers, thieves, and common criminals; political opponents; intellectual "enemies of the state"; religious dissenters; women and children; and people deemed guilty of simply associating with any of the above.

They were shipped to and from the camps in cattle cars and corralled behind towering barbed-wire fences into hovels pocked by filth and disease. With few resources, clothes, and tools, they faced extreme hunger and harsh, sub-zero climates where even fog would freeze.

The brutality they endured parallels the Holocaust.

Yet few people knew about their extreme suffering until publication in 1972 of Aleksandr I. Solzhenitsyn's epic oral history of the Soviet camps in three volumes.

It would be more than thirty years later before a fully documented, comprehensive history of the Gulag would be published: the Pulitzer Prize–winning *Gulag* by Anne Applebaum.

New details of the Gulag's horrors, as in Margaret Werner's extraordinary account, are being unveiled and documented even to this day.

Dancing Under the Red Star stands as a powerful story of a woman's survival.

PROLOGUE

E very person has considered at one time or another these eternally mysterious questions: Why am I here? Where did I come from? Where am I going?

As a child in the 1960s, I had no real ambition to find out the meaning or the history of my life. I was an average American boy, growing up in an urban, middle-class neighborhood in Cincinnati, too busy being a kid to care whether or not my history was unique. Yet I knew my roots were not commonplace.

As a young adult, I began to realize there was much that my mother, Margaret Werner, hadn't told me about her life during the decades she lived in Stalinist Russia. I knew she had suffered a great deal, but to what extent, I really didn't know. I had wondered at times but not all that much. I was a hard-living, wild young guy and didn't have the time to listen—or so I thought.

Besides, the past was the past, right? Why should I seek to

understand—and reckon with—something as strange and troubling as the past, which can pull at you, haunt you, hurt you? But then I learned, as the years progressed, that coming to terms with your past can also heal you—if you let it.

My feelings changed, and eventually I found myself consumed with knowing and understanding the whats, whens, and whys of my mother's life.

One afternoon during the early 1990s, as my mother peeled potatoes at the kitchen sink, I asked her many questions. And she began to tell me more about her life, certain things I had never heard from her before.

My mother spoke of her family's difficult times in Detroit during the Depression, a long ocean voyage to Europe, and a strange, new life in Gorky, Russia. She mentioned several people she had known in the Soviet Union, including a young man named Victor Herman.

As I stood up, ready to leave her house that day, she stopped me. "Wait." My mother left the room and returned carrying a book. "Here. This is Victor's story." I read the title, *Coming Out of the Ice: An Unexpected Life.* "In many ways, Victor's life was very similar to mine...but also different." She recalled that what they had in common was loss, injustice, and suffering...but then victory.

"Why don't you read this," she said, "and then let's talk again."

So I read the book. And I was stunned. Victor detailed his life in Russia. Maybe I was naive, but I could hardly believe that such horrible atrocities and human cruelty actually existed.

Some days later, when my mother and I spoke again, she asked if I had noticed Victor's comment, toward the end, where he wrote, "[I am] the only survivor of all those men and women and children who had gone from Detroit to Gorky and ended in Siberian camps all those many years ago. I am the one, the only one, who got back, who lived through it all."

I did, in fact, remember reading that.

"Karl," my mother said, "there is much I haven't told you about my life. Maybe now would be a good time to talk, while we still have the time."

I nodded, smiled. Of course, I had heard many details of her life throughout my years, but I wasn't entirely sure what she'd say next.

"Well, Victor's comment, that's not exactly how it went; that's not exactly what happened. There's a bit more to it that no one knows…" A tender, melancholy smile warmed her face as she continued. "Victor's father, like mine—your grandfather—was employed by the Ford Motor Company in Detroit and made the Gorky trip too. Both of our families were in the original four hundred or so chosen to go. Victor's story has been well documented over the years."

She paused. I waited eagerly for each word.

"Karl, just for the record, for the sake of accuracy as well as historical correctness… actually Victor Herman was one of two who made it back; he was the *second* one to return. I was the first. I'm sure Victor based his comment on presumption alone. Perhaps he just didn't know about me—almost no one did! When I got back to America, I certainly didn't want to publicize my life or my return to the States, because I was afraid of what they might do." Tears welled up in her eyes. "I never knew for sure if my battle was truly over or if my escape would ever be truly final."

I was dumbfounded. I sat speechless, listening intently, watching her blot the tears with the corner of her apron. She continued.

"I survived the unbelievable horror of the Siberian labor camps and prisons and came back to America, through Germany, despite incredible odds. But I did finally return home, with you and Mama, stepping back onto my native American soil on November 29, 1961. I remained quiet and kept a low profile, primarily for the sake of my family, for you and Mama. Victor followed some fifteen years later—in 1976."

Now I had tears of my own to wipe away as I tried to fathom the unspeakable suffering and the remarkable courage of my mother's life.

"Maybe I also have a story to tell?" she continued, an expression of curiosity and unspoken surrender on her face. "Maybe now is a good time for that? Things have changed. I am no longer afraid, and this is your family history, Karl."

I could only nod my head in sober agreement. I had always loved and respected my mother, but that day my admiration for her took on new significance.

Dancing Under the Red Star is the historic narrative and biographical account of a true American survivor. It is the poignant, often shocking, and always disturbing remembrance of the facts—the people, the passions, and the troubled years of Margaret Werner's life. My mother knew. She lived it.

Our journey beyond the iron curtain and back is a story of defiance, hope, inspiration, and personal triumph—those often unseen elements rooted in the deeper spiritual realities of the human experience.

Today I am a writer, yes—but yesterday, first, I was a son. And now I know where I came from and why I'm here. This is not really *my story,* but then again, maybe it is.

Based on her memories, this is my mother's story.

God must be out of Russia in five years.

JOSEPH STALIN

One

THE PAIN OF SEVENTEEN

If the comforting passage of time, coupled with God's gentle mercies, kindly erases the tragic memories of my life, even so, June 29, 1938, will still remain the one particular day that I will never forget as long as I live. I was seventeen years old, and destiny was coming, whether I liked it or not.

When I awoke that morning, I think I already knew. In my heart, or maybe it was the pit of my stomach, I sensed there would be something out of the ordinary about this day. It was an eerie premonition, something you could unmistakably identify but not necessarily explain. Just in my waking up, the day already felt strangely surreal and separate from all others.

It was an unusually splendid morning. The entire sky was uncommon, painted a crystal clear blue, with no clouds, and I felt oddly euphoric. And in the midst of the otherwise chaotic circumstances surrounding this time in my life, this day seemed filled with hope and promise, and I couldn't wait to get it started.

Peering out the window of our second-floor apartment in Gorky's American Village, I felt the warm and deceptively soothing rays of the Russian summer sunshine on my skin. I was eager to get outside, to meet my best friend, Maria, for a tennis match. I was surging with adrenaline and expectancy. My body, rather than my mind, was happy, perhaps outside of itself. And happy was not an easy thing to be in Russia, in those unpredictably turbulent days, when confusing changes were occurring all around us.

Through no choice of my own, Russia had become my home, although in my mind and in my heart, and sometimes even in my words, I still referred to it as a foreign country. This was not America, where I was born, and no matter how long I stayed, I simply did not belong here. This was not my true home! Here in Gorky, we feared that anything could happen at any moment, and no one ever really knew what to expect from one minute to the next.

I speedily ate a very light breakfast, mainly to satisfy my mother's demands, then grabbed my tennis racket and hurriedly kissed Mama good-bye, nearly tripping over her feet as I jolted down the stairs to meet Maria.

The brick wall and empty lot of an abandoned storefront around the corner from our tenement was a perfect place to practice tennis by myself or when Maria could not play. We had planned to meet there that morning and then walk to the nearby tennis courts together. She hadn't arrived yet, so I decided to stretch and loosen up on my own. Maria was eighteen—a beautiful, green-eyed Ukrainian girl who lived in our village because her father and older brother also worked in the automobile factory with my father. She was an excellent athlete and competitor, a renowned young gymnast in her hometown, and now a topnotch tennis player here in the village. We enjoyed each other's company and athletic competitiveness immensely. In fact, Maria was the only other girl my age in the entire village whose love for sports and general athletic prowess rivaled mine. I'm quite sure that's why we got along so well. Here in Gorky, Soviet sports had become my life. Athletic competition and organized sports were highly esteemed in Russia and taken very seriously. This suited me! Since early childhood back in Detroit, I had been raised to be athletic and physical, and my nature was to be competitive in everything.

Maria and I were highly touted swimmers for the Gorky region, having won several district and regional competitions together, and we were now ranked high in the national statistics. She swam the fastest 100- and 200-meter backstroke I had ever seen. She was absolutely phenomenal. I swam the best freestyle and butterfly sprint events in our region. Competitive sports made a positive place for us within this unfamiliar society. Russia was a place where we felt free to excel. But today was not a competition; we planned a day of relaxation, a day to dream of the future, a day for fun. My best friend and I were going to play tennis.

Maria soon showed up, and we began to chitchat, volleying back and forth against the wall, talking and giggling about school and sports and, of course, boys. Our voices made a little rhythm with the tapping rackets, the bouncing tennis balls, and the warm summer wind rustling the leaves overhead. I remember thinking what an absolutely perfect day this was. It was about ten o'clock. My papa was at work in the factory, Mama was at home doing her chores, and I planned to spend time with her later in the afternoon.

Mama was actually my best friend, and Maria came next. I always enjoyed the time I spent relaxing and talking with my mother, because she had an unassuming sort of tranquillity about her that made you want to be around her. She had an inner peace and a silent strength that simply refused to be managed by outside circumstances. I counted on her for stability in the confusing world in which we lived. My mother's gaze drew you in with piercingly light blue, nearly violet eyes. But more than her eyes, it was her heart she was giving you. It was her spirit that always drew you in without effort. When she took my hand in hers, there were no more problems and no more worries. She made you feel that everything would be okay. And that was difficult here in Gorky, to be sure. My papa's work was hard, and for six years we had been cut off from our American home. But my mama was something else. I always wanted to be just like her.

That summer day Maria and I were planning to play tennis for an hour or so, have a good workout, and then maybe go down to the river, the Oka, for a swim. Afterward I would come back home, help Mama with the chores, and wait for Papa to come home from work. We'd have dinner together, I'd bring him his pipe, and

Mama would make him some coffee. Night after night we'd sit and listen to him worry and complain about problems that agitated him so much at the factory, the things he could not change.

My father was an idealist at heart, and change was part of his very nature. He was in constant torment about what he saw at work: the organizational, bureaucratic management "nonsense," as he liked to say, in the factory. He would shake his head as he recounted the injustices he experienced at work, but then he would reassure us that a better day was coming, just ahead, on the horizon. "Just wait. You'll see. It won't be like this forever. I promise," he'd say, and I always believed him.

Sometimes he would read to me from one of our favorite books—*Black Beauty* or *Treasure Island*—and Mama would sit and smile, taking it all in. She enjoyed her family more than anything, and she was always trying to make life better for her husband. I had grown accustomed to these evenings. They were really no more complicated than that. We had made our own kind of adjustment to living in Russia, but beneath it all, I knew something was intrinsically wrong. I just didn't know how much.

Maria and I hit the tennis ball around and laughed hysterically about a boy named Boris, a Czech, from our high school. She was telling me about something crazy he did in class the day before, when she suddenly stopped in midsentence and almost dropped her racket. She stood as if paralyzed, looking past me toward my house. She whispered, "Margo, a car just pulled up in front of your building... I thought I saw your father in it."

My first thought was, *A car? Really?* I didn't understand why Papa would be home from work at this time, and I certainly didn't understand why he would be in a car or why a car would even be here. I was puzzled; automobiles were not a common sight in our village, except when there was trouble or something out of the ordinary. But I turned and saw the ominous-looking black sedan in front of our house, and then I saw its back door opening. I knew something was wrong—terribly, terribly wrong. And I knew my papa was in the car. I stood there for a moment and stared, unable to move.

Maria looked at my face, threw her arms around my neck, and began to cry. "Oh, Margo, not your father," she said in my ear. It was as if she already knew something I did not.

Maria was eighteen, going on thirty. Her mother had died under mysterious circumstances just a year earlier, and before that, her grandparents had been murdered during the Bolshevik Revolution. She was already more familiar with pain than I, and she carried a maturity beyond her years. They say, "Whatever doesn't kill you will make you stronger." Maria, despite our relative closeness in age, was already stronger than I was.

A strange man in a dark gray uniform stepped out of the car first and then reached back inside to pull my father out by his arm. Running toward them, I screamed, "Papa! Papa!" I saw the man grab my father's wrist and force him around the car, where another man got out. He seized my father by his other wrist, and they pushed him toward the apartment. Papa didn't seem to struggle, at least not much. I thought that was odd. I remember a look of agony on his face, but he didn't appear to be struggling. What I recall seeing was an uncharacteristic resignation and the absence of the fight that usually marked my father. That was strange to me, because he was a fighter—innately a fighter! For a moment he didn't seem like my father, my flesh and blood. I wanted this to be any other man but him. But it was not. It was my papa. And I knew he hadn't done anything wrong, so I couldn't understand what was happening.

I loved and admired my father, Carl Werner, more than I could ever describe. I thought he was what a man was all about and what a man should be. I compared every boy and every man I ever met to him. But what was happening here? Why were these men being so mean to him? My papa was foreman of the tool and die department at the Gorky automobile factory and a respected man. This couldn't be happening! I figured it was all a bad mistake—a terrible mistake—and certainly they would soon have this mess figured out, and things would be normal again. Of course, things in Gorky—in Russia, for that matter—were anything but normal.

About two years earlier, in 1936, Joseph Stalin had commenced infamous purges, instigated and carried out by his bloodthirsty associate Nikolai Yezhov and shortly thereafter by Lavrenti Beria, his notorious chief of the secret police. Beria was directly responsible for millions of deaths and unspeakable cruelty throughout Russia. The period in Soviet history known as the Bolshevik Revolution was over, but the Stalinist regime was at the height of its power and operating at full throttle. Throughout the land, it operated as a heartless killing machine, without conscience. In the period leading up to and during World War II, it took hundreds of thousands, even millions, of prisoners, often with no charges and no trials. You didn't have to be guilty of anything in Stalinist Russia to find yourself imprisoned or even killed. The Stalinist regime operated on paranoia, with no rational justification.

As my father was roughly pushed toward our building, he looked back over his shoulder, almost as if in confession, to see me running toward him. Then his face was practically shoved into the door by the two men. I was sprinting toward him but felt as if I was in slow motion, as if I would never get there. The other two men looked stone cold, without showing the slightest feeling or emotion, while my papa was being helplessly led to slaughter. How on earth could this be? The three of them disappeared through the building's front door as I raced just a few paces behind them, burning with fear and anguish. I flung open the normally cumbersome wooden door as if it were weightless. My heart was pounding right through my chest, and I was panting and crying. I ran up the narrow wooden stairway to see Papa just ahead of me, on the landing.

My papa, oh my dear papa! For the rest of my days, I will never forget his face as he turned to see me standing behind him. It was only a glance, but it was a look I had never seen before and one I wished I hadn't seen. I saw in his face the end—the end of his innocently blind optimism and the end of his hopes for our life in this country that was not ours. That look bespoke hopelessness, utter despair, and death.

The look haunted me. Tears welled up in his eyes, and I knew that they were more for me than anything else. In a voice that struggled to be firm and reassuring, he said, "Don't cry, my sweet girl. Everything will be all right." But his words were empty of faith. I knew at that moment he wanted me to believe his words, but his face told me he didn't believe them himself.

We knew something of Russia's brutality even to her own people, and yet my father always thought he could make a difference in this country. We had given up everything we had known in our beloved America and blindly left it all behind us when he brought us here. It was Papa's decision. And for what? During the hungry years of the Depression back home, he had actually pictured opportunity, livelihood, and financial stability in this country. That's why he came to Russia in the first place. That's why we came with him. That's why I was here. Didn't they know what our family had given up for Papa's commitment to this country, this Russia that was now stabbing him in the back as a "reward" for his faith?

The fear in his bewildered brown eyes drained them of all life. He quickly turned away, maybe ashamed that I had seen him that way. At that moment I knew this marked the end of his dream and the beginning of our nightmare.

The two men who had arrested my father at work were from

the NKVD. Under Stalin, the Soviet secret police had acquired vast punitive powers, and in 1934 the secret police were renamed the People's Commissariat for Internal Affairs, or NKVD. No longer subject to party control or restricted by law, the NKVD became a direct instrument for Stalin to use against the party and the country during the Great Terror of the 1930s. Now they had come to search our apartment.

My mind was racing, my heart pulsing uncontrollably. I didn't know what to do for him. This could not be happening; it just could not be happening! It had to be a mistake. My papa had done nothing wrong; I had to calm down. Once inside the apartment, I fumbled toward the kitchen, where I found some fresh strawberries from our garden. I poured some milk and sugar over them, and with feverishly shaking hands I tried to take them to Papa. I think at that moment they represented my love and much more. They represented everything I wanted to do for him but could not. I was completely helpless.

I set the bowl down before him, and again our eyes met. "Oh, Papa," I said, "how is this happening? Please tell me that everything is going to be all right…please, please, please!"

He looked down at the floor, then at the bowl, then at me and over to Mama, and then back at the floor. He said nothing, but he cried silently, violently, from the innermost part of his being. My papa was shaking and looked as though he was barely breathing. He seemed afraid to look up, afraid of what we would see in his eyes. I was scared to death, mainly because I had never seen my papa so fragile and so completely helpless. As for the symbolic strawberries, he could not force down a single bite. We were all speechless and terrified.

Mama was told she could pack him a few necessary items, and she did so with tears rolling down her cheeks. Not a word escaped her lips. I think she was too shaken to utter a sound. What on earth do you pack for your husband, an innocent man who is being ripped from your home before your very eyes while you can do nothing to stop it? I felt I was going mad inside! I wanted to scream, but more than that, I wanted to kill somebody!

My mother managed to pack a small suitcase, moving stiffly, zombielike—silent and pale. I had never seen her like this either. I think she didn't really believe this could be happening to us. How could it be? Papa's dream of Russia was turning into a nightmare. Look what they were doing to the dreamer. I didn't understand what was taking place in our house. Surely I would wake up soon.

I was shaking with rage and helplessness. I ran to my tiny bedroom and grabbed a photograph of myself and scribbled on the back "To my darling papa from his loving daughter, June 29, 1938." I ran back as they were forcing him up from the table. My mother groaned, an involuntary cry from deep within, but then she quickly covered her mouth with her trembling hand and, in German—my parents' language of love—softly whispered to him as if only the two of them could hear, *"Ich immer liebe dich"* (I love you always).

My father could not reply, and I tried to push the photo into his hand as they shoved him toward the door. One of the men put his hand against my chest and sternly said, "No, now back away!" I flung myself toward my papa and screamed, "Please...Papa... please! You leave him alone!" The other officer grabbed my arms and yanked me away from my father.

I was violently thrown to the unforgiving hardwood floor by a power that I didn't see coming. Strangely, I felt no physical pain; I think my heart absorbed it all. The photo lay beside me on the floor. Mama screamed as she saw me fall hard on my back, and she threw herself down to cover me.

The men dragged my precious father out the door.

I cried, "Please, let me kiss my father good-bye, please!" But they slammed the door shut behind them.

From the hall, the men yelled at my mother and me, "Do not leave this apartment!" Neither of us moved for several moments, but then, unable to contain my dread, I cracked open the door. My father was being pushed down the stairs, and even though he resisted, it was to no avail. One of the officers looked back at me and shouted, "Didn't I tell you to keep that door closed?"

I drew back inside our apartment, but through the door and from the bottom of the stairs, I heard my father calling, "I'll be back! You'll see!" Mama was still on the floor, on her knees, sobbing so hard that her shoulders and her whole body shook. My anger died down as I saw her like that, and I knelt to hug her with an urgency and desperation I had never felt before. She was now all I had, and I was now all she had...and we held on to each other.

Clutching each other tightly, we cried until I thought there were no more tears left in me. I don't know how long we stayed on the floor, but it surely must have been hours. It felt like days, an eternity—all in one Russian summer afternoon. We held on to each other, trying to grasp that Papa was gone and wondering if we would ever see him again. But he'd said, "I'll be back! You'll see!"

The sun was no longer shining through our window as it had on that perfect morning. Now it was dark, and not just because it was evening. We sat there forever, and we spoke no words. What was there to say? At seventeen, this new agony was beyond any of my words. Finally my mother asked if I was hungry, and I said, "No," but I glanced toward the table and saw my papa's untouched bowl of strawberries. Waves of pain seared me again, and Mama tenderly stroked my hair. Calling me by her favorite name for me, she said, "Maidie, you should eat something. You must hold on and try to be strong. This is not the end, I promise you. You must have faith and not lose hope. Never give up hope. God will get us through this."

I'm not sure that I believed her. Although she sounded convincing, I knew her words were as much for herself as for me. Papa was the love of her life, and I knew that her anguish cut deep— very, very deep! I don't know if we said anything else after that, but I recall lying in my bed and hearing my mama weeping well into the night. As I drifted in and out of sleep that troubled night, I kept hearing faint, muffled, whimpering sounds from the next room. My father was forty-six years old. My mother was forty-three. I had just turned seventeen. Our life, as we knew it, was over. I tossed and turned, trying to understand how this had happened.

The NKVD was the most powerful and feared Soviet institution under Stalin, who used it to eliminate all potential opposition to his leadership until he was the unchallenged leader of both party and state. Now he was purging the party rank and file and terrorizing the entire country with widespread arrests and executions. During the ensuing Great Terror, millions of innocent Soviet citizens were sent off to labor camps or executed in prison.

In Russia, this time from 1937 until mid-1938 was called *Yezhovshchina,* or the Yezhov Affair, the most severe stage of Nikolai Yezhov's great purges, when more than ten million lives were lost in the jails and labor camps that sprang up like wild mushrooms all over the country. Situated primarily in the Far North—in Siberia or central Asia, where the climates were most severe—these camps were filled with multitudes of free laborers, peasants, and poor people, all unable to defend themselves. To the Soviet regime, human beings were only the means of production—numbers, items, things to count—expendable.

Countless fathers and mothers of my friends were suddenly and savagely arrested under trumped-up charges, taken from their homes in front of their parents and children—even during their evening meals—and never heard of or heard from again. And this country-wide brutality didn't seem to distinguish nationality or ethnic origin; it had no bias, no favorites. No one was exempt. I don't even think the Stalinist agenda was particularly anti-Semitic at its root; the Jews were certainly victims, openly targeted perhaps more than the rest of the population. But the fear was universal. Families in untold numbers, of all ethnicities, were irreparably devastated at the snap of a finger, the signing of another false arrest warrant.

Betrayal in its most primitive form was a common way of life during this period in 1930s Russia, even among family members. Mothers, fathers, brothers, and sisters routinely and sometimes falsely informed on one another to the police. I suppose it was a last-ditch effort to survive. The pervasive fear of arrest undermined everything. One day you saw your friends, you spoke with them, and the next day someone asked you where they were. It was as if they had suddenly vanished from the planet. "What happened to so-and-so?" was an all-too-regular occurrence. Your neighbor was here one day, gone the next, and no one knew anything about it.

Personal suffering at the very core of the human spirit swept the community like wildfire, and not many were able to escape. The whole world of human experience was driven by pain and fueled by fear. I thought, *If there's really a devil...I mean if he really exists, then surely this has got to be it; he must live here in Russia!*

By the time the terror subsided in 1939, Stalin had managed to bring both the party and the public into complete submission to his rule. Soviet society was so atomized and the people so fearful of reprisals that mass arrests were no longer necessary, but that had not happened yet—not today, not on June 29, 1938, not in time to save my father.

In the summer of 1938, this was my life: my father ripped away from me, my mother's husband gone, a good man taken from his family. Just like that, it was all over. Dreams shattered and hopes forsaken in one strangely beautiful but wicked Gorky summer day. Now Mama and I were left in this country that was not our own…with no way out. We never wanted to come here in the first place, and now our future was nothing but a matter of Mama's blind faith.

Thus began the darkest time in our lives. We suddenly had to find a way to go on without Papa, who until this black day had provided us with a better-than-average way of life, at least by Gorky's simple standards. We had no support or financial means, no savings and no protection. Though I felt a full-blown anger taking control of my heart, I was also hit by a physical sense of hopelessness and despair. They walked in uninvited, as if they were people or something I could actually touch. And right behind them came a powerful new fear.

My sleep that night was anything but peaceful; it came in agonizing increments when my mind was too tired to think. I slept only by default, for sporadic and lurid spurts a few minutes at a time, and I would fearfully awaken between my terrifying dreams to find that my new reality was much worse than any nightmare.

I kept hearing my mama's words: "Have faith; be strong; do not lose hope." I didn't feel much comfort from them now. A stronger force outside of me—fear—was controlling my heart and my thoughts. I thought hard about Mama's faith in God. God would get us through this? I questioned. How could that be? How could anything or anybody wipe away the horror? How could I be sure God even existed? Was God stronger than fear? That was a good question, because I had no idea what to believe in, but I knew that fear was real, as I now felt fear like a three-alarm fire burning out of control. And I could not help but think, *Where is God in all of this?* as my mind replayed Papa's words, "I'll be back. You'll see," over and over again.

Two

PAPA DECIDED

I t was Papa's decision to move our little family from Detroit to Gorky. Mama and I had never wanted to come, and now we were in a very precarious position without him.

I was their only child, born on May 28, 1921, just outside the city limits of Detroit. My parents and two other couples were desperately trying to eke out a living on a small and unproductive beet farm, waiting for the Depression to end. As it turned out, they would wait for quite some time. During my parents' early years near Detroit, they did all they could to make ends meet, raising chickens and various vegetables for their own consumption, along with whatever else they could rummage or produce. The land was unfruitful, but sometimes the men hunted skunk, for the pelts, which they were able to sell for a few dollars when there was an interested buyer. And when there were no skunks, their cupboard was bare. Their lives were simple and austere, with no excess in any area, except perhaps their love for one another.

My mother, Elisabeth Rausch-Werner, was of German stock, originally from the Black Forest region in southern Germany. In the 1700s her people, seeking religious freedom and better educational opportunities for their children, had immigrated to Austria, to a region that was later annexed by Hungary. They were called *Donauschwaben,* essentially German-speaking Hungarians, speaking a unique form of the German language. Elisabeth's father owned the village inn and was also the village cabinetmaker. Her mother was in poor health, and as the eldest of five children, my mother bore the brunt of the household chores and child-rearing responsibilities. Consequently, she received only four years of formal education and schooling in Austria.

In 1912, when my mother was seventeen years old, she immigrated to America with her aunt. They arrived in Cincinnati, Ohio, where my mother held numerous jobs: first as a barmaid, then as a housekeeper in several affluent homes, including that of Walton Bachrach, who would later become mayor of Cincinnati. A few years later Mother moved to Detroit, where she again found employment as a housekeeper. Her talent in the kitchen as a wonderful cook and baker kept her steadily employed. She had a thin, wiry frame but a surprising degree of physical strength for her meager size. Mama's eyes were the purest, most stunning light blue I have ever seen, at times a solid violet color. She soon joined an amateur

German drama club called the Thalia, since acting was a true passion as well as an undeniable talent. It was here that she met Carl Werner, the club's stage manager. In August 1920 they were wed.

Carl Werner, my father, was an Austrian Jew from the city of Linz. The family was fairly affluent, and he had two brothers—Richard and Friedrich—and one sister, Eva. Their father died when Carl was only four years old, so Carl was reared by his mother and the servants. His brothers and sister all finished high school and went on to the university. My father, however, had other ideas about his future. He opted to work with his hands, and so he attended a technical school to learn the skill of tool and die making. He soon mastered the trade, and upon completion of this technical education, he immigrated to the United States, where he immediately found work in the automotive industry.

In 1917, during World War I, he refused to be drafted, choosing prison instead. He was a true patriot, but he had to draw the line—*his line*. It was that invisible line in the sand that he could not cross without compromising his sense of decency, integrity, and morality. Although he was not a financial success, he loved his American home and his life. However, my father did not believe in war. Losing his life would mean losing his family, and that would be an unacceptable sacrifice to Carl Werner. That's just who he was. He consequently paid the price, but not for a lack of loyalty to America. Papa thought if a man had no personal integrity, he had absolutely nothing! He was conscientious and he was an idealist, so maybe he was a conscientious idealist rather than a war objector.

During his approximately three-year imprisonment, he spent one year in solitary confinement. Later he described that experience to me as the most significant and deeply revealing time in his life. This serious internal reflection led to a time of personal awakening, when his determination grew in conjunction with his outrage. He said he got to know his inner self, which confirmed his cherished ideals and destroyed his false beliefs. My father kept most personal things tightly concealed. I don't know what he would have said about some of the later circumstances of his life, the twists of fate and other unforeseen detours, including his arrest, but I suspect his U.S. prison confinement was a walk in the park in comparison to his imprisonment by the NKVD.

Regardless, the American jail did not soften his resolve. Perhaps his opinionated and outspoken nature contributed to some extent to his fate. Who knows? He believed strongly in a pure socialist reform system, and based upon what I have learned, I'd have to say he was right, in a purely idealistic and untainted sense, if this were a perfect world. But as we later came to know, evil exists in this world, in humans as well as in systems; it is inherent in the very core of fallen humankind. Carl Werner said that no political system is ever flawless, but his goal was to "always seek out that which seems to make sense." He had radical tendencies—those that made sense to him. He was a unionist and an active member of the Proletarian Party during those days. My father wholeheartedly believed in people, and he always took the side of the underdog and the oppressed, because he felt someone had to stand up for them.

He approached his job and his career responsibilities with the Ford Motor Company in exactly the same fashion.

Many meetings were held in our small Detroit home at that time, with friends and neighbors and even total strangers. I would guess all of them had to do with the pivotal role he played in the Proletarian agenda in Detroit as well as the controversial employee and labor issues at the automobile plant.

I was an ordinary, fun-loving, ten-year-old American schoolgirl in 1931 when my carefree existence took an abrupt turn for the worse. It was in the middle of the Depression, and everyone around us felt its grave effects. Factories and businesses were closing almost daily; friends of my parents were losing their jobs; whole families had no income; people had a strangely distant and lifeless look about them. Sometimes I even heard Mama and Papa speak of someone committing suicide. Poverty, sadness, and emotional upheaval devastated nearly every family we knew, and we were no exception. The atmosphere seemed thick with this unpredictable lingering gloom that was heavy like a fog and unspoken yet visible in the faces we met. Yes, *depression* was fitting, not only for the state of the economy and social life, but also for the emotional state of my mother and father and most people we knew. *Depression* was the right word.

My earliest childhood recollections take me back to the time when I was an adventurous three-year-old—in 1924, when my parents and I lived in a second-floor apartment in Detroit. I distinctly remember waiting until it was my mandatory nap time, then sneaking down the back steps of our apartment. I was headed to the house across the street so I could play with Adam, the little boy who lived there. That particular day the attraction was his shiny red pedal car. I didn't see a dairy delivery wagon approaching at the same time I decided to dart into the street. I had no time to react.

I woke up in an all-white bed in an all-white room with a very bright light hanging from the ceiling. My mother and father were pale and frightened by my bedside. I particularly remember the look on my father's face as he worriedly hovered over me. I was in a hospital, with bandages on my face, but I was lucky to have escaped with only minor nicks and scratches. After that little escapade, my father concocted a brilliant idea; he decided to tie me to the back porch on a dog leash, long enough for playing, but short enough to prevent me from crawling under the fence to join my friends in the next yard. I remember his face as he looked at me, on that leash and in that predicament. He was proud of himself, and I could see that he thought he was quite ingenious. That memory makes me smile, and it makes me miss my papa all the more.

Later our family moved into a newly built red brick house at 14452 Rochedale Avenue, a dead-end street. My "boyfriend," Tommy Natress, lived down the block. At the end of our street was a great playground for all the kids—a vacant field bordered at the rear by a large wooded area with many trees and narrow winding paths disappearing into the brush. It was the perfect place for a child's imagination, and we often pretended we were far, far away.

This mysterious wooded paradise was also just the place for all the exciting and scary stories kids love to tell. We would try to out-frighten one another with wide eyes and softly whispered details about the infamous bogeyman and other such fictitious elements of our overactive imaginations. But those chills were nothing compared to the story of my own life. In fact, the scariest story I know is the one I'm beginning to tell you now.

This innocent time in Detroit was as far from Gorky as the east is from the west. I remember this as the most joyous time of my life: a time of peace, happiness, and comfort, with no responsibilities. And for children, that's exactly how it was meant to be. Despite the economy, there was definitely no pain on my horizon, at least none that I could see.

Once a week my parents played pinochle with their friends. On one such night, I became restless and bored from being confined to my bedroom upstairs, so I quietly crept out of bed and went exploring in my parents' bedroom. The top of my mother's dresser was covered with many intriguing items, but what I coveted most was her perfume! In reaching for the prize, I accidentally tipped it over, spilling the entire bottle onto my nightgown. Sheepishly I padded silently down the stairs and reluctantly made my appearance, standing under the archway that divided the living room and dining room. Suddenly the living-room audience was silenced. And I can still hear that silence as I replay the scene in my mind.

My father's reaction to my escapade was, as always, animated and playful. He got up, turned slowly and deliberately—for dramatic impact—and walked robotically toward me in slow motion, wanting me to fear the consequences of my actions, saying, "What has my sweet little girl gotten into now?" He quickly packed me under his arm, took me up the stairs, and put me in the bathtub, where he turned the shower on me. I could tell that his sour exterior was feigned strictly for my benefit, in his customarily theatrical way. Underneath, he was dying to burst out laughing, but he couldn't let me know. "What should I do with you?" he said sternly. "I'll just have to think about it, I guess."

Why do I so distinctly remember that look of loving humor on my father's face that day? Does it hold a treasure meant only for me, yet undiscovered, whose secret location I alone could find? Was it something I had to hold on to, because such future memories of him would be few? I didn't know. He was in the prime of his life then, with bright brown eyes, filled with joy, adventure, and vibrancy. He was a powerful man for his moderate size: a strong, chiseled European chin, rough hands, wide forearms, and a strength that rejoiced in physical labor. He wanted nothing but the best for his family. I knew that.

I never doubted my parents' love. One day I became deathly ill. I had been exposed to scarlet fever as a result of being bathed in the same tub with my infected cousin, Robert. He and his parents had stopped in Detroit to see us on their way to Canada. I overheard the doctor telling my parents that I had, in fact, contracted the disease and we had two choices: I could either remain at home under quarantine (my father would have to live elsewhere for twenty-eight days), or I could spend those same twenty-eight days in a hospital. Of course I wanted to stay home, but I was immediately taken to the hospital. I remember that my favorite nightgown and robe were quickly taken away from me; I was given a separate bath on each of three floors, dressed in new hospital attire, and then rushed to a fourth-floor isolation ward.

This ward contained nine or ten beds, and mine was next to a window, where the view stretched off into the distance, far away from the hospital grounds. This was the first time in my life that I had to share a room with anyone. It was also the first time I recall being separated from my mother and father, which was much worse. I remember my discomfort in this room and my dismay at having to live twenty-eight days without my parents. It was dark for me there, almost otherworldly, and I was frightened to death.

Fortunately, I had only a mild case of the disease, and though I missed my parents, I ended up having a relatively good time in the hospital. I celebrated my sixth birthday; my parents brought me cake and ice cream, which was shared by all of my new friends in the isolation ward. The worst part was that I couldn't touch or hug or kiss my parents, nor could I hear their voices. They could only see me through the glass. I couldn't hear my mama call me "Maidie" or hear Papa call me his "sweet girl" and say, "Don't worry, baby. Everything will be all right." I felt all alone, and that was an unfamiliar feeling.

Such experiences were exceptional in my otherwise happy

childhood. Every day I merrily skipped to and from my elementary school, which was about three blocks away. I had many friends, got straight A's, and was especially popular with the young boys, because I could run and play and compete with them on their level in their sports and games. Whenever they chose sides for kickball, the most popular game at school, my favorite boys—Tommy Natress and Billy Graves—always chose me first or second, even before the boys. I had a normal height and build for my age, I suppose, perhaps on the slender side, but I had a physically aggressive mind-set and a highly competitive spirit. I didn't mind getting hurt, if necessary, and I think that's what the boys liked about me.

Dodge ball was another favorite. Not many girls my age took an interest in sports or seemed able to compete with the boys. But I absolutely loved it; I lived for it! Even at ten, I was a competitive athlete, though I could not imagine how this drive would shape me in the years ahead. During that time, I don't remember having a worry in the world. My life was indeed good, it was pure fun, and it was all for the taking!

I admired my favorite schoolteacher, Miss Lovejoy, who made school a genuine pleasure. She had pretty blond hair, beautiful clothes and jewelry, and an effervescent personality. My favorite subjects were social studies and history, though I really enjoyed them all. I just enjoyed learning—at least at school, but maybe not as much at home. Although I was an excellent student, my father demanded absolute perfection at all times, and he ensured that I never settled for anything less than that from myself.

DANCING UNDER THE RED STAR

He was a strict disciplinarian when it came to school, my grades, and my studies. "How do you expect to ever get anywhere if you don't give it the best that you have right now?" was a typical response. "If you work hard now, you will excel, and later in your life you will be happy that you did!" He did not believe in learning from mistakes. Sometimes he was a bit hard to bear, but I knew that he was motivated by love.

He said that failure was impossible if I was not careless and if I applied 100 percent of my effort toward my work. I was not permitted to use an eraser while doing my homework at home. He reasoned that if an eraser had to be used, then the whole assignment could just as easily be redone, avoiding all mistakes the second time. "That will teach you to think more carefully next time...before you begin to write, won't it?" he would ask in calculating fashion. Then he would wait for my response. No one other than Mama could ever disagree with my father, so my response was always, "Yes, Papa."

I brought erasers home from school on several occasions, used them very carefully and only when I had to, and then hid them from Papa. But I never hid them well enough. Though he never said a word, when I went to look for them again, they were nowhere to be found. I always knew exactly where I had put them, but they would mysteriously disappear, as if they never should have been there in the first place. It wasn't easy to put anything over on Papa, and consequently I didn't spend a lot of time trying. I also didn't use erasers much. Instead, I usually redid my work in its entirety until I got smart and learned to do it right the first time.

Consequently, I always did my best to complete my homework during the school day, while I could use an eraser if necessary. Some might consider such measures extreme, but I knew Papa's objectives and the spirit behind them. "Life is too short for mistakes," he would say. "This way you will learn."

I attended a nearby summer camp when I was about seven or eight years old. Among the many activities I enjoyed at this camp, swimming and diving in the immense man-made lake were by far my favorites. Papa taught me how to swim when I was six, an experience I'll never forget. He nearly drowned me in the process! He held me tightly to his chest while he walked out into the lake until the water was at his neck and well over my head. Then, with a warm but mischievous smile, he pushed me out into the deep unknown. I desperately tried to clutch him, and he began to back away slowly while he encouraged, "You can do it… You can do it… Now swim!"

My arms flailed helplessly as fear enveloped me. I must have swallowed half the lake in the process. I was scared, crying and choking, struggling for breath and kicking my arms and legs wildly to survive. Somehow I made it back to shore, to see my father doubled over in laughter. "I hate you, Papa," I sobbed, which made him laugh all the more. Naturally I didn't mean it, and it was that single day, then and there, that I learned how to swim. A few minutes later I went back out on my own, and the process seemed to automatically make sense. I could swim! And from that moment on, regardless of the fearful initiation, I lived to swim. That's all I wanted to do.

A natural passion for athletic competition—whatever the sport—was birthed in me at that time and grew stronger in the years to come. My parents always seemed to know how to bring out the best in me. Mama's style was a bit different, but both of my parents wanted me to be athletically equipped. For me, the great thrill was the event—the sport itself, the opportunity to compete against others, to match my skill with theirs, and theirs with mine. Competitive excellence, I believe, comes largely from within—unseen, intangible—and has little to do with one's physical ability. But I had both, an above-average degree of physical ability coupled with a competitive desire, the heart to win.

Every Saturday morning Mama took me downtown for my weekly acrobatic training and gymnastics classes. I couldn't wait for those Saturday mornings to arrive! I always tried very hard, earnestly desiring to be not only the best I could be but also the best in the class or on the block or in school or anywhere else. That was my goal. Mama always told people I had no fear, and that made me feel good. And I was a natural acrobat. I especially loved the more difficult routines and was often used as the class example by my instructor, Mrs. White. "Now, class, watch how Margaret does it," Mrs. White would say as I demonstrated tumbling routines. I even thought about becoming a ballerina, a ballerina with great acrobatic skills. Perhaps I could even run off and become an accomplished acrobat in a touring circus.

The beauty of my childhood was that, with an active imagination, I could be anything or anybody I ever wanted to be. My mind knew no limitations. Everything was possible. Papa often said, "Nothing is impossible if you only believe! You can do anything you want to do." One only needed enough time to think, to dream, and I certainly had that, even more than my fair share. I would lie on my back and daydream in the warm summer grass of a nearby playground.

It's amazing the things a kid can ponder while lying in the grass. Maybe that's what grass is for. Given enough time, could I have solved the problem of world peace or prevented my father from being taken away? But my fantasies focused for hours upon end on this theme of success and variations of it: how I would be the object of much public admiration, performing death-defying and amazing feats for all to see and enjoy. Perhaps I would be a world-class ballerina, just like the Russians. Before I knew anything about Russia or that I would one day live there, I imagined myself dancing there. It was always easy to be a ballerina in the grass.

My mother could not have known how my acrobatic skill and training would benefit me in the days to come, but perhaps her deepest desire for my strength made it a kind of preliminary equipping for me, for what would be an entirely unpredictable future with many setbacks. Did she have a prophetic sense of preparing me for the road ahead, the road so remote from my growing up in Detroit?

Dear Lord, why couldn't we have just stayed in Detroit? Why didn't Papa listen to us years ago?

My father, Carl Werner, was a highly skilled and valued laborer with the Ford Motor Company and was quickly promoted into their supervisory ranks within the Detroit plant. There he heard speculation, then rumor, then actual discussions, and finally, concrete plans about Ford signing a one-year contract with a Russian automobile factory. Autostroy, in Gorky, was seeking to establish a modern, streamlined automotive production facility and needed specialists in various fields, including my father's specialty: tool and die making. In essence, it was almost a Ford factory; Henry Ford wanted it to be a model and replica of his highly regarded Detroit plant.

During the 1920s and early 1930s, tensions between the Soviet Union and the West had eased somewhat, particularly in economic cooperation. Russia's new challenge was to organize its vast natural and human resources efficiently. For a variety of reasons—compassion for the sufferings of the Soviet peoples, sympathy for the great "socialist experiment," but primarily for the pursuit of profit—American businessmen and diplomats began signing business contracts with various Russian officials.

Henry Ford sold tractors to the Soviet Union. But he was not alone. Other leading American capitalists and financiers were also involved in Russian trade and business financing, including Averell Harriman and Armand Hammer. These commercial ties between the Soviet Union and the United States established the basis for further cooperation, dialogue, and diplomatic relations between the two countries. This era of cooperation was never solidly established, however, and it diminished as Joseph Stalin attempted to eradicate all vestiges of capitalism and to make the Soviet Union economically self-sufficient. Any Americans who were left in Russia were considered expendable.

As a Ford employee, my father faced a difficult and fateful decision. In Detroit, Ford was going through major cutbacks and sizable employee layoffs, and no one knew for sure whose head would roll next. He could stay in Detroit, under difficult conditions, and simply make the best of bad times. Or he could opt for the opportunity of a temporary, one-year move (as it was presented to us) to Gorky. That would be an economic advance for us and a fresh beginning. Staying offered uncertainty at best, while going offered immediate financial relief and perhaps some future stability for his family. Perhaps a move even suggested to him the realization of a dream, the fulfillment of a vision.

I have no doubt that he always had his family's best interest in mind. I thought my father always knew what was best. I'm certain he spoke at length with my mother about this potential move, such a drastic change in our lives, carefully weighing the factors and considering all the possibilities. But in our family, he was a strong man, a decisive man, a man's man, and would ultimately decide for us all.

Some of them were dreamers

And some of them were fools

Who were making plans and thinking of the future

With the energy of the innocent

They were gathering the tools

They would need to make their journey….

Carl Werner was a good man to the very heart and fiber of his soul, much loved by Mama and me. But he was making a decision that would impact not only his own life but ours for the remainder of our days.

I loved America, and I loved my young life. I didn't understand my father's plight or what he really had in mind, but I wondered if we didn't have other choices. Had Papa thought this thing through carefully? It seemed a ridiculous notion. In hindsight, it seems to me that he rushed to judgment, that he made a rash decision not entirely supported by his wife. Even as a child, I knew it, and I wholeheartedly agreed with her that we should not go to Russia. Why was Papa so stubborn? Why didn't he give credence to the intuitive things Mama and I felt? He was the only one who really wanted to go to Russia. Mother and I simply had no choice in the matter.

I could not reconcile myself to the thought of leaving. I absolutely did not want to go. Not for any reason, not under any circumstances. My heart sank to new lows as I tried to consider what would become of my life in this strange new place I hadn't even seen yet. And just what on earth were we doing, anyway? What was my father thinking? We already lived in America, capital of the free world. What else could a person ever want?

Although reluctant to accept the inevitable—this destined journey east—and trying my best to avoid it, I still had to face reality. With the help of many friends, my father collected, greased, and packed more than a ton of instruments, tools, and parts to take with us. I sat speechless as I watched friends carry off more and more of our furniture and personal things prior to our departure. Our couch, upon which Papa had spent hundreds of hours reading to me; the crib that I had slept in, with the pink and yellow ruffled lace trim Mama had made just for me; my toys and games—all were suddenly no more. These were more than just things to me. They were part of me, my life, and they were gone.

Reality was quickly sinking in, and there was no escaping it. We were leaving, and that was that. Papa couldn't be persuaded otherwise. It was useless; his mind had long since been made up. We were leaving it all behind and venturing out into the wild unknown, my papa, Mama, and me.

Three

DESPERATE EYES

Bound for Russia, our family of three left the United States in April 1932. We embarked on the ocean liner *Hamburg* from the port of New York, along with approximately four hundred other Americans—Ford employees and their families.

I had dreamed of taking a vacation on a huge ocean liner with my family, but this wasn't the trip I had imagined. I pictured traveling to the Caribbean or the Bahamas, not Russia. I was now compelled to go on this voyage to the other side of creation—not on vacation, but, according to my father, "to make a better life."

My mother was unusually reserved as we made our final preparations on the morning of our departure. She was unhappy about our move, but she was Papa's wife, obligated to support him. My father's disposition was the opposite; his spirits were noticeably high. I could see on his face that he had a vision and was energized by his plans and goals. He looked youthful, almost euphoric.

The three of us barely spoke that entire morning, preoccupied with our own opinions and feelings: my father anticipating a fantasyland, Mama adrift in uncertainty, and I already missing my friends, our home, and our neighborhood. We traveled together, but on three uniquely separate journeys.

Papa insisted that we take only "absolutely necessary" personal belongings. There was no room for things of mere sentimental value. We took only the bare bones of what we owned, not much more than we would have packed for a two-week vacation.

"Margaret, we barely have enough room to take you along," he chuckled.

"That's okay, Papa. I'll just stay here, then. Maybe I'll join the circus and come see you in Russia," I half-jokingly replied.

With a wide smile, he tenderly patted my cheek and promised, "We'll be just fine."

I had my small diary, a personal journal I'd kept for about two years, and not much more of value other than my clothes. Oh, and I carried Maggie, one of my dolls. I spoke with Maggie a lot, especially this morning. She always seemed to understand me when no one else did.

I pleaded with her, "Oh, Maggie, where on earth are we going, and what will we do? What will become of us when we get there?"

I wanted her to say, "Don't worry, Margaret. We are going to a new place—to Russia—where they have the best and most beautiful dancers in the whole world, just like we used to talk about. And I will be with you. We will have a grand time!" But today Maggie didn't answer me.

Despite my objections, we boarded the *Hamburg* and headed to Russia, the great unknown. The Atlantic Ocean felt more like the sea of uncertainty to me, because I had no idea where we were going or what we would do when we got there. I wondered if Papa really knew either, although he acted as though he did. Only God knew what was truly in store, I supposed, but *he* wasn't telling.

An announcement blared from the ship's intercom shortly after we departed: "There's a good chance we'll encounter heavy winds and rough seas during our voyage. March is the season for Atlantic storms." Though we didn't encounter dangerous weather, the ship rolled and pitched a lot.

Each of my parents reacted differently to our time at sea. Papa wasn't a sailor. He was miserably nauseated for the first half of our trip. When he wasn't throwing up in our cabin, he was playing cards down below with the deckhands and some men he knew from the Ford factory. This nautical adventure may have sickened him physically, but he remained enthusiastic about his decision.

Mama was a better sailor, showing no signs of seasickness, but I could tell that her mind was somewhere else. She kept to herself, immersed in thought, or was it prayer? It was clear she wasn't happy about the journey. I sided with my mama; I hated leaving America.

I was a pretty good sailor, just mildly seasick for the first couple of days. I spent some time on the upper deck, playing jacks and hopscotch with a boy about my age—Joey, from Long Island, who was headed for Germany with his parents. He was only going for a month-long vacation and then would return to the United States. I would live in Russia for at least a year—that's what "they" said— and hopefully no longer.

The food on board was the best thing about the trip. After our stomachs adjusted to the state of buoyancy, Papa and I made the dining room our headquarters. We couldn't get enough to eat. After the scarcities of the Depression, we were thrilled to dine on home-fried potatoes and hamburgers or steak and eggs—as much as we could pack away! Life was a joy again, however briefly. I stuffed myself with food, perhaps to fill the emptiness I felt about leaving home.

In our stuffy cabin, I pestered Mama with incessant questions: "What will we do in Russia, Mama? What language will we speak there? Will we have to speak Russian? What will my school be like? Mama, do you think I'll be able to find any friends over there? And what about my sports? Will I still be able to swim and do gymnastics?"

She didn't exactly answer my questions. Mama always said more to me with silence than others did with many words. As we sat talking on the bed, she gently held the sides of my face with her warm hands. Looking tenderly into my eyes, she said, "Maidie, I don't know what tomorrow will bring, but one thing I promise you: we will be okay. God has a plan for us!" Her smile comforted me, and she spoke with such conviction that I believed her.

"And, Mama, will Papa finally be happy there?" I asked. She didn't answer. She sat quietly beside me, staring at the wall, holding me tight as I drifted off to sleep.

Each day at sea started with a bugle call on the main deck, a melody that made me feel nauseated. Those notes woke me every morning with a huge knot of anxiety twisting inside my stomach. I was fully awake but immersed in a nagging dream, overwhelmed with uncertainty. What were we getting into? When we eventually docked in Hamburg, Germany, I hated to leave the ship. Perhaps intuition told me that life would never be this good again.

I noticed that the German children acted just like the kids I knew in America. They all seemed confident, quick witted, and high spirited. I was naively amazed at the ease with which the little children spoke German, which was my first language as well. I had learned the language at home because German was my parents' language of choice. It wasn't until I entered kindergarten in Detroit that I learned to speak English well. So I didn't feel like a foreigner in Germany and would have been happy if Papa had decided to stop our journey right there. But that was not to be.

After staying a day and night, we left Hamburg by train and first passed through Poland before entering Russia and arriving in Moscow on a brutally cold winter day in April. Dirty snow, piled at least waist-high, lined the rutted streets. Horse-drawn sleighs and decrepit streetcars were the only visible means of public transportation.

"Why are there so few cars in a big city like Moscow?" I asked Papa.

"Most of the people don't need cars, and not everyone can afford a car, sweetheart," he explained. "If they must go somewhere, they take the streetcar. Automobiles are a luxury, not a necessity. And that's why we're here. We're going to make more cars for them and make them more affordable."

Something about that answer bothered me. I had trouble making sense of it. I thought that he was trying to avoid my question, that he didn't want to give me a direct and honest answer. I said nothing else but thought, *Papa, didn't we come here to improve our lives?*

Poverty and hopelessness were apparent everywhere we looked. Almost every building in Moscow seemed in urgent need of reconstruction or demolition. The people were poorly dressed, wearing long sheepskin coats or homemade, padded cotton jackets. As they sat or stood on the ice-covered streets, their feet and legs were protected only by woven straw shoes and burlap leggings. They looked as if they were starving. Why were they all out on the streets? Where did these people live? It was like a hard slap in the face as I immediately realized that our life back in Detroit had been luxurious compared to this.

The children, many my age and younger, looked pitiful. Their clothing was too thin and ragged for this climate. As they stared at us, their eyes looked like empty canyons yearning to be filled. A terrible sadness enveloped me, and I began to cry. With their sad eyes, the children cried out for help. I saw no hope in their gray faces. I wanted to help them, but I had no idea how.

The elderly Russians seemed to carry an innate sense of resignation, as if they were waiting to die. Their faces, drawn tight by the severe cold, showed no emotion yet spoke volumes of their miserable life. We had barely arrived in this land, and in spite of my own pain, my heart broke for these innocent people.

"Papa, can we do something for them?" I asked.

He did not reply.

Over time I began to understand what had produced the ghastly conditions we saw in Moscow. In November 1927 Joseph Stalin had launched his "revolution from above" by setting two extraordinary goals for Soviet domestic policy: rapid industrialization and the collectivization of agriculture. He aimed to erase all traces of the capitalism that had entered under the former "New Economic Policy." He planned to transform the Soviet Union as quickly as possible into an industrialized socialist state without regard for cost.

Stalin's first Five-Year Plan, adopted by the party in 1928, put these goals into action. With an emphasis on heavy industry and productive agriculture, individual farms were absorbed into a system of large collective farms, or kolkhozes. The Communist regime believed that collectivization would build up large grain reserves to feed the growing urban labor force and pay for industrialization. Many peasants would become available for general labor and factory work in the cities, and the Stalinist regime would extend its political dominance over rural areas.

Stalin first targeted the wealthier peasants, or kulaks. Their property was seized, and about one million kulak households (approximately five million people) were deported to remote Siberian regions and never heard from again. All other peasants were forced into collective farms, where they worked the fields with the collective's equipment and were paid with grain and other basic agricultural products. The remainder of the harvest became the property of the state.

Although the first Five-Year Plan called for the collectivization of 20 percent of peasant households, by 1940 virtually all peasant households had been collectivized. The ownership of private property was almost eliminated.

Many peasants fiercely resisted collectivization, resulting in a disastrous disruption of agricultural productivity. Nevertheless, in 1932 Stalin raised Ukraine's grain procurement quotas by 44 percent. This meant there would not be enough grain to feed the peasants, since Soviet law required that no grain from a collective farm could be given to the members of the farm until the government's quota had been met. Even indispensable seed grain was confiscated from peasant households. Stalin's decision, and the methods used to implement it, condemned millions of peasants to death by starvation.

With the aid of regular troops and secret police units, party officials waged a merciless war of attrition against peasants who refused to give up their grain. Any man, woman, or child caught taking even a handful of grain from a collective farm could be executed or deported. Those who did not appear to be starving were often suspected of hoarding grain and consequently interrogated. Forced collectivization helped achieve Stalin's goal of rapid national industrialization, but the human cost was incalculable.

When my family arrived in Russia, the entire Soviet Union was suffering a massive famine. In the Ukraine alone, the death toll from the 1932–33 famine exceeded six million. According to a Soviet author, "Before they died, people often lost their senses and ceased to be human beings." Yet one of Stalin's lieutenants in the Ukraine stated in 1933 that the famine was "a great success" because it showed the peasants "who is the real master here. Sure, it cost millions of lives, but the collective farm system is here to stay."*

---

* "Revelations from the Russian Archives," Library of Congress, http://www.loc.gov/exhibits/archives/intro.html.

As we prepared to leave Moscow after a layover of several days, I was haunted by the misery I had witnessed there. Russia didn't feel like America at all. I was only eleven years old, yet I felt the full weight of the hopelessness of the Russian people. *Will they ever hope again?* I wondered. For the rest of my days, I shall never forget the darkened, desperate, and dead eyes of the people of Moscow.

Four

GORKY BEGINNINGS

As we departed Moscow, our train passed through countless miles of icy snow chambers, at least five feet high on both sides. I had never felt this kind of cold before. It was cold enough to freeze your brain! After traveling along the frozen steel rail at a painfully slow pace, we finally arrived at midday in Gorky, the city originally called Nizhni Novgorod.

Upon our arrival we received a relatively warm welcome from a Ford factory representative, who promptly escorted us to a large old hotel in the center of town. This hotel was a check-in point where all foreigners stayed before they were assigned to permanent residency elsewhere. Our cold room had only one bed and no toilet; we used the filthy, reeking communal bathroom at the end of the corridor as little and as quickly as possible.

Our escort led us to the hotel dining room, where lunch consisted of buckwheat cereal, salted fish, black bread, tea and lemon, with sugar in large chunks. My mother was the only one who ate anything. She deflected disappointment better than Papa and I did. We both wore our hearts on our sleeves, but not Mama. I envied her ability to detach from adversity.

Papa's face looked sullen, unlike his exuberant expression just days before. Perhaps he didn't eat because he was appalled at the things he was seeing here. I didn't eat because I felt sick. Just the very thought of eating, coupled with the horrible smell of the food, turned my stomach.

After a few days in the transit hotel, our group assembled at the train station, where we were met by the Gorky factory officials. It was April 28, 1932—my father's birthday. We boarded a bus and headed to the American Village, about ten kilometers away. As we jolted along the furrowed road, I was thrilled to see mountains in the distance. I had always longed to live near mountains, so I was soon disappointed to learn that these "mountains" were just high bluffs across the Oka River. Other visions, once alive and strong, were quickly disappearing as well.

Gorky's American Village housed all of the foreign specialists who were under contract with the Ford automobile factory, situated about two kilometers away. More than a hundred families—from countries including the United States, Germany, Poland, Italy, Czechoslovakia, Hungary, and Austria—populated the village, crowding into about forty two-story wooden structures. The eight apartments in each building were alike: single-room flats that consisted of a bedroom with access to a communal kitchen, complete with a wood-burning stove, and a communal toilet. Washroom facilities were in a separate building. (Later, during World War II, many of these apartments were occupied by at least three families each.)

When we arrived, the village was surrounded by water. A winter of unusually heavy snow had caused the nearby Oka, a tributary of the larger Volga River ten kilometers away, to swell over its banks. Much to my delight, we had to board a rowboat to reach our apartment building. Once there, a short, white-haired man showed us to our quarters. As we looked them over, I saw Papa's shoulders sink as he mumbled, "You've got to be kidding."

We were assigned one room for our family. Sure enough, there was a communal kitchen and a communal toilet on each floor but no bathtubs or shower facilities. To bathe, we had to walk to a nearby public bathhouse, where men and women were assigned alternate days. We washed and rinsed with a wooden pail that was provided there; everyone bathed in the nude in a large washroom.

Oh, Papa, what have you done to us? I thought. *I love you so very much, and I know you meant well, but can our temporary trip to Russia be over? Please, today? Can we go back to Detroit now?*

I believed Papa had made a dire mistake, but there was nothing I could do about it. I knew my father's pride would never allow him to admit he'd made a mistake. And if Mama shared any of these thoughts, she never spoke them. She was always devoted to Papa. But I always knew that look in her eyes, the look that never lied to me, the look that said she agreed with me.

We had special passes for three meals a day in a dining room that was open only to foreigners connected with the factory. The menu never changed: buckwheat cereal, salted herring, an unidentified meat submerged in the darkest gravy I'd ever seen, a weird berry drink, and tea with lemon.

Within a few weeks, my father lost so much weight that he went to a doctor. His "illness" was diagnosed as starvation. To our surprise, the doctor provided some valuable coupons for white bread, butter, milk, and coffee. This brightened Papa's mood, if only slightly, and he began to eat and regain some weight. Mama and I were thankful to see his health improve, but his recovery was short lived. Following a shave in the village barbershop, Papa's face broke out with sores from a dreadful skin disease. That was his last visit to the barber. With disdain for our new life in Gorky, Papa grumbled, "To hell with them all."

After several months we received a rare treat one day—a meat we could identify: roast pork. Unfortunately, the pigs had been fed rotten fish, which contaminated the meat. Despite Mama's best attempts to disguise the bad taste, we couldn't eat the pork. We survived on eggs and vegetables, which Mama cooked for us in the communal kitchen. As usual, Mama masked her disappointment.

I entered school in Gorky at the third-grade level, the approximate equivalent of American fifth grade. Our teachers were all Americans, with the exception of one woman from England. Classes were taught in English, and we studied Russian only as a foreign language.

In Gorky, our small community of children and teenagers lived together harmoniously, but outside of school we did not associate with the Russian children much. When weather permitted, we held regular baseball games and other outdoor athletic competitions. In the evenings the kids in the village danced and played billiards in the clubhouse. I learned how to pole-vault and eventually became a fairly accomplished vaulter. Sports, or anything involving athletic skill, were my main interests—in fact, my life! The thrill of victory over another talented opponent fueled my competitive athletic drive, no matter what the sport.

The Russians never took anything quite as seriously as their sports, except perhaps their anger. Oppressed by the totalitarian state, they showed their hopelessness in their contempt for the system that dictated their way of life. Athletic competition was an important diversion for the people of the Soviet Union; the more accomplished you were at one or more sports, the easier your life would be.

Like the Russians, I thrived on the spirit of head-to-head competition. I already excelled in virtually every competition of skill that I attempted. Papa had carefully groomed me to be a winner at everything in life. I hated to lose, no matter what.

If I wasn't practicing or competing in sports, I could be found volunteering in the village library. Books were scarce in the Soviet Union, but there I was able to read to my heart's content. Since damaged books were not easily replaced, I also learned the art of repairing them. The only thing I enjoyed more than reading was sports.

As a highly qualified tool and die designer, my father's first advisory job at the factory was that of foreman. But from the outset, Papa was as disappointed with his work situation as he had been with our housing. He wanted the Ford automobile factory to excel in its Soviet production through honest, quality workmanship, and he expected integrity in his workplace. But he was alone in his vision.

Papa came home one day with tears in his eyes and told my mother of the atrocities he had seen in the factory. He said the Russian workers were stealing the leather conveyor belts from the expensive imported machines in order to repair their boots. He sat with his elbows on his knees and his chin in his hands, and he said, "Elsie, what can I do? I just don't know. They come to work but never to really work, only to steal. There is no integrity with them. They are all infidels and idiots! This can't continue."

With her usual calm strength, Mama listened very carefully, then spoke softly: "Carl, my husband, you mustn't let it get to you so. All you can do is to do what you can. Time will take care of the rest. It is not always your job to turn everything upside down. You are only one man. Please don't make anyone angry there. Remember that you have a family here who loves you and believes in you.

Just do your job and then come home to us. I want us all to be happy, that's all."

Carl Werner was a man on a mission, but he was misunderstood by his supervisors and the factory hands alike. His views were strong and his words uncompromising. Over time, Papa's face revealed that he was losing the vision that originally had brought him to Russia. He forgot how to smile; he began to look so frail that Mama and I feared for his life. His outrage escalated to uncharacteristic fury. "They are all renegades, rebels, and hypocrites," he would rage. One day he came home and told us, "The traitors are everywhere—liars and thieves, selling themselves and everyone else for pennies."

"Papa, just be careful, okay?" I often urged, but I don't know if he ever listened.

Both of my parents aged rapidly under the pressure. Life was very hard, but some things improved in time. We were finally given a two-room apartment in the village, with a kitchen and a bath and a small garden behind the building that included a shed where I could house a few pet rabbits.

My father was later promoted to chief instructor of the tool and die design shop, so he became more involved in training and oversight and less involved in daily production activities. Sam Herman, another Ford employee from Detroit, became foreman in the body shop, and he and my father became good friends.

The Herman family—Sam and Rose and their children, Victor, Leo, and Miriam—lived in our apartment building in Gorky's

American Village. Victor worked in the tool and die department at the factory with my father. He was about eight years older than I was, and though we would exchange casual pleasantries in the village now and then, we had separate activities and groups of friends. Victor eventually became an aviator and sky diver, was dubbed "the Lindbergh of Russia," and later broke the world free-fall record. In 1936 he was sent to Spain with the Russian military to participate in their civil war. One year later he returned to the Soviet Union, where, less than thirty days after my father's arrest, he was arrested for treason and anti-Soviet propaganda.

We also met two American brothers, Victor and Walter Reuther from Detroit, who lived temporarily in the apartment above ours. I developed a younger-sister, older-brother friendship with Walter. We took a liking to each other from the very beginning. He was an extremely kind and thoughtful man, and I always enjoyed his company. Mama and Papa spoke with him quite often too; they thought he was a wonderful man.

Walter always looked as if he knew something below the surface of things, something no one else knew. It was clear he was a man of forethought, with something definite in mind. I could tell he always had a secret or knew something out of the ordinary. His eyes had a certain gleam about them.

We often ice-skated together in the village. And before he returned to America, he gave me his skates because they were better than mine.

"And since I'm going back to the States anyway," he flashed a warm-hearted smile, "keep these skates until you no longer need them, and then you can return them when you get back to Detroit. Call me when you come back home, and we'll go skating." But I recall the look on his face that day; Walter never really expected to see his skates, or me, again.

Many friendships in Gorky during this time formed quickly and then ended abruptly. One day life was normal, and in the following weeks and months, people literally disappeared. Just like Papa, many were arrested for no apparent reason. Even as a child, I realized that Gorky had too many abrupt changes. Many times there would be no warning before a person, or even an entire family, simply moved under cover of night, sometimes escorted elsewhere with no explanation. I lost many friends this way. There were too many people, too many human tragedies to adequately detail them all. But I will never forget.

We had been in Gorky for a year when my father was granted a one-month vacation in 1933. We were allowed to visit relatives in Austria and Czechoslovakia. And Papa would see his mother for the first time in twenty-one years. We were all excited to have a break in our drab routine. Joyfully we packed and left Gorky by train.

A stop in Moscow provided time for us to purchase a few small gifts to take to our relatives. Papa chose a beautiful filigree antique vase for his brother, a well-known collector of antiques. But the vase was confiscated at the border and held until our return because the export of antiques was strictly forbidden. Papa silently rolled his eyes in disgust. Nevertheless, the trip renewed our spirits immensely. Mama was exuberant, Papa was revitalized, and I hoped this time would last forever.

We finally arrived in Vienna, home to my father's sister, Eva, his other brother, Richard, and their families. For the only time in my life, I got to meet some of my aunts, uncles, and several cousins. I immediately felt at home, relaxed and comforted. I was too young to remember everyone. Although I have no records left, and the names have escaped me, I vividly remember the happy, loving faces. I could play the memories back right now, as if they were scenes from a heartwarming movie.

With a new joy in his heart, if but for a season, my father proudly gave us a grand tour of his beloved city. We visited a very famous amusement park called The Prater, which also had a museum of natural history. We were thrilled by the wonderful food and pastries, for which Vienna is known. The whole city was breathtakingly beautiful, radiating majesty and splendor; it is one of the most gorgeous cities of the world, and I did not want to leave. "Papa, can we stay?" I pleaded to no avail. So after two short weeks, we bid our dear relatives a reluctant farewell, and sending a telegram ahead, we left Austria for Brno, Czechoslovakia, where my grandmother and Uncle Friedrich lived.

No one met us when we arrived at the train station in Brno, so we took a taxi to my uncle's home. It turned out to be a penthouse apartment with a wonderful wrought-iron balcony around all four sides of the building. The garden on the balcony was filled with plants, primarily cacti. Gardening was the hobby of my eighty-five-year-old grandmother. When we rang, a maid promptly opened the door and showed us inside. She explained that my uncle was not home yet but grandmother was here, alone in her room, playing cards. At the entrance to her room, my mother and I waited in the background, permitting Papa to approach his mother by himself.

"Mama?" he called.

She slowly turned from her game of solitaire. "Who's there?" she asked.

Then my father, in his extremely dramatic and animated fashion, crept up behind her and softly whispered in her ear, "Your ssson, Caaarrrl." A most profound frozen silence filled the room.

The old lady sat there motionless for what felt like an eternity, stunned, visibly overwhelmed, and noticeably shaking. The advance telegram had not yet been delivered. It finally arrived later that afternoon, after emotions began to settle. Now Papa's mother had tears rolling down her wrinkled cheeks and could only say, "Oh, my son, my Carl. Where have you been so long?" It was an unforgettable reunion, and I was so happy to meet my only surviving grandparent! I wanted to stay there and live with her forever.

Uncle Friedrich was the vice president of a very successful cosmetics factory. When he finally arrived home from work that day, he was speechless and deeply glad to see us. He was quite an emotional man, like my father. "Ahhh, and this is your beautiful little pumpkin, I guess," he said to Papa, hugging me as if there were no tomorrow. I instantly fell in love with Uncle Friedrich! We spent a very close and loving two weeks with them in their home in Brno. Again, I did not want to leave; neither did Mama. "Papa, let's stay here... Let's stay, please."

"Carl," Mama added, "we could stay, you know. Friedrich said there's room for us. What do you think?" But despite my many pleadings and Mama's hopeful eyes, despite Uncle Friedrich's offer, Papa's mind had long since been made up. He paused, with signs of serious consideration on his face, but after a long sigh, he shook his head slowly and said, "I'm sorry, but we must leave in the morning."

Perhaps it would have been difficult for us to return to the United States at this time because of Papa's prison record—his 1917 refusal to be drafted during World War I. Perhaps not. We didn't know. But we could have easily stayed in Czechoslovakia with *family* that loved us. I was sure Papa wanted to stay too. Why did he fight against his inner man, his spirit, which must have been warning him about returning to Russia? But we did not stay, and we never saw either of these dear ones again. My grandmother died in her sleep about five years later. Uncle Friedrich, I later learned, committed suicide when the Nazis occupied his beloved country. Fear of certain death by execution drove him to choose his own fate.

We went back to Russia to stay. Returning to Gorky, we moved into a housing commune and were given two rooms, one directly across the hall from the other. It was far from comfortable, but still

I felt satisfied to some degree, because once again I had a room all to myself. Mama joined the kitchen crew and did everything imaginable to improve the daily menu and to make the most of the food and supplements available to her. She had a God-given flair for making something out of nothing. And she never complained.

Mama spent much of her free time gardening and cultivating, and she managed to provide us with a fairly decent assortment of food. In 1934 some of the residents created a "closed" food store within the village, available only to foreigners who had the necessary passes. It stocked such rare items as white bread, butter, eggs, meat, sugar, candy, flour, and cereals. Usually my family could not afford these luxuries. When we had a few extra dollars not slated for other necessities, a very rare and special treat was to purchase some *real coffee* from a store in the city about twenty kilometers away. Coffee never tasted better to me.

In the meantime, I graduated to the fifth grade. One day we were abruptly informed that all our classes taught in English were being immediately terminated. From then on, we were going to take our classes with the Russian students...and *in Russian!* Henceforth, we would take English as a foreign language. We were dumbfounded. The news felt like being hit hard in the stomach and having the wind knocked out of you. I was just thirteen at this time, but I remember feeling that a major season of change was beginning. They were only talking about the language for now, but I wondered what changes would invade our lives next.

None of us really understood the language sufficiently to cope with the complexities of studying mathematics, science, physics, literature, history, and geography. We soon discovered that the Russians are not a very subtle people, and sensitivity to our needs was not a pressing concern to them. Compassion was not a strong suit with most Russians I knew. Most of us kids struggled greatly. All in all, there were about twelve subjects in our new school curriculum. Since we were being forcibly merged with existing Russian classes, already numbering more than thirty students each, there was no time for individual tutoring or attention for us foreigners.

We drifted along for the first few weeks, barely holding on, while most of the Russian kids snickered at how we were struggling to learn their language. I remember it seemed overwhelming at first, but eventually it somehow made sense, and learning Russian actually turned out to be faster and easier than I had feared.

After a few months, things seemed to lighten up a bit for us in school, except that the Russian children genuinely hated us with a sort of vengeful and jealous disdain that we couldn't ignore. Mama said it was probably because of our well-nourished appearance and the ample lunches we brought to school. For Russian children, lunches were just a bit of black bread and perhaps a raw onion, if they were lucky. Their clothes were crude, not very clean, and smelly; it was clear they also envied us for our usually clean and fresh attire.

"We should have pity on them, Maidie, and help them with

whatever we can, for this is what God would want. And be thankful for all you have, for we have been blessed," Mama would say. Sometimes I'd say it, and sometimes I wouldn't, but the question I wanted to ask her was, "What do you mean, 'blessed,' Mama?"

What I remember most about this time is feeling constantly deprived. Compared to the Russian children, my life must have been filled with good things, but you couldn't have convinced me of that then. The Russian girls in particular didn't care much for me, because the boys usually picked me first for their games. No other girl seemed to have the level of agility, stamina, or ability to keep up with the boys that I had. And all of the Russian boys liked me pretty well, so I was shoved and bullied around plenty during school—mainly by jealous girls—but I was tough enough to endure it.

As time went by, a major improvement began in our relationships with them. The transformation was astonishing, inexplicable. The Russian children seemed to realize that we didn't have any personal animosity toward them, and their attitudes changed for the better. We began to get along quite nicely, and I even became good friends with many of them. I noticed that the most hardened kids also seemed to be the most impoverished. Perhaps they needed the most healing, but some of them turned out to be my best friends. I believe that was God in action, bringing forth healing—a grand human reconciliation of some kind—long before I really knew him or what he was capable of doing in people's lives.

Once I got to know some of them, I began to understand the

Russian kids and grow very fond of most of them, and they of me. In the final analysis, the reality was that all of us, foreigners and Russians alike, were pretty much in the same boat. So we might as well get along. In the meantime, food became more plentiful for the Russians; their meat and bread were no longer rationed, and their entire outlook and demeanor changed almost miraculously with their improved diets. Clothing was becoming more readily available in their stores as well, and there appeared to be a generally more prosperous season just up the road.

While I was still in elementary school, I spent two consecutive summers at a children's recreation camp, about twenty-five kilometers from our village. The camp was a mix of children from various ethic backgrounds and countries, but most of them were Russian. The first summer I was quite homesick, but by the time my parents came to visit and brought my pet kitten, Popcorn, to see me, I had settled down a bit. However, I hated the food.

The first morning for breakfast I found two large smoked herring on my plate, along with some bread and tea. I ate just the bread and drank the tea. Then for lunch we had mashed potatoes and fish, so I gladly traded my fish for more potatoes. Supper was the same: fish, cereal, bread, tea. By the third day I was so incredibly hungry that I had no choice but to try the herring. To my surprise, it was delicious. From then on, I had no more problems with the meals at camp. Herring became my favorite thing to eat. Every chance I could get, I finagled more and more fish from the head chef, who had taken a liking to me.

I made many friends at a month-long summer camp the year I turned fifteen. There I participated in all social activities and sporting events available. Probably because of athletics, I became a favorite of the camp officials. When I returned home, however, my mother was frantic—I brought with me a head full of lice! She drenched me with kerosene, which burned like the dickens but seemed to work well in killing the critters. It was a small price to pay for the attention and friendship I had received at camp.

My best friend in those years was not an American but the son of another expatriate family, the Dubceks from Czechoslovakia. Their son, Alexander, whom we all affectionately called Sanya, was a sensitive young man with a flamboyant, comical nature. He had an overly active imagination and a keen wit. Sometimes he was moody, but mostly he was fun to be around. He often told stories, embellished and animated, about the people we would become in the years ahead and the lives we would lead. Everyone in the village loved to listen to Sanya's stories. He became the village story-teller and comedian.

One day he said to me, "Margaret, after you have won all of your medals, you will eventually decide to remain here in this country. You will marry a notorious Russian politician with thick, black eyebrows, and you will live with him and his eyebrows in the Kremlin. You will have many red-haired, freckle-faced babies who will also grow up to become politicians—some with thick, black eyebrows—and they will have many red-haired, freckle-faced babies. And you will then be a fat grandmother—with thick eyebrows—of so many red-haired, freckle-faced babies that you will scream!"

I laughed so hard my sides began to ache. The funniest part was that I wondered how accurate he might be. My youthful freckles had faded during my early teen years, but could they return on the faces of my children? Could my thick, wavy auburn hair be passed along to the next generation in a brighter shade of red? Or worse, as thick, black eyebrows?

I playfully slapped Sanya's face, and he knew his story had accomplished his goal—gaining my undivided attention. Everyone in the village knew that Sanya had a crush on me, and our circle of friends teased the two of us relentlessly. I thought it was funny. I had no time for boyfriends, but there was no other boy in the village whom I liked as much as Sanya Dubcek. He would always be my friend.

In 1936, even at the age of fifteen, Sanya wore ambition proudly. He was convinced he was born to be a leader who would one day conquer the world and do something of social significance. "Someday you'll be proud you knew me." He would laugh and boldly proclaim, "You'll tell your friends, 'Hey, I used to know him; I used to know Sanya Dubcek!' "

During summer vacations, which lasted from the end of June to the first of September, my friends and I spent most days at the Oka River, which was a good twenty-minute walk from our village. The river's beach was a beautifully brilliant white sand, and on hot days I loved to bury my feet inside the comforting warm sand. It gave me a feeling of peace and tranquillity. This was my secret place, my getaway. At one favorite spot, the river was about one kilometer wide, and I would continually swim back and forth until I was exhausted. A swimming area had been outlined with pontoons on the river, a large rectangle of water about fifty meters out from the beach. It was equipped with three-meter and ten-meter diving platforms, along with four starting posts for swimming races. The swimming area also had water polo equipment. I loved every moment of my time here, and this is where my serious indoctrination to swimming actually began.

Without exception, all of us took swimming and diving lessons from Nikolai, our young Russian instructor from Moscow. He was still in high school at the time but worked here as a lifeguard during the summers. Everyone looked up to him; not only was he tanned, well built, and handsome, but he also had a character and personality of gold. His smiling eyes lit up the whole place. Nikolai was extraordinary; you could tell he was a natural winner. It was like magic when he spoke, and all the girls' hearts melted. When his blue eyes looked at me, my heart melted too. Sanya, the comedian, was my friend, but Nik, the handsome lifeguard, was my hero. I figured that if I ever did get married, someone like Nikolai would be a great choice! He was everyone's favorite, and something in me began to hope that maybe, just maybe, I could one day be his.

On the Oka, with ample motivation and countless hours of practicing, I soon became an accomplished swimmer and diver.

During these summer months, if I was not eating or sleeping, I could be found in the water or close to Nikolai. Life was good and as close to normal as I could have expected. I loved Nikolai, for what I then knew of love. And he probably thought that all I cared about was my swimming.

A retired pleasure steamship was towed up to our swimming area and anchored as a permanent swimming and boating club-house, which we treated as our own. It had an antique billiard table on board, where we played for hours on end. This ship was where we always wanted to be, by far the best place in Gorky for a young teenager like me to socialize! The swimming club also owned six sailboats: three class 20s, two 30s, and one very large one—a 45, which we called *The Pelican,* seating twelve people. We spent many wonderfully carefree days on the water, under the water, in sailboats, in rowboats, or in canoes…with Nikolai.

I became a champion swimmer for the American Village and for the entire Gorky region, traveling to different meets and tournaments in surrounding cities. Throughout the region and provinces, I became known as the one to beat, and I enjoyed the popularity immeasurably. In typical Soviet fashion, regardless of your nationality or ethnicity, you received an extra helping of social favor based on your God-given athletic prowess. That blunt reality of Russian life didn't bother me in the least. I excelled in all athletics and was delighted to receive some small extra considerations, maybe not amounting to much more than a good dose of pride and ego enhancer.

Papa was very proud of me, especially when he'd come to see me compete. Ever since that traumatic day in Detroit when Papa had taught me how to swim, "You can do it, my sweet girl. Now swim! And always be the best!" were the words that played in my ears and in my mind before I swam. I just loved to compete.

We also learned folk dancing at classes in the village clubhouse, exclusively for the foreigners, and we also staged musical concerts. My mother sang a solo once, but she forgot part of the lyrics, making me want to crawl under my seat from embarrassment. Another time I was performing a Spanish dance with my partner, when our accompanist—who was thoroughly drunk—totally ruined our performance by erroneously repeating the first passage of our music. My partner and I gawked at each other in sheer terror until I sheepishly turned and ran off the stage in tears. My partner floundered alone on stage for a few moments more, then he also fled. My father, who was sitting in the audience, took these things rather seriously. He ran backstage and dragged the so-called pianist outside by the seat of his pants. That guy never again showed up to play piano in our club.

In school I was also an active member of the Gymnastics and Athletics Club. Here, too, I was said to be the one to beat in our competitions. I especially excelled in the 100-meter dash and in both high and broad jumping (now called long jumping). I've always thought that the great thing about competitive sports is it acts as the great equalizer, not favoring any nationality, race, religion, social, or economic status. You just compete in your event, and the best—whoever that might be—generally wins, with no politics involved. You simply let your performance do the talking. Why couldn't everything in life be like the Olympic Games, I wondered.

The extreme winters in Gorky lasted for at least five months of every year. With all the snow and ice we could possibly handle, there were plenty of winter events and sporting activities. My favorites were skiing and ice skating, and I skated at the village outdoor rink for hours on end. The Oka River also froze almost two meters thick; you could drive a bus across it, but the ice was usually too choppy to skate on. We'd cross the river on foot and then climb to the top of the steep snow-covered hill on the other side, dragging our homemade toboggans crafted from sheets of veneer. Then, with the uninhibited excitement that only a child knows, we'd come flying down the mountain without a care in the world! Then we'd go back up and do it all over again! What a thrill on those days to come home completely exhausted, famished, chilled to the bone, faces flushed red as a beet, but elated through and through. Even now, if I close my eyes and relax, I can almost go back to the sights, the sounds, the smells, and the emotions of that time!

It's true that our little circle of friends was heavily involved in sports, but we also went to the movies whenever we could, especially when they featured foreign (American) films. We had a very crude, quaint, but functional little theater in the village. During this time I developed a serious and increasing passion for drama. My whole family had it to some degree. Although Papa surely helped with the genes, my love for drama was probably inherited from Mama.

Dating was never a problem either, because we didn't do it on an individual basis. Instead, we always did things within the group, although old-fashioned flirting certainly went on at every opportunity. I already belonged to Nikolai, at least in my heart. But we were truly just one big healthy group of kids trying hard to make the best of less-than-favorable circumstances.

Those snapshots of my early years in Gorky were pleasant fragments of life as we adapted to living in this place where we did not really belong. It all seemed surreal, because we were caught between two different worlds, consciously and not.

The idyllic aspects of Russia ended for me when Papa was arrested. The harsh and fearful aspects of life in Gorky loomed ahead.

CONSEQUENCES

Barely one month after Papa's arrest, Mama and I were evicted from our home. The only space available to us was a single room that looked and felt more like a closet—a tiny living area only five feet by twelve feet. This room had been used as a small storage facility in the basement of a building where we lived when we first arrived in Gorky. It was right next door to the public toilet and washroom, which was used by all of the building's residents.

This was our new home. We were barely able to squeeze in two mini-cots, a small bookcase-desk that my father had built for my room, and two stools. I could reach out and touch the opposite walls with my fingers. In these cramped, sardinelike conditions, we also had to tolerate the nauseating stench and noise from the facilities next door.

My mother eventually found a job as a janitor in a metal shop, sweeping up the metal shavings from the floor. She came home every day with her hands cut up and bleeding from the shavings, until she was able to make herself some sturdy canvas gloves for better protection. I hated watching her suffer, day after day after dreadful day, and I hated everything about my own life. But the worst part was not our squalid living arrangements, the horrible stench, our dreadful poverty, or even the uncertainty. These hardships would've been bearable if we'd only had Papa with us. His absence was a permanent pain of the worst kind.

My constant thought was, *Where is my papa?* We had no idea where to turn or what to do next, but Mama told me more than once, "God will see us through this." I didn't know, but I sure hoped she was right!

She didn't sound very convincing, because a part of Mama died on the day they took her husband away. She was still emotionally strong but only a splinter of her former self. Only God knew what was happening to Papa. Was he still alive? They didn't take just him on that horrible day in June; they also took our peace. We had no hint of where he was, how he was, or what was happening with him. I thought of ways to find my papa, but we were not allowed to have any contact with him due to his status as a *vrag naroda* (enemy of the state). And unlike in America, here we could not demand our rights. We had none.

During Stalin's Great Terror of 1938–39, there were no outside avenues of help. We could not present our case to the American Embassy in the Soviet Union; if there was one at this time, it was only a ploy. All foreign mail was inspected and filtered. Nothing insinuating the horrors of Soviet life to the outside world would be tolerated by the NKVD; instead, it would be harshly dealt with. The worst thing Mama and I could have done would have been to draw attention to our situation.

So we forged ahead as best we could. We had little money and no material resources, so we struggled for everything. I tried to help Mama stretch the measly wages she earned, but we lacked even the bare essentials. Gradually we became accustomed to having just enough food to survive. Some days were better than others. A few potatoes and an occasional loaf of stale black bread was our usual portion; it was day-to-day survival. And despite Mama's strong appearance, she was not the same woman she had been before they stole from the bank of our family's future memories, before they took my future children's grandfather away. *I hated Russia.*

I wanted my precious mama back. I wanted to see joy in her face and that lovely sparkle in her eyes. She still had great faith that God would somehow see us through this. She was trying to stay firm not so much for herself but so I would not lose hope.

I had one more year of high school remaining. Russian education required ten years in all, compared to twelve in America. This year, with my papa missing, I didn't have the same attitude and motivation as a student. But I would not let the barbaric Russian system kill my spirit. I was determined never to be a victim. Instead, I wanted revenge for what they'd done to Papa!

One day in September, all of the schoolchildren in Gorky were summoned by Communist party officials to the school auditorium for a youth rally. Such events were designed to support Stalinist ideology and to instill pride and patriotism in the country's youth. How ridiculous! From my perspective, and I was certain the other children felt the same way, the rally organizers had their work cut out for them. This assembly was a political ruse intended to put the party's positive spin on the cruelty everyone knew was taking place throughout the country.

We were all Young Pioneers, the national Soviet youth organization that prepared children for their future roles in the country's political life. I was an American and had always despised the Pioneers organization, even before Papa's arrest. Now I felt no desire to pretend for their benefit. Not today!

I was only seventeen, highly skeptical, and certainly not a fool. I saw that in Russia events happened unpredictably and uncontrollably. There were no individual rights, liberties, or personal freedoms. If you questioned anything or made adverse comments, you were labeled "treasonous." Trying to gather information, to act as your own detective, was not only stupid but suicidal. You had to walk cautiously in order to preserve your next breath.

I was no idiot; I had learned by experience to watch my back at all times. And I was no puppet; I was not and would not become their blind and "faithful daughter." I was becoming a rebel, a rebel with a just cause, a trapped "American in Russia" rebel.

According to standard Soviet protocol, our assembly commenced with the playing of the Russian anthem. I chose not to participate. I sat there, angry, on the hard wooden bench while most of the students, perhaps sixty in all, participated in the coerced escapade. The teachers and school officials sang heartily and vigorously clapped their approval—mainly, I thought, for fear of being observed doing otherwise. The crude schoolhouse, built of gray brick and wood, always seemed cold to me, but today it was deathly frigid.

As the last notes of the anthem subsided, the chairman took his place at the podium. In a brusque and condescending tone, he began to speak of our "highly esteemed Comrade Stalin" and our "blessed motherland." I grew nauseated, even though I'd heard this ridiculous jargon before. His cunningly contrived speech referred to "criminals," "lack of patriotism in the heartland," "anti-Soviets," and most ironically to me, "intruders in our midst." This was nothing new to me, but I was not prepared for what came next.

The chairman declared that we students, as "loyal comrades," now had to personally and individually take a stand for the nation. We had to officially denounce and totally separate ourselves from anyone convicted of treason or crimes against the state. Family members were no exceptions. We Young Pioneers were ordered to "publicly denounce our fathers and mothers for being traitors of their country." We had no alternative. They intended to force us to declare that our first loyalty was to the party. Even neutrality would not be tolerated.

I tried to absorb the words he spoke, but I felt numb, almost paralyzed. The man's words were like carving knives—big Russian ones—stuck deep into my gut and twisted slowly from side to side. *They were directly ordering me to denounce my father!* Rage, fear, and a host of other emotions welled up in me at once, battling one another for supremacy. I knew I would never say anything so preposterous against my parents, regardless of what these people might do to me.

I wanted to get up and storm out of the assembly, but I knew that would not be wise. Trying to be inconspicuous, I quickly looked around, eying my friends and Russian "comrades" for confirmation of this absurdity. Did anyone else feel this outrage? I suspected so, but I wasn't sure. Maria was there, but we didn't sit together. I saw her across the aisle, several people between us. When our eyes accidentally met, she shook her head from side to side in repugnance and disbelief. Would anyone be willing to stand up and speak the truth at this farcical meeting—and face the cost?

As was customary, we were not allowed to speak until called upon. The entire student body was dead silent, but I could see fearful eyes darting about, trying not to be obvious. Who would go first? Who was the lucky one? I saw hatred and bewilderment on every face. We were all scared to death, our anxiety surging. We looked like helpless victims awaiting execution.

I gazed around cautiously. Most of the students were the children of immigrants to Russia from other European countries. Several had also experienced the abduction of parents and loved ones. In a sense, we were all in the same boat, but I was different. I was the only American. If these children felt as I did, they were too afraid to show it. I was frightened but also furious. Strangely, I felt no real connection with any of them except Maria. Were they all going to succumb to this coercion and speak this demonic lie? Were we really going to consent to this lunacy, what Papa would call "nonsense"?

The rally leaders began a roll call, demanding that each child make a public declaration. "Stand up and make your feelings known. Confess and denounce the activities of your parents, and proclaim your allegiance to Comrade Stalin and Mother Russia!" they barked. Anxiety covered me like a blanket. I felt as if my mind would explode. Many of the students were small children, age twelve or even younger, who couldn't possibly understand the implications of these commands. But the others clearly understood what they were being required to do.

The procession began. Like sheep they followed, one after another after another. Each child spoke on cue, robotically repeating the same words said by the person before them. I thought, *If life and death are in our words, then this is massive, verbal homicide.*

And then it was my turn. "Comrade Werner?" As I heard my name, I thought, *Oh Lord, if you can hear me, please don't let this happen!* The presiding chairman politely asked me again, "Miss

Margaret Werner, what do you have to say about the character and deeds of your father, Carl Werner? Will you please tell us of his unpatriotic ways and his crimes against our country?"

Time suddenly crashed to a complete halt. I froze. My heart beat wildly. *What will I say? What will I do? Oh, my papa, what should I do? Why am I here instead of back home in Detroit?* I prayed, *Let me be wise, let me be discerning, and let me measure with care the words I am about to speak. O God, I need you right now. Please help me!*

I carefully weighed my options for several long seconds. Then I chose, despite my fear, to stand up and blast them. I chose to speak out against their blasphemous insinuations. Instead of denouncing my father as instructed, I decided to speak the truth.

I began, "*We*, the families, have never been told what alleged crimes our parents were charged with. Furthermore, *we* do not believe they are criminals at all." I purposely used the word *we* instead of *I*, knowing that I was speaking for everybody, whether anyone else would join me or not.

"How dare you tell me to speak that way against my own father, the one you took away from me," I said, my voice shaking with indignation. "This country is filled with ruthless murderers seeking their own perversions at the expense of innocent people! My father thought of you as mindless renegades. I can easily see that he was right!"

My words shot forth like the fierce backdraft of a raging fire. "After all that my mother and I have already endured, you now have the gall to ask me publicly to murder my father—perhaps again—right here? Are you out of your minds? Carl Werner was the best man who ever set foot on Russian soil! All he ever did here was good, and you dare to call him a traitor?" I paused, emotion swelling my throat.

"My father has more true courage and patriotism in his little finger than any of you will ever have!" I spat out, my eyes now full of tears as anger consumed me.

As I finished, I began to weep uncontrollably. Adrenaline gushed through me. I had said the exact opposite of what they had expected me to say. And, embittered emotions aside, I felt stronger for it. My words had been so forceful that it felt as though someone bigger and more powerful than I had spoken. This was a moment to be savored—a moment of personal victory. My speech had stunned the audience. I saw bewildered faces with mouths wide open; wild, unbelieving eyes; some silent cheers. I didn't jump on the party bandwagon that day or any day thereafter. I also knew there would be a price to pay for my indiscretion, my "unfaithfulness" to Comrade Stalin and his loyal henchmen; I just didn't know when. *But today I didn't care.* I had no fear or concern about my own safety or what they might do to me. I was confident in the moment, in the outrage, and in my defiance.

After I finished, a small, gray-haired woman who had been sitting on the stage stood up and walked purposefully toward me. She stopped at the end of my aisle and with a pleasant smile said, "Come, Margaret," motioning for me to move toward her. I complied, and she walked me out of the auditorium and into an adjacent hall where another woman and a man stood talking.

I had never seen any of them before. The man spoke softly but matter-of-factly to me: "I guess you know that you have left us with no other choice but to expel you from the Young Pioneers? You made certain choices today, and now you will have to live with those choices."

I had expected something worse than that and actually felt a little relieved. Was that really all I would have to face? Was this the extent of my punishment—I would be expelled from the Young Pioneers? *Ha!* I thought. *That's no big deal; I was getting ready to quit anyway!* I laughed internally as they spoke.

Less gently, the elderly woman said, "You must leave the premises immediately and report back to the school office first thing in the morning." I didn't expect serious disciplinary action, at least not now, for I was only seventeen and an honor student. I had never created a disturbance of any kind and wasn't a trouble-maker at school.

I didn't think they would take me out back and shoot me or anything quite that severe. They wouldn't execute a seventeen-year-old American citizen living as a Russian schoolgirl. While subtlety and human compassion were not their strong suits, party members were much too aware of public opinion for anything that blatant, especially in public. I assumed such things happened in prison cells or maybe in Siberia but not to teenagers attending school in Gorky.

As I learned later, after I was ushered out of the auditorium, many of the other children, including my friends, denounced their parents as ordered. My heart broke for them and for their anguished families, whatever was left of them.

I went to Maria's house for moral support that afternoon. She was still fuming from the day's proceedings, having chosen to remain seated and silent when asked to denounce her family. I did not fault her for that choice; it was her way of protecting not only herself but also the ones she loved. Such a decision was not made carelessly or taken lightly.

Maria shrugged apologetically. "I just couldn't do it. I froze. I couldn't say a word. I'm not like you, Margo. It's so natural for you to stand up and speak what is right. When you spoke up today, my heart wanted to leap out of my chest for joy!" Her eyes met mine. "Everyone knows what great courage it took to do what you did. Margo, do you realize what you said? You said exactly the words that everyone else wanted to say—the things they knew were true—but were afraid to say. That's a great thing! I am so proud of you!"

I was thankful for Maria's affirmation, but I didn't open my heart until I returned home that evening. Then I told Mama all that had happened. She listened quietly, her eyes steady, full of warmth and compassion. My shock and sadness surfaced in a wave of tears. Exhausted, I collapsed on my small bed and cried and cried. Mama lay down beside me. I felt her tears on my neck. We huddled together until sleep finally claimed us and the early morning hours came around again.

Mama was my best friend.

I got up earlier than usual, still charged with energy from yesterday's events. I washed my face, got dressed, and ate a slice of dry bread, then departed for school. I wasn't fearful or worried. Perhaps I should have been and just didn't know any better. I was ready to hear the reactions, face the music, and confront the day. You can afford to be reckless when it feels as though you have nothing left to lose.

Things seemed peculiarly normal when I arrived at school. Had yesterday really happened? No one—neither school officials nor fellow students—said a thing about the previous day. Hadn't I, uncharacteristically, said horrific things about Russia? It all felt surreal.

As instructed, I reported to the school office. The staff workers smiled, said little, and went about their usual business as if yesterday had been nothing out of the ordinary. I wondered why they would pretend it was not a big deal. Was it because I was an American? Perhaps they had something else in store for me, something worse, and they were just waiting for the appropriate time. Whatever the reasons, nothing happened…that day.

The school day ended, and I returned to our shabby room feeling more exhausted than I had the night before. I sank down on my bed and fell asleep without eating. My body, racked by stress and fear, cried out for rest. Yesterday's crisis in the school auditorium had been the culmination of six years of personal and social conflict.

Only a few weeks ago the sun was still shining, and I had a loving father who came home to me every evening. I was different now; my friends were different. Memories of good times, formerly so vivid, were now like the pages of a book, ripped apart and blowing away in a strong wind. I cannot describe how much I missed my papa, my daddy.

Since my family had left America so long ago, I had learned much about this strange land. But there was much more to learn.

Six

LIFE WITHOUT PAPA

Hard as we tried, Mama and I never became accustomed to living on our own. It never seemed natural since we were here only because of Papa, and now he was gone. Some days seemed easier than others, but really, all of them were next to impossible. You lived because you had to. The two of us were now trying to live the life of three. Papa was still very much with us, only we couldn't see him, and he couldn't see us. He was still our world, and Mama clearly believed, more than I did, that he would return. That was the measure of faith she had.

We had to sell most of our belongings. We kept only a few things: our sewing machine, Papa's precious tools, and certainly his beloved drafting table. Mama wasn't ready to abandon the possibility that he would one day return by the grace of God. Sometimes I daydreamed that he would walk back in through the door, right into our outstretched arms, and things would be as they used to be, as they were supposed to be. Thinking that way was fantasy, obsession, and personal torture, but it was the only remnant of hope we had. Mama continued to say, "Have faith, be strong, and God will get us through this."

We didn't have room to store even the few things we kept, so we gave many of these items to friends for safekeeping. It was hard parting with them, even temporarily; each of Papa's things brought him back to mind just as we were saying a more permanent good-bye. In one case, a friend decided to sell my father's tools to pay for a visit from her son, Alec, who was in the Russian army. That infuriated me, but I saw that her actions were driven by necessity. The system preyed upon and played upon the weaknesses and vulnerabilities of the human condition. She had nothing else to barter with, and we had inadvertently handed her some bargaining power. What else could she have done? Arrangements such as this were routine, not the exception. We were all too weak and ill equipped to initiate change. I felt more compassion for Alec's mother later, when he was killed in the intense fighting in Gorky during the German occupation of the area in World War II.

I finally finished school in 1939 *with honors,* all A's and B's. My goal and dream was to attend medical school at Moscow University and to practice medicine one day—back in America, should God or fate bless me with that opportunity. But we did not have the funds or friends in high places who could pull the necessary strings to help us get back to the United States, and I eventually had to accept that I had no real chance at further education. We had no money at all. I had to work to help support myself and Mama, because there was no other option.

Just after graduation, I went to Moscow for the first time on my own. For two weeks I visited with friends who had lived near us in the American Village. They were renting a room in a peasant's house on a kolkhoz on the outskirts of Moscow. Our small reunion included some other acquaintances from my earlier years in Gorky. For many hours in the peaceful evenings, seven or eight of us talked together in that living room. Most of them were about my age, and some were a bit older, in their early twenties. When it came to discussing the future—destiny or even hope—there was mostly silence and quiet reflection in the room. That was okay, because anything peaceful was rare and valuable to us. But it was as if no one knew what to say, as if the future was unanimously understood to be a forbidden subject. Many of our collective hopes had already been dashed beyond repair.

One day I saw the owner of the kolkhoz, a man who looked about sixty years old, eating his midday meal on the front steps. He was pouring his four-year-old son a stiff shot of vodka. When I questioned him, the father laughed and proudly proclaimed, "He's been drinking vodka since he was one year old! He can drink a glass of vodka faster than you can drink a glass of water!"

"But what will that do to his liver as he grows older?" I asked.

"What do you mean what will happen to him? He's just fine! Look at me. I'm thirty-four years old and the strongest man on this kolkhoz!"

My jaw dropped when he blurted out his age. I couldn't believe it. My question had just been answered. This poor man held no hope for the future either. Hopelessness was evidently a common thread for all who lived in this depraved country.

When I returned to our village, I landed a job in the chemical laboratory of the factory's foundry. I stayed there for about three months and then earned a transfer, a promotion of sorts, to the foreign archives. I was chosen for my knowledge of English and my previous experience in the library. Vast piles of records, blueprints, and plans from the Detroit Ford Motor Company were haphazardly stored in those archives. I learned how Ford had sold plans for the factory to the city of Gorky, making it an exact duplicate of the Detroit plant. And this would have been quite a find, I reckoned, for certain interested parties, had these documents inadvertently slipped into the wrong hands. Since Henry Ford was simultaneously working both sides of the fence by supplying cars, technology, and financing to archenemies Russia and Germany, the people overseeing plant security and operations wanted this information secure. English, German, and British spies were everywhere, so secrecy about everything was always top priority.

All things considered, I enjoyed my job there, doing translations and keeping things in order. My boss and manager of the archives was Norissa Plotnov, an older woman not really qualified for her job. She spoke no languages other than her native Russian, nor was she able to read the blueprints. I took over virtually her entire workload. Unexpectedly, one day she told me that her sickly father, whom she had cared for most of her life, had just died, and she was spreading the news of her recent engagement and plans to wed. I was surprised that she was confiding these personal matters to me, even that she was in the process of quitting her job. She had never been very chummy with me before, so I suspected some kind of setup.

About a week later, purely by accident, I saw Norissa again in Kanavino, a Gorky suburb. As the two of us waited in line to board the streetcar, she was delirious with excitement, talking about her upcoming marriage and honeymoon. She was the happiest I had ever seen her, but soon she grew impatient in the waiting, then noticeably agitated, and she decided to take a crowded gypsy taxi-cab to her destination instead.

"Come on, Margaret. I don't have time to wait. I'll pay for us both, okay? Besides, there's so much I want to tell you!" she pleaded.

I'm not sure why I chose to decline her offer. It would have saved me considerable time, cost me nothing, and been a significantly more comfortable ride. But something inside me said no. It was feeling over logic, instinct over intellect, faith over knowledge. Who knows? A simple premonition, like an inaudible voice, made me listen to my heart instead of my head.

Norissa and I said our good-byes, and she rode away in her taxi.

When the streetcar came along minutes later, I was able to secure a good window seat. We traveled just a few miles and then suddenly came to a jarring halt. There was mass confusion on the pavement ahead, gathering a large crowd of onlookers. I speculated that there had been an accident. Just then, a gap opened in the crowd, and I could see. Clutching my heart, I recognized Norissa's taxicab entangled with another car. There had been a terrible collision—parts of cars and parts of people lay all over the street. Everyone in both vehicles was dead. Never in my life had I seen anything so ghastly! I recognized the body of my former boss, but her head had been totally severed and was lying in the middle of the street. Norissa Plotnov, who in her exhilaration had tried to convince me to ride with her. Other bodies were also strewn about.

I could hardly breathe.

There was no earthly reason why I should not have ridden with Norissa. Was this an indisputable instance in my life when maybe I heard the still, small voice of God? What else could it have been? I had no other explanation…but I knew that Mama prayed.

We still had no word of Papa and could not know whether he was alive or dead. At my job I eventually met several people who had seen him. They all spoke very highly of him but only in the strictest confidence. It was dangerous to express any sympathy for the family of an arrested vrag naroda, or "enemy of the people," as they were so callously and conveniently labeled. You carefully guarded your thoughts and, better yet, your lips. People were blatantly encouraged and sometimes coerced to inform on one another to the NKVD. Even family members were forced to become informers, turning in mothers, fathers, sisters, brothers, and relatives in order to survive. Very rarely would anyone risk telling us anything.

Mama and I tried over and over to determine what had happened to Father, what he was charged with, and where he was being detained, but all information was denied to us on every attempt and approach we made. Russians could learn nothing about their fellow citizens. All of the Soviet newspapers were operated and manipulated by the Communist government—the spinners of political darkness. They did not permit any information from beyond the borders of this morally ravaged country, either. Like physical darkness, the Soviet system had to be kept closed off in order to perpetuate itself; it could never admit the light of day that exposes the evil deeds of men. We had to wait in this darkness as did all the other families affected by this national ruthlessness and mindless cruelty. The first thing we heard, several months after his arrest, was that Papa was being held in the Gorky city prison, some twenty-five kilometers away.

I remember having the strong expectation that I would be reunited with him. Perhaps I was foolish, but faith is why we choose to press on, despite the odds. I loved him and missed him beyond words. We packed a box of permissible items for him: some small bits and pieces of food, a toothbrush, underwear, a pair of shoes, a shirt, a warm sweater, and some cigarettes.

Along with hundreds of frightened families on similar missions, we waited for several hours in a large hall. Then our name was called, and it was our turn to submit our package. "Werner," called the blank-faced woman in charge. I quickly jumped to my feet and ran up to her desk. Handing her the box, I looked at her anxiously for some sign of confirmation, but she wouldn't show me her eyes. She just went about her business, staring downward, avoiding looking at me, saying nothing. "Nowitski," she then grumbled and went on with her mechanical roll call. Some two hours later we were privileged to see a receipt Papa had signed. With hope still alive in our hearts, we could only trust that he had received our gifts, but we didn't know for sure. Of course we wanted to believe, so believe we did.

On a bitterly cold day in November 1939, wearing my father's sheepskin jacket and other warm clothing, I went out into the city again in search of more information. At the Gorky city prison, a tiny man standing inside a huge booth curtly informed me that Papa had been "sentenced to an indeterminate term" and "shipped out without the right to correspond with his family." He would or could say no more; that was the official response. No lawyers would touch the case, as was the situation for millions throughout the country. For Mother Russia, this was business as usual, just another day when there was no place for protest or demonstration, no one to get angry with, no one who cared about your civil complaint. If you were smart, you wouldn't try to learn more than the authorities wanted you to know.

A year or so later we talked to one of the Italian men from the village who had also been arrested but then later released. He told us he had accidentally seen my father in prison but had not been permitted to speak with him. I probed him for more, but he was either unwilling or unable to elaborate. He was another person who would not look me in the eyes when he spoke. Another time, a complete stranger contacted us and reported that he had been in a crowded cell with my father for a time before his trial. This man expressed his genuine admiration for Papa, for his good spirits—despite his surroundings—and for his encouragement to others. "Everybody loved Carl," he said. "We all looked to him for strength." That news sounded indeed like my precious father. I remember feeling much better with that report, even somewhat relieved.

From another source we heard that all the prisoners had been sick with extreme diarrhea, caused by the filthy food and the unsanitary living conditions. This type of diarrhea doubled people over in agony for days, and there was no medical care or treatment of any kind. The bread they received was moldy; so, as the news went, my father hung the bread out to dry through the window bars, and the bread became palatable. Somehow this gradually cured the prisoners of their ailments.

Mama and I gathered these random tidbits of information and hoarded them in our memories. They were all we had. They became cherished remnants of Mama's husband, my father, the head of our family—golden treasures no one could take away.

We continued our daily struggle to survive. My mother took a short nursing course at a nearby vocational school in Gorky and finally found more suitable work as a nurse and receptionist in a local medical clinic about a mile from our apartment. For a short time, I worked as a typist in a secretarial pool in the factory, and then I began working in the drafting department, making copies of industrial prints in ink. The days were gray and depressing. They passed with agonizing lethargy. I thought many of them would never end.

Seven

WAR: ENEMIES AND ALLIES

In 1940 I had a vacation at a resort about sixty miles from Gorky. It was set deep in a dense pine forest, along a meandering river. The peaceful beauty of the landscape was marred, however, by mosquitoes that were as large as my thumbnail. I'd never seen anything like them.

At night I slept completely covered by my sheets because the open-air tents had no nets. Everyone at the resort kept in constant motion during the days, frantically playing volleyball or tennis to avoid being stationary victims of the insidious insects. Even swimming in the river provided no relief. The exposed skin along the part in my hair turned a bright red from the painful, swollen bites. I often wished I could breathe underwater. But, miniature vampires aside, the camp was pleasant, the food was good and plentiful, and I enjoyed meeting a few other vacationers.

I often walked in the woods, where it was cooler and the mosquitoes were not quite as fierce. One day I came out of the forest into a small open meadow completely covered with countless lilies of the valley in bloom—my favorite flower. They stood a foot high or taller, and oh, how exquisite they were! Sprays of delicate fragrant stars hung above the thick green leaf blades all around me. It was such a lovely sight, I thought I was close to heaven. *Could it be there is a God after all?* I pondered.

A unique feeling of peace enveloped me in this open field of lilies, as if *peace* were actually a place. The flowers smelled of purity to me, of comfort and freshness, but they also spoke of separation and departure. They represented newness, a utopian dream, a rebirth away from the awful realities of my life. Except for my friendship with Nikolai, I had never felt this good about anything in Gorky; this was entirely different from anything I had known in Russia. And I wondered, *How could this be, these extremes?* I wanted to never leave. How could I keep this feeling in my heart? How could I take it back with me?

Looking back, I remember feeling as though this experience of beauty and hope was an encounter with the world's Creator. I did not think of myself as religious; in fact, religion was seldom brought up in our family. We did not attend church back in Detroit, nor did I ever hear my mother and father speak to each other or with others about God, religion, or the church. Papa was a good man of unwavering character, conscience, and principle, but he wasn't religious. I never heard him openly deny God or question his existence; it would have been out of character for him to do so.

But I never heard him outwardly express a belief in God, either. Mama was different. There were times I saw her praying silently, and there were things she said only to me, words I'll never forget. "Spirit knows spirit." My mother and father loved each other dearly, but they were cut from distinct cloth; they had different sensitivities to God and the deeper, timeless considerations of the human heart. That was okay with me. I loved both of them for who they were.

But the field of lilies startled me into an awareness of something beyond myself, a goodness deeply different from my everyday life. Something in me responded with love and hope. I could tell it moved like my mama's heart. Mama was not "religious," according to any textbook definition. But did she believe in God? Absolutely! She was content with what she knew inside and with how she lived her life. From start to finish, her life was a daily example of love, peace, and abounding faith. My mother didn't feel it was right for people to display their religion, as they would wear a garment.

"There are far too many crusaders already," she said to me one day. "Their speech is not based in truth. They are best left alone to preach to themselves. Let your heart tell you what is right, Maidie. Sometimes it's good to just be silent and content with what you know."

I longed for Papa, and I often cried myself to sleep thinking about him. I saw Mama's grief too, and I often prayed in my inner thoughts, although I had never been taught how to pray. The friends I had grown to love and trust were no longer constant: Sanya and his family had moved away, Maria seemed strangely distant after the incident at school, and Nikolai went back to Moscow. The unpredictable times dashed my hopes for a normal life. And deep down inside, although I certainly never admitted it or spoke it aloud, especially to Mama, I felt that Papa was already dead.

I imagined I was talking to God, a God I didn't really know up close and a God I wasn't quite sure heard me. But somewhere along the line, through my simple prayers, I knew I had made a connection. Something or someone had broken through to my heart. Maybe that's why I felt as though I recognized him in that flowery meadow. By calling out to him, I had begun to see him. I was longing for an inner place of peace like that.

The next year I had only begun my vacation when, literally, all hell broke loose in Russia. One morning at camp, in June 1941, we were having a late breakfast when the loudspeaker suddenly announced, "All men and women are to depart for home and report to their workstations immediately." We were told that Finland had just attacked Russia, so we were now at war. Certainly, we all *knew* it had to be the other way around, that Russia had invaded Finland, but no one dared to say this. We weren't idiots; to speak our minds would have been suicidal. Regardless of the endless military and political propaganda constantly spread by this regime, we all knew the real truth: Stalin was the oppressor, a perpetrator of evil. I considered him a devil.

All shortwave radios and private cars were confiscated, because the state saw them as tools for the discovery and dissemination of privileged information. We were permitted to receive news only via loudspeakers, which broadcast nothing but politically filtered and heavily censored local programs. Soviet leaders had no use for democracy or freedom, much less freedom of speech. Truth was alien to them. They were, instead, masters of deception. The party hated truth; it is too much like light. In fact, truth *is* light.

In August 1941 all of the village youth from the factories and the younger teachers, along with their high-school students, were mobilized to dig antitank trenches. We were told that the German invasion of Russia was now under way, as evidenced by the screeching planes overhead. Several hundred of us were strategically assigned to various locations along the road from Gorky to Moscow. The militia sent us about fifty miles down the Oka River toward Moscow. We were inching closer to the advancing Germans, and monstrous, paralyzing fear loomed in our hearts.

Three other girls and I were assigned to live in a small kolkhoz—a hut belonging to a young woman who worked in the bakery of a village near the river. She had a child, so that night six of us cramped together in one tiny room. The front lines were nearby, and we heard gunfire all night long. We were too scared to sleep.

At six o'clock the following morning, we were issued shovels and, in strict military fashion, marched more than six miles toward Moscow to our appointed work detail. There we learned everything we never wanted to know about digging trenches, entirely by hand, and carting away the dirt in small, flimsy wooden trolleys.

We were constantly under the suspicious eyes of harsh military officers, as if we and the students—instead of the Germans—were Russia's actual enemy. They must have expected escape attempts or a massive group desertion, but most of us were too afraid even to look at the officers the wrong way, much less to attempt a getaway. Under this dark, watchful command, we labored until our hands were blistered and bleeding. After only the first day, my hands looked like raw meat.

They gave us a half-hour break for lunch: a small piece of hard black bread, a chunk of unheated sausage of questionable origin, and a sip of water. We also had two ten-minute cigarette breaks during the day.

At about six that evening, we started an excruciatingly painful journey toward our temporary home. We were all overcome with weariness, near the point of collapse, with feet so tired and sore that they dragged as we tried to inch forward. Our meat-red hands were covered with blisters, and anything we touched adhered to our sticky, raw skin.

When we finally reached the kolkhoz late that evening, we collapsed on the floor, famished but too fatigued to eat. The lucky ones immediately fell asleep. I lay awake, thinking of Papa, Mama, and my anguish. Through half-open eyes, I watched the others as they slept. Waking up sometime after midnight, we went out to the well for water to heat on the stove so we could wash and treat our poor hands. We cooked millet cereal and potatoes and ate everything with our hands, like animals. Then, still fully clothed, we slept as if we had died.

The next day was the same. And the next. Aching, stiff, and sore beyond description, we got up to the early-morning calls that always came too soon. Without much complaint, we bandaged our bloody hands and started out again, day after day after day. This went on for several weeks with little diversion. The only good thing about our work was that we gradually developed heavy calluses on our hands, which helped us cope with the strenuous work assignments.

The military authorities allowed no malingering within the ranks, but many workers began to fail from the unbearably harsh physical, emotional, mental, and spiritual conditions. I was learning, through blood and toil, that hardship offers a chance at personal growth and character development. And through no choice of my own, I stretched my capacity to handle more than I ever thought I could. I was overwhelmed, exhausted, and yet still working. And sometimes, when we got into a rhythm of digging and shoveling and loading earth, I felt proud of working together to protect the people we loved.

One morning marching out to our work detail, we noticed a dense grouping of airplanes heading over us toward Gorky. None of us thought it too peculiar at the time, but later that afternoon we began to see flames and smoke on the horizon. Those airplanes were German bombers attacking Gorky. We were stricken with fear for our families and could not concentrate on our work. Many of us broke down and cried for our loved ones at home. I kept thinking of my mama and wondering and worrying—was she okay? I prayed for her, and I hoped that God heard me. Despite our anxiety, we had to work our full shift, and at quitting time, it was a very subdued and troubled column, about four hundred in all, who shouldered shovels and began our three-day journey back to Gorky, with no idea what we'd find when we got there.

We were walking in a small gully beside the road, following a meandering creek with reed-lined banks, when suddenly the German planes returned. They passed directly over us, but this time they strafed us with tracer bullets. I heard, "Quick! Dive!" then felt myself falling as a man's arm pushed me down a hill into the tall brush. Our hearts beat wildly with panic as we flattened out among the reeds of the creek. The assault began in the air with a dense spray of bullets that spread out as they struck the earth, making muffled noises as the projectiles penetrated the ground around us. I guess I was just *lucky* again that day, because the gunfire missed me by no more than three feet in any direction.

When the planes were gone and we began to get up, I was still so frightened I could no longer walk straight. My body shook involuntarily as I tried to move my feet along the road. Only a few in the group were slightly wounded from the gunfire that day— nothing serious, by the grace of God. No fatalities.

None of us slept that night—not a wink! We were not allowed to return home, and there was no information, except from the radio, which confirmed our fears that Gorky had been heavily bombed and damaged, along with the automobile factory and surrounding areas. There was no mention of casualties, but we all assumed that many lives and families were destroyed that day. Days later, much to my relief, I found out that Mama was okay. There had been only one casualty from our village, Ramona Rushton, an American woman. I was deeply saddened to learn of her fate, but I was also amazed and grateful that many more had not perished. I was learning not to look too far up the road, not to plan too far ahead, to take only one day at a time and then move on.

Our task grew even more difficult. That fall the days grew drastically colder, and that winter eventually developed into the coldest on record. It is said that Russia's brutal winter of 1941–42, the coldest of the century for that region, was instrumental in the Russians' repelling the German advances, leading to the eventual German defeat and Allied victory of 1945. The German attacks on Gorky continued coming from the air; the endless stretches of antitank trenches we dug with our hands were never put to the test.

But we kept digging in the bitter weather. I didn't know such cold existed, and it was very hard on even the strongest of us. I developed a severely inflamed instep from walking long miles in an ill-fitting felt boot. By great good fortune, I was granted some sick leave to have it treated at home, and the doctor gave me a pass to travel. My mother was then working in a hospital in our village, in charge of the linen supply, and I was again fortunate that the head doctor gave me a thorough examination and x-ray. He found my foot to be in extremely bad shape and prescribed extensive bed rest, which suited me just fine. He then gave me a document releasing me from further work in the trenches, at least for the time being.

Is this, too, an element of the divine? I speculated.

I recovered rather quickly and returned to my job in the Gorky auto factory, Autostroy, as the intensity of the war seemed to settle a bit. I had a fresh perspective about factory work now as I remembered my trench-digging days and my aching feet. Adversity is an amazing phenomenon.

I held a variety of jobs in Gorky. In 1942 I began working as secretary to the head of the tank-building department in the Gorky factory. Russia had started building its first tanks, the T (Tiger) series, the year before. I only worked there for a few weeks, but the experience was a bright spot for me. My boss, a Russian nicknamed Domino, was a man of genuine sensitivity and compassion. He took me under his wing, in a sense, and went out of his way to be considerate to me. He also provided a fine job for my former math teacher, whom I happened to find one day, starving to death on the streets of Gorky. Domino's generosity toward me and my teacher was a rare humane occurrence.

Then I found a new job as clerk and secretary of the people's court. This was the civil court, where people charged with crimes other than political ones would stand trial. It was convenient— right in the village, just a few houses away from ours. But if my own life and circumstances were bad, in the court I saw more of the same and worse.

The prisoners were mostly Russian nationals, the motherland's own, everyday hardworking people just trying to get by, causing no one harm. Most had been arrested on trumped-up charges of petty crime. And even when an actual crime had been committed, the punishment always outweighed the offense; execution or deportation were routine sentences for the least alleged infraction. The officials never listened to the defendants' explanations or cries for justice; in fact, the officials actually laughed in the defendants' faces at these hearings. Each story of suffering and injustice was different, but each was also the same. I could only stand this for about nine months, and then I left voluntarily. I could not be impartial to the pitiful prisoners I saw brought into court from the prison. So much human misery marched in front of me every day that my heart couldn't take it any longer. Why such unnecessary ruthlessness and cruelty? I didn't understand. The only answer I ever found was the evil that dwells in the hearts of men.

After my brief stint with the court, I returned to the factory as a secretary again. This position involved traveling from our village into the city, which I enjoyed, but traveling also caused new problems. Every morning I walked about twenty minutes to a streetcar stop so I could take a short ride, then transfer to a second streetcar, which took me the rest of the way to work. It sounds simple, but the streetcars often didn't run, or they ran terribly late, and they were always crowded. Like many others in the same predicament, I often hitchhiked to arrive at work on time.

Being late for work was considered a crime, and absences from work required a written and verifiable excuse from a doctor. During the war, infractions were sometimes severely punished, including by imprisonment. Since everyone was under the same constraints, the Russian people were generally willing to help others. On several occasions, when I could see the streetcar was already overcrowded, I'd wait until it stopped, and then I'd climb up the back and in through one of the rear windows. This usually required assistance, and someone already on board helped me every time. When the streetcar moved, people literally hung outside the door, on the steps, holding on to wherever they could, to ensure they would not be late for work. These episodes must have looked like a circus.

When hitchhiking or bus climbing didn't work, I would sometimes jump onto the back of a passing truck and then leap off in the next town. It was very tricky as well as dangerous. But I was successful; I lived. My gymnastics background proved quite useful.

I thanked God for my early childhood athletic experience, and I was able to get to work on time in most instances. My exploits brought plenty of personal exhilaration to my otherwise despondent life. I lost many buttons and sometimes arrived disheveled and scraped, but I always arrived smiling. If Mama had known the risks I took, I'm sure she'd have had a heart attack. But then again, Mama prayed.

☆

Later in 1942, at a dance in Gorky, I met two British officers—Mac and Leslie. They were delighted to find someone who spoke English. Mac was short, stout, and muscular with black hair and a thick black beard. Leslie was tall, thin, and clean shaven with pale features. They were part of a crew of instructors who were teaching Russian soldiers how to operate the English tanks, a contractual part of the Allies' lease-lend pact with Russia. Leslie was the quiet, reserved type who did most of the thinking, while Mac was a confident jokester who was never at a loss for words.

The three of us struck up a unique bond and friendship. They lived in a hotel in the city and had no other friends. These guys were a breath of fresh air to me in the midst of my galling life. I admired and respected them for their frank compassion, integrity, and unconditional friendship, and I think I kept them from being so lonely. Mac and Leslie provided me with support, encouragement, and amusement. They were funny, best friends, like Laurel and Hardy, and as wildly different as America and Russia. Unsuspectingly, they would also play a pivotal role in my future.

One day Mac asked if he and Leslie could visit me at my home in the village. "Please, Margie. There's nothing to worry about, really!" he said.

I hesitated. I didn't want them to see our living conditions. We had moved from that abominable little room to another, which was not much less abominable. Reluctantly, though, I agreed; I trusted them and wanted them to meet my mother and my other friends.

So Leslie and Mac came for a visit. In spite of our humble conditions and my sadness that I had no treats to offer them, we had a great time. My fears seemed unfounded, for these deficiencies didn't matter to them. They were really happy to be with us; we talked and laughed and even danced to some old American records that I borrowed from a neighbor. And I treasured my relationship with them all the more.

Our time together ended much too quickly. I was broken-hearted when I learned that we'd have to say our permanent good-byes. They were due to leave Russia in just a few days, returning to England upon completion of their military tour.

"Margie, what can we do for you? Whatever it is, just name it. If there's anything we can do…," Mac generously offered while Leslie stood back and nodded in sad agreement. They both knew that, more than anything, Mama and I wanted to return to the States. Papa had been gone nearly five years now, and we didn't have much hope that he was still alive. They promised to help us in any way they could.

Those fine men kept their promise. A month or so after their departure, Leslie and Mac sent us a telegram from England. It said, in effect, "Dear Margaret: We went to the American Consulate in London and told them about your case. They said they would look into it, but they were not sure what they could do to help. I have other ideas. I will be in touch soon. Best regards, Mac."

They had tried all possible avenues to help but couldn't find any practical solution to our plight. Although my friends could not have known it, this telegram would forever alter the course of my life. I know they meant well and only tried to help us, but their good intentions were miscalculated. The Russians, of course, censored all foreign mail.

I have only myself to blame for this serious lack of foresight. This incident would become the primary reason for my misfortunes, which began in 1945. However, there were no immediate repercussions. For the time being, life went on as usual. And despite the outcome, I was always grateful to my British friends for their support and genuine kindness to Mama and me.

1932, the ocean liner *Hamburg* carrying the Ford employees and their families toward Russia. Margaret (second row, fourth from right in scarf) with Elisabeth behind her (to right of woman waving) and Carl Werner (identified with arrow)

Margaret (age 4),
Detroit, 1925

Carl, Elisabeth, and Margaret
on board the *Hamburg,* April 1932

Margaret (seated in
front), Carl (third
from right),
Elisabeth (fourth
from right),
Gorky's American
Village, 1934

Carl, Gorky, between 1933 and 1938

Margaret, in the photo she tried to give her father on the day of his arrest, "For Papa Darling from your loving daughter, June 29, 1938"

Carl (first row, second from right), Ford's Autostroy tool and die design shop, Gorky, 1933

Margaret (on chair, bottom right), Sanya Dubcek (front row, far left),
high school graduation class, Gorky, 1939

Margaret (age 19),
Gorky, November 1940

Margaret (age 21),
working in Gorky, 1942

Margaret (top right), Tamara (center, with book), "Flower Waltz,"
the Inta ballet group, 1955

Margaret, "Snake Dance,"
the Inta ballet group, 1955

Margaret (soon after her release)
and Elisabeth, Russia, 1955

Newly wed Margaret and
Günter Tobien, Inta, 1955

Margaret and Karl (four months old),
Inta, 1956

Günter, Inta, November 1956

Karl, Hanover, Germany,
September 1959

Karlie and Grandma Elisabeth,
coming home! SS *Statendam,* 1961

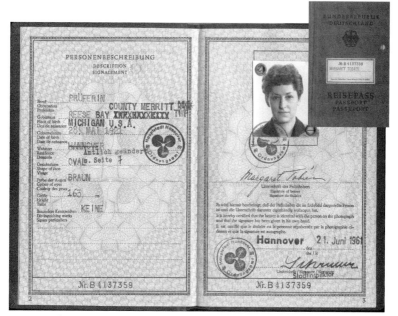

Margaret's West German passport

Margaret (still an acrobat at age 53) Orlando, Florida, 1974

Karl and Günter, father-son reunion, Cincinnati, 1995

Margaret Werner Tobien, Cincinnati, 1996: "My life has come full circle."

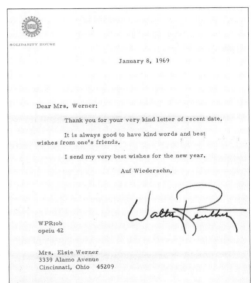

SOLIDARITY HOUSE

January 8, 1969

Dear Mrs. Werner:

Thank you for your very kind letter of recent date.

It is always good to have kind words and best wishes from one's friends.

I send my very best wishes for the new year.

Auf Wiedersehn,

WPR:ob
opeiu 42

Mrs. Elsie Werner
3339 Alamo Avenue
Cincinnati, Ohio 45209

Letter from Walter Reuther, January 8, 1969

Walter Reuther's skates: "Call me when you come back home, and we'll go skating."

Eight

POTATOES AND PRAYERS

In the terrible first winter of the war, Mama took an authorized two-week vacation from her job at the clinic. She walked almost ten miles to a kolkhoz that needed immediate help with potato harvesting since all the men had been drafted into the war. There was no time to spare; the potatoes needed to be taken from the ground to prevent rotting. The crop was very important, because many people were starving to death. Potatoes were a major staple, and we needed them desperately ourselves. The deal was this: first fill three sacks of potatoes for the kolkhoz, and then the fourth one is yours.

Because nothing was mechanized, potato harvesting was very hard work. Stooping, lifting, carrying, Mama managed to earn four sacks of potatoes; she filled a total of sixteen sacks. When she finished, however, she could bring only one sack home with her at a time. It was a six-mile walk, and she had to strap one sack of potatoes to her back and leave the other three sacks at the farm. She was frustrated that she could manage only one sack and worried that the others would be stolen before she could return for them. But Mama prayed—even for those sacks of potatoes—that they would not be found until she returned to get them.

Depending on who you were, in Russia a sack of potatoes could mean life or death. Those potatoes meant the world to us! We tried to find a way to transport the three remaining sacks, which were hidden in an old storage shed under some farming supplies. We found no one willing or able to help us bring them back. Before we could return for them, the full brunt of Russian winter struck, and all of our hidden potatoes froze solid. They were still untouched, however—according to Mama's prayers—in the place she had hidden them.

During the next month, Mama made three trips back there, all alone, braving the deadly cold Soviet winter, to claim her hidden treasures. She dragged a sled across the wide and frozen Oka River. With her hands and feet void of all sensation, she was nearly frostbitten on those journeys. But her heart warmed to find that her frozen potatoes, by God's providence, were still where she had hidden them. Then, at the same frigid snail's pace, numbed to the bone, she returned home—one agonizing trip and sack at a time.

Her return trips were doubly treacherous, because she had to drag the sled loaded with frozen potatoes. Entering our room from those trips in that insane cold, suffering from the loss of muscular control, she would have fallen across the doorway and onto the floor if I hadn't helped her. Each time she would rest for a few minutes and then begin preparing our potato feast for two. (We always wished it was dinner for three, as we were ever aware of someone missing from our evening table.) Mama didn't complain about those journeys; she just continued as if everything were normal. And I didn't complain either, because I was so happy to see her return safely. I never told her, but every time she went after those precious potatoes, I also prayed.

The flavor of those potatoes could be described only two ways: bad and worse. The two of us cooked them in every way imaginable, but nothing disguised their horrid taste. Improvisation and creativity didn't matter. They were always the same; they were always horrible! But Mama would smile and say, "Maidie, they might not taste worth a plug nickel, but now we have more potatoes to eat! And don't forget to thank God for all he has provided."

Mama and I sometimes told potato jokes to each other, just to take the edge off, and then we'd laugh. It made it easier to face those hideous things. They were just too bad to be taken seriously.

"Tonight I'm going to make you the best potatoes you've ever had in your life," Mama would announce.

I'd look at her and answer, "Right, Mama, I know!" and then we'd both laugh uncontrollably.

"And tomorrow, Maidie, what if I made you some mashed potatoes? Or would you like them fried instead?"

I'd answer, "No, Mama, but let's make a big pot to send to Stalin! He will surely appreciate them!"

No matter what we did to them, those nasty potatoes caused a painful throat irritation that wouldn't go away for days. But since we had little else, we ate more potatoes and laughed at more potato jokes. We never seemed to run out of them. But horrible as they were, I think they saved our lives. I'll never forget them, ever!

During the war, food became supremely important. We never threw out even the smallest speck of food, no matter what it was or how bad it was. We treasured every bite. We didn't peel the potatoes, carrots, or any other vegetables we could get our hands on; we ate every bit as is. We couldn't afford to lose even the smallest morsel of food, so we ate every breadcrumb that fell on or off the table.

We ate things we'd never considered to be food. A friend of ours worked in the factory's chemical lab, and occasionally he smuggled out glycerin. When we added that to our supply of cranberries, we produced a crude form of jelly. The taste was tolerable, but the stuff caused intestinal problems. Castor oil, purchased at the drugstore, was used to lightly coat a frying pan. We made omelets from an egg powder, which the store routinely issued as a meat substitute. We ate these things in desperation. The harsh reality was that we were both starving, but we were still obliged to work very hard at our jobs, seven days a week, without vacations or holidays, while our city was increasingly targeted by German bombings.

Not everyone survived these conditions; we saw neighbors and friends dying. At first I thought my increasing stomach pains were from tension, but finally I saw a doctor and was diagnosed with severe stomach ulcers. The doctor could do nothing other than prescribe a mild diet with plenty of milk and plenty of rest. The irony didn't escape any of us. But I was issued a meal card that allowed me to get one meal a day at the factory's dietary dining room. There I was able to eat some meat, and I received a half loaf of white bread with sweetened condensed milk. I dug a hole in the loaf and poured the milk inside, then wrapped it inside my coat so I could take it back to Mama. Like me, Mama craved sweets, and the condensed milk was as close as we could get.

"But, Maidie, this is for you. You must eat. You need your strength! I can do without it," was her usual response, although she too was thin and weak.

And as we struggled to survive, we also struggled to hope. Where, oh, where on earth was my dear papa? Was he still alive?

Around this time a stranger came to see us, saying he had just been released from the brutal labor camp in Krasnoyarsk, in Siberia. Mama and I already knew something of the dreaded camp. Krasnoyarsk was commonly known as the place where men went to die. But this man had survived, he said, and now had a job outside the camp. He told us, "I knew your father...and your husband, Mrs. Werner. I knew Carl well. He was...er, um, I mean...he *is* a fine man. I liked him very much. All he ever spoke about was his wife and his daughter, and now I have met them. He works at chopping trees in the forests."

I was beside myself with excitement. "Well, when did you see him? How does he look? And did he say anything else? Tell me...tell me, please," I urged him, unable to get my questions out fast enough.

The man just smiled at us very kindly, reassured us that he indeed knew my father, and added, "I'm going back to Krasno-yarsk in a couple of days. I would be happy to take him anything you would like to send."

We wanted very much to believe this guy, but there was some-thing about him that didn't seem quite right. Something was disin-genuous about him. His mannerisms seemed too polished for someone who had recently been released from such a villainous labor camp. He seemed too clean and maybe too sane to have just returned from the ill-famed Krasnoyarsk. I suspected he was a con man who didn't know my father at all. Or perhaps he'd actually been there with Papa, but maybe my father was dead by now, and this man wanted to take advantage of Papa's family. That was a dis-tinct possibility; we knew such things had happened to people. Maybe we should ignore his cunning request.

But Mama didn't want to chance it. And deep down, neither did I.

Accepting the stranger's report, we packed all my father's warm clothing, his leather boots, sheepskin jacket, sweaters, socks, and underwear. We even gave the man some money for his trip back. Of course there was no way we could be sure these items were ever delivered to Papa. Con men often appeared out of nowhere, tak-ing advantage of bereaved families as opportunities arose. It was a way of life for some, getting one over on good-natured and honest people when their guard was down. But as for Mama and me, even if this was just another human vulture with a smooth, silver-tongued delivery, we *had* to believe him! If faith is, in fact, "being sure of what we hope for," then we certainly had faith.

That first year of the war was by far the most difficult. The civilian population was caught by surprise, unprepared to endure the hardships. By the second year, however, Gorky was better equipped; many of us had planted gardens, which provided us with fresh vegetables and potatoes—the edible kind. This produce was especially important because rarely did we get the rations we were promised. Food rations quickly became black-market items, too costly for our meager earnings. Nothing was available in the stores, aside from leaden bread, baked with frozen potatoes mixed with flour. If we wanted the bread, we had to wait in line for hours. It tasted horrible, but it provided some nutrition.

Starving people are desperate. In Russia we did what we had to do in order to endure. We traded whatever we had—clothes, fabrics, curtains, pots and pans—on the black market for food that was brought into the city by peasants working on the collective farms. We knew others who traded much more than their belongings. Multitudes of women sold themselves in order to survive. They wandered the streets of the main city and would stand in front of the factory, especially on paydays, looking for prospects. Many women felt this choice was necessary; many of them were keeping their families alive. Still, I knew in my heart that prostitution was out of the question; Mama and I were prepared to accept death as the alternative.

Both of us donated blood about once a month just to get the hot meal that was served to the donors on those days and the much-coveted worker's class-ration card, issued to a fortunate few. Mama donated four pints of blood, and I donated eight, until we both began to suffer from severe anemia. Eventually we were both turned down from donating more.

Our building no longer had central heating, because a bomb had destroyed the city's power station, but we were able to keep our room relatively warm. We had acquired a small tin stove, about one foot in diameter, which we stationed in the middle of the room. This stove, a small but treasured gift, doubled as our cooking unit, burning wood, coal, or peat as fuel. But in the middle of this brutal winter, it was nearly impossible to find something to burn. We routinely risked our lives to steal bits of wooden fences in the middle of the night or to swipe some coal and peat from the coal yard, which was usually under armed guard. Had we been caught trying to preserve our lives this way, we would have been executed.

One night I was returning to our apartment. As always, I was looking for any kind of fuel. In the almost total darkness of the street, I noticed some scraps of wood. Very discreetly, I placed three or four small pieces in the inner part of my coat lining, completely hidden from view. I knew it was safe, because there were no lights, no one was around, and I was only a hundred yards from our apartment. I would be safely inside in no time at all. Walking down the street toward my building, with my wood secretly tucked inside my coat, I heard a shout from behind.

"Lady! Stop in your tracks and do not move!"

I stopped immediately, paralyzed with fear.

"Now turn around slowly and walk toward me." About thirty yards away, a military guard approached me with his revolver drawn.

I was fully aware of my surroundings; there was no one else in sight. I had absolutely no idea where this guard could have come from. Like the devil, he simply appeared out of nowhere. *Surely this is it!* My mind raced. I already knew what the penalty would be. I was even too scared to pray.

I was most afraid of looking the guard in the face. I was sure he'd see or smell the fear I was radiating. All I could do was hope that God would blind him or render him stupid so he wouldn't know what I'd done.

I stood frozen, thinking, *Should I confess my crime and appeal to his sense of mercy? Or should I make a break for it and see if I can outrun him?* Those were my two options. Running didn't make any sense; he had a gun. So I just stood there like a puppet, in shock, ready to accept my penalty.

The cold black steel barrel of his revolver stared right at my nose. He spoke harshly, "Your name, citizen? And what are you doing here?" I figured he would search me.

"My naaame…," I began to reply. Then suddenly a voice rang out in the distance, calling him as if there was an emergency.

I was stunned. I saw no one else there. I heard the voice call the guard, but I couldn't detect where the voice came from. The guard, the one I thought would surely seal my fate, turned away as I was in midsentence, and he went crashing off into the icy Gorky night. It was as if he had forgotten me, as if I were no longer there. Was it the voice of a friend I could not see? Was it an angel assigned to watch over me? Did God answer my unspoken prayer?

What I know is that only moments earlier no one else had been there, as far as the eye could see in any direction. Then the guard appeared out of nowhere to confront me, and then, beyond explanation, he was gone. I couldn't deny what had just happened. I stood there for another minute, looking up in utter astonishment at the dark, silent heavens.

Though I didn't understand what had just taken place, I was deeply thankful. I felt strongly that it was supernatural, miraculous. I knew it more in my heart than in my head. I was humbled and grateful in a way I hadn't felt in a long time, remembering Mama's words and her constant, fervent prayer, "Don't worry, Maidie. God will get us through this!"

I whispered, "Thank you," and began to sob.

I felt my way home, shaking and crying, walked through the

door of our apartment, and fell to my knees. Mama ran over to see what was wrong. "What is it, Maidie? What happened to you?" she asked. I couldn't speak for a while. When we put the wood pieces into the stove and lit them, I cried, and then Mama cried and thanked God the rest of that night for sparing my life.

Rumor had it that an old friend, a Czech woman I hadn't seen in a couple of years, had recently been executed for that very infraction, for stealing wood for her own survival.

In the daily ritual with our stove, within minutes of finishing our cooking, the room became deathly cold, so we quickly climbed into our beds, clothes and all, and tried to keep as warm as possible. We were fortunate to have a feather bed, purchased from a German family who left the country before the war. It helped, but the word *cold* was an awful understatement for what we felt in this place, especially at night!

After we survived that dreadful winter, we faced a new threat. In June 1942 the Germans began a massive aerial bombardment of the Gorky factory and all the surrounding villages. For thirty days straight, they employed the same tactics and ran exactly the same missions, night after night. Every night, precisely at midnight, they attacked the same targets as the night before. They never deviated from this regimen, but we always feared that their attack strategies might change. We were on constant alert, prepared at all times, our eyes always wide open, because our very lives were forever at risk. We learned to grab a minute's sleep whenever and wherever we could.

By the initial element of surprise and the steady pressure of superior military weaponry and tactics, the Germans all but obliterated Gorky. Despite the havoc, I wasn't specifically afraid of dying. Perhaps I was just naive, but something inside told me not to panic. I certainly had reason to fear: destruction and human agony were everywhere. But somehow I knew I'd get through. I didn't fear my own death; I feared more for the lives of others. Somehow I knew that Mama and I would live to see another day and another time.

As the nightly bombings mounted and took their toll on Gorky and the surrounding areas, we happened upon a perfectly inconspicuous and safe place to hide. About two miles outside the village, along the river, obscured by a thicket of trees and brush, was a small, partially underground, dugout trench. A man from the village had accidentally found the opening, heavily covered by vines and summer overgrowth, while hunting rabbits with his dog. We thought it might have been a former war bunker, but no one knew for sure. It was a hole, in essence—a room about fifteen feet by ten feet, reinforced throughout by heavy wooden support beams and floorboards that had been carved into the side of a river knoll. No one lived nearby, and even a stray German bomb would never find this location.

About fifty of us knew of the place, and we were sworn to

secrecy. Mama and I headed there about ten o'clock every night, and we would stay there until the bombings ended. Our building in the village remained intact, but we didn't know how long that would last. Many houses were destroyed daily and nightly as the village was slowly reduced to rubble. Since we could pretty accurately predict the nightly attacks, it made sense to get out of the way if at all possible. But some villagers stayed in their homes. And some lost their lives as a result.

By now even the most basic foods, like the bread we could formerly rely upon, were becoming less and less plentiful. We all tried harder to improvise and find alternative foods, but often there were no alternatives. Many people, especially the small children, became deathly ill from starvation and the extreme cold. The "very little" they had counted on to get by was replaced by "none." The war persisted, ruthless and uncaring. Men, women, and children died daily by the thousands. I'll never forget the shrieking sound of the bombs falling around us, the endless miles of burning debris, carrying the injured and the dead to the clinic where Mama worked, or the sickening smell of burning flesh. It is said that Leningrad suffered the worst; there the bodies of small children were piled up on the streets and pulled through the snow on sleds for burial by other small children, who might soon follow them.

Beyond my comprehension, my mother seemed barely fazed by it all. It sometimes seemed she was living another life in another place, as if she was here, but yet she wasn't. I thought she was a consummate actress, but I knew she had to be feeling all this horror somewhere deep inside, in a place no one except God knew about. She always stayed firm. I think her own personal hell had occurred in 1938 when the NKVD took away her husband, and perhaps no other hell could ever be quite as bad.

During the raids, when Mama had to report for duty to her clinic, I usually stayed at home to rescue the few belongings we had in case of a direct hit. Sometimes I took cover in a nearby trench, which served as a makeshift bomb shelter, and covered myself with boards or whatever I could find for protection. I preferred to stand in our building's entranceway, watching the skies in nervous anticipation. We came to know the nightly raids well, but we could never predict their results. One terrifying night came after another, and we never knew how many more of them we would live to see.

The attacks always lasted exactly three hours, and then we faced a massive cleanup. Across the street from us lived a married couple, my former biology teacher and the principal. One night an incendiary bomb struck their apartment house; it could have easily been ours instead. The building was instantly reduced to a heap of rubble. A small alarm clock, a wicker laundry basket, and a book were the only things left intact. Amazingly though, their lives were spared. And judging from the look of their former building, this must have been a miracle, a circumstance of inexplicable mercy. Violence and trauma were so widespread, so unfathomable, that anything good came as a blessed surprise.

Nine

NIKOLAI'S DANCE

While the sand slipped through the opening
And their hands reached for the golden ring
With their hearts they turned to each other's hearts for refuge,
In the troubled years that came before the deluge....
Now let the music keep our spirits high
And let the buildings keep our children dry
Let creation reveal its secrets by and by
By and by—
When the light that's lost within us reaches the sky.
—Jackson Browne, *Before the Deluge*

t had been five long years since I'd last seen my former camp swimming instructor, Nikolai. Even then I had seen him only during the summers, because he lived in Kiev. In the dreadful days of the war, I often recalled the times we spent together before Papa was taken, when we'd swim in the Oka and be with our friends at the clubhouse. They were by far the happiest days of my life. Nik would often point out a plane overhead, pull me close, and say, "I'll be up there one day, Margaret. Just watch. I'll be flying just like that!" I remembered him with longing and delight. Maybe it really was love, because throughout all the difficult years that ensued, Nikolai never left my mind. I always hoped that maybe, just maybe, he loved me too. But I never knew for sure.

When he graduated from high school, Nikolai entered a select military flight academy in the Urals to begin intensive training. His dream was to become a fighter pilot. We had corresponded a few times, but after he left for the Urals, we wrote each other regularly, and it was through those letters that we both realized how much we cared for each other, though we had never even exchanged a kiss. Nikolai's letters gave me hope for a better future. Except for wanting Papa to come home, I longed for Nikolai's letters more than anything.

I dreamed about him constantly, especially during the bad times. I imagined being with him, holding him. I pictured a life in the future, with Nikolai and children and peace. In the middle of all the muck of our life in Gorky, those thoughts helped to get me through. Along with the dreams of seeing my papa come through the door, these happy visions sustained me through some terrible days. I sensed that God was with me, and I knew that Mama always prayed. But dreaming of Nikolai helped me separate myself from the chaos and horror. He gave me something personal, something beautiful to hope for.

In those waking dreams, he was the love of my life, my husband, and the father of my children. We'd walk along the river together, laughing and holding hands, in the thick green grass of summer, hearing the birds sing while our two children frolicked behind. I didn't know if Nik had dreams like that; I only hoped he did. I'm sure I needed the mental and emotional preoccupation of those dreams, but I felt they were much more than daydreams. My heart felt there was truly something special between us.

When the war began, Nik and I lost contact. I didn't know where he was or what he was doing. His military obligations took first priority and prevented him from contacting me. During that time, because of the war, Stalin's madness, and the political machinery everywhere, everyone's life was in utter disarray.

In my heart I believed that Nikolai truly loved me, but basic survival needs overwhelmed my sensitivities, though they never lessened my feelings for him. In the few precious solitary times I had, I made the most of the imaginings, longings, and fantasies of my mind. Those dreams always featured an athletic, blue-eyed Russian boy who loved me.

My friends and I grew accustomed to the incessant bombings, lack of sleep, and lack of food. These were a part of our everyday lives. Eventually we even went to the movies and the city dances again. These facilities were still operating, despite the constant dangers. While we could never completely forget the painful reality of the war, we were determined to have some fun. One evening, through a friend of mine at work, four of us girls obtained tickets to a very special ball in town, about six miles away. We borrowed and traded the prettiest clothes we could find and did each other's hair. For one night, we wanted to look like the young women we were.

It was a bitterly cold evening, and we had to walk so far to the streetcar stop that our feet were nearly frostbitten when we arrived at the club. This was not a sophisticated nightclub but an old, damaged public building in the center of town. We shoved our way through the crowds of people in the lobby who had no tickets and finally, through much commotion, squeezed our way inside. My friend Rudolph met us there, took us upstairs, and hung up our heavy coats. He then walked us to another room with an old upright piano. He sat down and played us the latest hit from America but with German lyrics: *Bei Mir Bist Du Schön* (You Are Beautiful to Me). We loved it! Of course, I loved anything that came from America, because that was *home*!

Downstairs in the ballroom, a small band was playing courageously, and my girlfriends and I began to dance with one another. The war made available men scarce, so Rudolph dutifully danced with each of us in turn. The music got inside us as we twirled in our pretty dresses. Even with little Rudolph, I felt young, alive, beautiful. We were having such a grand time that we almost forgot about the war, Russia, and the subzero night outside. Suddenly Rudolph stopped on the dance floor, facing me. He raised his eyebrows and blurted out, "So…how long have you known Nikolai, and where did you meet?"

His question caught me completely off guard. I was bewildered. Why was he talking about my dream hero in this improbable place? Rudolph calmly explained, "Oh yeah, Maidie, Nik and I grew up and went to school together. Didn't I tell you?" I stood still, my mouth wide open, wondering why he was telling me this now.

Then Rudolph winked and continued, "And did I neglect to tell you that he is upstairs waiting for you right now?"

Everything stopped.

My heart skipped a few beats, and I thought, *Surely I'm dreaming. Did I hear him correctly, or am I imagining things?*

Slowly, as if in a trance, I walked up the wide marble stairs, one step after the other, until, at the very top of the staircase, I saw a man in an air force officer's uniform waiting for me. I stopped, holding the handrail, and stared up at him. Those wide blue eyes locked with mine. It *was* Nikolai! Only he looked so different. His hair was darker and his face paler than in our days on the water. The bones in his face were more prominent, and his shoulders were wider. He had become a man since our eyes last met.

Nik leaned down and took my hand. He drew me up the last few steps, never turning away his gaze. I saw in his face that I was different too. As if in a mirror, I saw my face flushed with dancing, my hair swept up for the party, my whole body alive. We wrapped our arms around each other and stood there, speechless, holding on tightly for what seemed like an eternity. Words were not necessary. Shock, amazement, joy, and hope passed through me like electric currents. I could feel his heart beating through the thick wool of the uniform.

Long moments passed, and when our bottled-up emotions began to subside, we managed to walk to the refreshment room. There we sat and talked, our arms around each other. We did dance together a bit, but we wanted to talk and look at each other and embrace. *Bei Mir Bist Du Schön.*

We had so many things to learn! He told me about his family, his brothers and sister, and his own papa. His family had nearly been destroyed by the regime's cruel, forced collectivization in the farmlands of Kiev, where his father had owned land. "They butchered our lives," he said.

Nik also remembered my family. He asked, "Maidie, how is your mama? How is she doing? Is there any news about your father?"

"Everything is still the same, Nikolai. Mama's fine," I answered, "and we've heard nothing yet about Papa that has made any sense. Let's just talk about us, okay?"

The hours passed like minutes. The dance ended. The musicians closed up their cases. Soon we were the only ones left in the building, paying no attention to the time, not even noticing the others depart. We were the last to leave. We didn't want to separate—ever! Life felt complete, perfect, even if we had died there that night in each other's arms.

Nik walked me all the way back to our building in the village at about three o'clock, both of us completely exhausted. I could hardly stand to let him go, to let go of this vision of happiness. We made plans for him to come back the next evening to meet my mother. I had already told him so much about her, and Mama had listened to me chatter enthusiastically about Nik for years. He said good-bye and kissed me softly once more.

The next day was Sunday, and time couldn't pass quickly enough for me! I couldn't eat a thing all day. I just sat and watched the door, waiting for *the knock,* as I recited to Mama all the details about the previous night with Nik. Mama was thrilled for me, as I knew she would be. She couldn't wait to meet him. She even primped a little bit, more than I had seen since Papa's days, putting on her best dress and asking, "How do I look, Maidie?"

"Oh, Mama, don't worry. You look just fine," I responded, never turning my eyes from the door.

When we finally heard Nikolai's knock, I flung open the door and fell into his arms. He filled our tiny room with his gladness, strength, and energy. Mama was taken with him right away. She didn't have to say a word. As Nikolai talked and laughed with her, her open smile of approval said it all.

"You were right, Maidie," said Nikolai, smiling at Mama. "She's even lovelier than I imagined!" That was the clincher. Mama was usually a tough sell, but Nik's genuine, magnetic personality reeled her in. He was naturally generous and outgoing. It was an overwhelming thumbs-up approval from my mother; she loved Nikolai too. I knew she would!

Among the three of us there was an unspoken mutual affirmation. Future plans were made, formalized, and confirmed within minutes, and not a word had to be spoken; our hearts knew. We didn't need a rehearsal for our unspoken exchange. I felt it was a divine appointment that Nik felt exactly as I did. When we looked at each other, we knew we were destined for one another. And our relationship was clear to all three hearts. As we began to talk together, I saw that Nik's affection for me included Mama; he wanted to care for her too. Dazed and happy, I noticed I was thinking again in terms of three!

Nik and I sat on the couch with Mama and excitedly discussed our future: marriage, children, the United States, in no particular order but in complete agreement. How Mama smiled, how Nik laughed, with his arm around me, and how my heart soared on the wings of love and joy. This was another evening of absolute bliss, two marvelous days in a row. *Bei Mir Bist Du Schön.*

Early the next morning Nikolai had to return to Leningrad, where he was stationed. There he would make arrangements with his unit commander for me to come see him the following weekend so we could finalize our wedding plans. I kissed him once more at the door, my heart full of joy. Now I had to tend to all the details and make as many advance preparations as I could. Just how and when could we finally get married? And where? Oh my, there was so much to do and so many things to consider, and all in the middle of a brutal war. I had no idea how we'd be able to pull it off.

I didn't expect to hear from Nik for a few days, but no letter had come by the end of the week. Two weeks passed, and I hadn't heard a word. I was frantic with worry and fear. The waiting became too much. I paced the floors for days. I paced our street. I paced the entire village, and still there was no word. I was ready to pull my hair out, because I needed my dear Nikolai, and I didn't know why I hadn't heard from him after all this time.

Finally I received a letter from Nikolai's commanding officer. Nikolai had been flying an aid mission north of Moscow as air support for the weakened Soviet resistance. His plane had been shot down. In that moment my hope was severed, my dream killed, and my world destroyed. My Nikolai was gone, and so was my reason for living.

When I phoned and pleaded for more information, I was told that the wreckage of his plane had been found and his body identified. The part of my heart that was reserved for Nikolai was ripped out. He was shot down only two days after he had returned to Leningrad from Gorky, from being with me. Only four nights before he died, the two of us danced to our hearts' content and dreamed the night away, as if we would live forever, as if Nik and I were already one, as if the world would never end.

After reading the letter, I crawled into a ball in the corner of the room and wept with an agony I'd never felt before and haven't felt since. Mama sat on the floor and cried with me. *Devastated* doesn't begin to describe the pain that consumed me for weeks afterward. When I lost Papa, I lost the security and joy of our family life, the past and the present. But when I lost Nikolai, I lost my future, the prospect of any happiness to come. And I have never felt love for a man the way I did for Nikolai. *Bei Mir Bist Du Schön.*

I did not know how I could go on. Blindly, I went to work again, came home again, tried to stay alive, but a deep new sorrow settled in my heart that never completely left. How do you forge ahead when your heart has been shattered? For a very long time I could not enjoy any kind of leisure or recreation. Russia, along with this evil war, had killed my smile.

I had planned to join Nikolai in Leningrad. Later I heard what had happened to the people of that city, trapped there during the nine-hundred-day German blockade. Ten thousand people died there every day from starvation, disease, and cold. No city or area of the country suffered more. More than one million Leningraders died during the siege of their city. In fact, Leningrad became a symbol of the unbearable suffering all of Russia experienced during the war with Germany.

If I'd gone to Leningrad as planned, I would probably have died there. This drastic realization seemed like a sign, something that maybe God used to bring me back around again after my sudden and tragic loss of Nikolai.

I began working again in the automotive factory as a secretary. I did well in my job and got along with my boss, Andre, though others thought he was an ogre. I'd worked for him earlier in the tank department, and he asked me to begin teaching English to his nine-year-old son, Sasha. Once a week, before work, I was driven to Andre's apartment to have a light breakfast with Sasha and his mother and to give him an English lesson. Then they would drive me back to work. Sasha was a delightful little boy, a joy to me in this joyless time. His bright face and eager ways raised my spirits; we'd even laugh over his jokes and English pronunciations. I've wondered for years whatever became of him. His smile could light up an entire room, and it put a spark in the darkness of my heart.

Mama and I finally moved out of that hateful little room, which was suitable only for a small family of cockroaches, into a larger room of another building, part of a three-room apartment with a communal kitchen, bathtub, and toilet. The two other rooms were occupied by the head doctor and gynecologist of the clinic where Mama worked. Now we at least had a kitchen, bathtub, and toilet, even though they were shared with the other two tenants. This was as close to privacy as we would ever come during these precarious times in Gorky.

We struggled on through the war years. Many men—actually just boys at the time—who had come over with us from Detroit and others from the village were killed, exiled, imprisoned, or disappeared mysteriously during the war. The population I had known changed drastically after I graduated from high school in 1939. I kept a class photograph, and within five years most of the handsome young men in the picture had been killed; only two of them returned, with nearly fatal wounds. My former gym teacher lost both legs. I was numb with grief for the lost men of my generation, but most of all I mourned for Nikolai. Though I was still alive, my future was gone.

Ten

ARRESTED

On May 7, 1945, we heard on the radio that the war was finally over. People spilled out of their apartments and danced in the streets, cheering wildly until they were hoarse. Russians celebrated their survival even as they mourned the millions—approximately twenty-seven million people, military and civilians—who had been killed in some of the most brutal and intense fighting the world has ever seen. But even at peace, Russia was still ruthlessly ruled by Stalin.

On a cold night in December 1945, I was visiting some friends only a few houses away from where I still lived with Mama. We chatted and relaxed after work. We were all wishing out loud for a few new clothes and some much-needed shoes, since nearly everything was still scarce after the war. About ten thirty I left my friends' apartment to walk home. Approaching our building, I noticed a car parked outside. This was odd, because no one in our village owned a car. My mind immediately raced back to the only other time I had seen a car parked in front of our building. As I climbed the stairs to the second floor, I was trying hard to remain calm. When I opened the door to our room, I saw two strange, unfriendly-looking men standing near my mother. She was deathly pale, with dread in her eyes. That look is embedded forever in my mind. *What now?* I asked myself as I stepped woodenly inside.

These men had arrived about an hour earlier, claiming they were my co-workers. They said they'd come to get a key I had inadvertently taken home from work. Mama knew better, so she had tried to distract them, saying she thought I wouldn't be home that night, that I was spending the night at a friend's apartment. But they didn't believe her and waited for me anyway. We had heard of their many stories, such as "the key," invented by these people to mask their unlawful entry and secret agendas.

The first man spoke: "Citizen Werner..." As soon as I heard the term *citizen,* I knew he was my enemy and I was his victim. Under normal circumstances, his greeting would have been "Comrade Werner."

"You are under arrest." I didn't grasp what he meant at first; it didn't entirely sink in. This was like the nightmare when you can't run or scream. He glared at me, pointing to a spot on the floor, and barked, "Now stand right here and don't move."

The two of them began to search the room, tearing up the bed-covers, dumping out boxes, turning everything upside down. I tried to talk to them. "Bu-but what did I do? What is this all about? I didn't do anything! I am innocent," I pleaded. They paid no attention to a word I said and continued to ransack our apartment, looking high and low and for what…I had no idea. I had nothing of interest to them, nothing at all.

I looked at Mama. Her normally reserved features were twisted with anger and fear. She cried, "What are you looking for? There is nothing here that concerns you. My daughter is innocent. She hasn't done a thing! Can't you just leave us alone? Haven't you done enough damage already?" Again the strangers gave no sign of having heard her. An awful feeling of déjà vu came over me. This was just like the day seven and a half years earlier when they had taken Papa.

I was more concerned for Mama than for myself. First they had taken away her loving husband and now her only child, her daughter—me. It was more than a person should have to bear. I would gladly have died for her right there if it could have spared her from suffering.

But me? I was outraged. Didn't they know that I was, I mean, *I am* an American citizen, from Detroit? That I have been a champion swimmer and track star right here in Gorky? That I could be an acrobat or a ballerina and could eventually become a doctor? That I had dug trenches to protect our city and had loved a Russian pilot? Didn't they understand or care?

One of the thugs said to Mama, "You can pack her a small bag—just some underwear, a few clothes, a toothbrush, and a comb. That is all." Mama had been trying hard to control herself, but now she began to shudder and cry. As she stumbled and collapsed over the couch, I ran to hold her. With my arms around her limp body, I held my face to her cheek, trying to revive her. The younger man tried to push me away rather gently. It was a small but discernible act of compassion.

"She'll be okay," the younger one said in an apparent attempt to comfort me as I tended to my mother. He didn't want to be here, I could tell; it was written all over his face and in his eyes. I kept asking, "Why am I being arrested?" And the older man, who had been issuing the commands, responded arrogantly in a stern, unfeeling voice, "Don't worry. You will soon find out."

Mama was sitting upright now, her head back, her eyes blankly staring at the ceiling. The NKVD men completed their search, finding nothing of a "suspicious or controversial nature," so they filled out a form and had it witnessed by our downstairs neighbor. She was an American from New York whose husband had also been arrested but then released after several years of imprisonment. Getting her signature was strictly a formality, carried out only because they felt like it.

The walls seemed to be closing in around me. I was short of breath, suffocating.

The older NKVD man stuffed the form into his coat. Then he seized my wrist. They allowed Mama to hug me one last time. She was sick with fright but more composed now. I kissed her with completely numb lips, saying, as my father had, "Don't worry. I'll be back soon. I promise."

Mama looked straight at me and spoke in a voice that combined confidence and concern. "I know you will, Maidie. God is good, and God is faithful. I will be here, waiting and praying for you, until I die. Don't ever forget that!"

Holding me tightly by the wrists, the two led me outside to the parked car. And just like my father before me, I was locked in the backseat and driven into the malevolent Soviet unknown.

They took me to a jail in Gorky for political prisoners, called the Vorobyo'vka, which had a dreadful reputation. Everyone knew about it. I was taken into a large room where a female guard, a supervisor, immediately ordered me to undress. She was a stumpy, crude sort of woman who enjoyed her duties far too much. She gave me an extensive physical examination, including all body cavities and private parts. "Now bend over," she demanded, grinning, paying more attention to some areas of my body than was necessary. I was shivering from head to toe, furious, entirely helpless. She took my watch and ring, removed all of my hairpins, examined my clothes, and removed all belts, zippers, elastic, and even shoestrings. I had nothing left on my person that I hadn't come into this world with. I felt like garbage.

I stood there humiliated, my hair hanging down my back, my underwear at my ankles (with no elastic waistband), and my shoes without ties. My tooth powder, which had been in a cardboard box, was dumped into my handkerchief. She left me a few cigarettes but confiscated my matches. All Russians smoked as regularly as breathing, so cigarettes were not considered impermissible items—even for prisoners.

Demoralized and naked, I was marched to a tiny cell at the end of a long, winding corridor. It was windowless, damp, dreadfully cold, and gray. There was no bed or chair, just a slimy, narrow wooden bench built into the moldy wall. The bench was more like a shelf, just long enough for me to sit sideways with my knees bent up to my chest. The floor was a wooden platform, with slats, through which I could see water below. I thought, *Well, it won't be long now; I won't last long in here.* A guard slammed the heavy steel-grated cell door, and I was left alone with my thoughts.

I thought of my dear helpless father. I wondered if he was also in a place like this one or maybe even worse. Was he still alive? I doubted it. I thought about his many luminous dreams and his shattered hopes about life in Russia. Did Papa know God? Did he find any comfort in faith or hope? I didn't know the nature of his relationship with his Maker, but I prayed that Papa knew the same God that Mama did.

I thought about God myself. Was there a God? If so, who was he? How could he have allowed all this misery? Had he totally abandoned our helpless family? Had he forsaken me? Would I live to see my precious mama again? And now that I was a political prisoner, what would become of me?

We were not political people by any stretch of the imagination.

We had no formal agenda in Russia, nothing other than Papa's desire to live an ordinary, peaceful life with his family. We were ordinary folk, Americans, who had unwittingly walked into a trap, a lifelong disaster for which there seemed to be no remedy. Would I ever get another chance at a new beginning? I prayed, "God, if you're here, please help me."

About five o'clock someone opened the door and gave me a cup of hot water, a lump of sugar, and a piece of bread. I couldn't eat, but I drank the water. They also lit a cigarette for me. Now I only thought about my mama's situation, her not knowing where I was or what was happening to me. It was a living nightmare for me, thinking of the horror my mama must be feeling.

Later that morning I discovered that this was not my cell at all; it was the entryway to the prison's bathhouse. A guard opened my door and ordered, "Gather your belongings now, Citizen Werner, and follow me." He led me down the hall and up a flight of stairs to a regular cell. It was furnished with two cots that folded up into the wall, a night table for two, two chairs, and a large wooden pail with a lid, conspicuous even in the corner. The walls were dark gray, and there was one tiny barred window, nearly covered by a metal shield outside, so I could see only a minute patch of the gray Russian sky. Everything to me was gray: this prison, Russia, my thoughts, my heart.

An elderly woman dressed entirely in black was the other occupant of the cell. She was kneeling on the floor, hunched over as if in prayer or some other form of devout communication. When I tried to talk to her, she seemed to be chanting something under her breath. Her demeanor was very odd; everything about her seemed to carry an eerie glint of otherworldliness. There was something frightening about her eyes. They had an evil, petrified look about them. I thought that she might be a gypsy or maybe a witch. She said her name was Anastasia.

I understood the misery that someone else might feel in this wretched place. I tried to speak with her, but she was unresponsive. Perhaps this old woman was demon possessed; I was very uncomfortable in her presence. *Spirit knows spirit.*

When the guard left, I put away my clothes but was not permitted to lie down. As I learned all too quickly, there would be no lying around during the day, except for one hour after lunch. That was the rule, and it was strictly enforced. I asked Anastasia how I could get to the bathroom. Without looking up at me from her stooping position on the floor, she jerked her head toward the wooden pail in the corner. This vulgar thing called a *parasha* nearly made me heave; the smell was absolutely sickening.

The cell door had a small spy hole about halfway up so that the guards could watch us at all times. Depending on the guard, every three minutes or so, we would hear the cover of the spy hole slowly slide open. I always pretended not to notice, but I knew when eyes were watching me.

Some guards had a quiet, creepy way of sneaking along the corridor; others marched along clanging their heels as loudly as possible. But we did have a few guards who didn't seem to go out of their way to make our lives more difficult or miserable than they already were. They were a nice departure from the norm. I learned to appreciate the simple things that made prison life more bearable.

I quickly became familiar with the different guards and their ways and could usually anticipate their moves. I actually became very good at predicting the human (or inhuman) behavior of specific individuals. It was almost funny to me sometimes to see how conventional these people were. Hardly anything shocked me: I had learned to expect the unexpected. At a mere twenty-four years of age, I was already unfazed by most of the lunacy around me.

Later that same morning I was summoned upstairs for my first interrogation. I was ordered to hold my hands behind my back, and the guard gripped my wrists and pushed me down the corridor. I was instructed what to do if we met anyone approaching from the other direction: I was to stop immediately and face the wall with my eyes shut so I would not accidentally recognize another prisoner or be recognized by them. This was standard prison protocol. If prisoners ever met face to face, the guards would panic, and you didn't want to be the offending party of such a serious procedural breach.

I was pushed into a little gray office, furnished with the barest essentials. It was the first of many such offices I would enter. The only noteworthy things in this room were a man and a desk. He sat with his hands calmly folded on the desktop. He was neither impressive nor intimidating, but he was an officer of the Ministry of Internal Affairs (MVD). He asked my name and address and very carefully wrote them down, as if taking pains to avoid a mistake. He then handed me a paper, which listed my accusations under specific paragraph numbers of the Soviet criminal code. The numbers were unfamiliar to me, so I very politely asked for an explanation.

He appeared to be intelligent, tranquil, and collected, as he courteously pointed out, "Article #58-6 is espionage, and Article #58-10 is anti-Soviet propaganda." Espionage? In my drab, unassuming life? This was certainly overly dramatic. I erupted in uncontrollable laughter when I heard this preposterous accusation. Really, I laughed out loud, perhaps partly from shock but mostly at the sheer absurdity of the charges. I could tell it wasn't the response the officer was expecting. But it was natural and unrehearsed. What else could I have done? *Espionage, right! As if I had spent my time perfecting the art of gathering intelligence!*

He waited for me to finish, coolly licked his lips, and serenely said, "What is so funny? Why are you laughing?"

I told him, "Those charges are utterly ridiculous. What else can I do but laugh?"

His eyes peered kindly into mine as he responded, "Well, then, suit yourself and have a good laugh, because soon you will not be laughing."

The officer's name was Fidoli. He was Russian but had a

superb command of the English language. We spoke mainly in Russian, but every once in a while, he would throw in a statement or two in English, I think to let me know how articulate he was and to make sure I was paying attention. Strangely enough, I liked him. He had a certain gentleness I admired and respected, regardless of what he did for a living. Fidoli could have passed for a kindly English professor at an American university, I thought. He told me that this was just an initial get-acquainted session. There would be more. Then I was escorted back to my cell.

My orientation to the world of prisons was only beginning. The Soviet system of prisons and forced-labor camps was established in 1919, but it was not until the early 1930s that the camp population reached significant numbers. By 1934 the Gulag, or Main Directorate for Corrective Labor Camps throughout Russia, then under the command of the NKVD, had several million inmates. Prisoners included murderers, thieves, and other common criminals along with political and religious dissenters. And I was there, a prisoner of the political variety, along with Anastasia.

Many others in the Vorobyo'vka were political prisoners awaiting trial or being held for exile and deportation. People accused of other crimes were held in the Gorky city prison. Gradually I gained a better sense of how many people were imprisoned here: many Russians and even more foreigners, all seized on political grounds. But I was the only American.

Prison mornings started with a nerve-racking shrill bell at five o'clock. Then we received our daily ration of bread and sugar. As news about Papa had suggested, the bread was terrible, almost inedible. But Mama had taught me to make the best of what was available, and I came to discover a little prison culinary secret. One of the guards showed me how to remove the bread crust and pour some slightly discolored hot water on it. This produced a not-too-unpleasant toastlike flavor, much better than the plain bread. Necessity is the mother of invention—we could have coined that expression in Gorky's Vorobyo'vka prison.

The noon meal was not much better. I soon learned that its quality depended upon who was cooking that day and what mood they were in. We always tried to avoid angering the cooks. Lunch was often soup made with unpeeled, nearly raw potatoes, some carrots, and small herring floating about here and there. Again we had a kettle of hot water. The food was horrible, but I had to eat; I was famished. All the prisoners were—always. And I already knew how to deal with the most hideous-tasting potatoes on the planet. Even these prison potatoes were better than the four sacks of frozen ones Mama and I had lived on.

After lunch I would often open my bed to prepare for a long-awaited and much-needed nap in that single permitted hour—only to have a guard burst in and march me off harshly for another interrogation. I always hoped it would be Fidoli who interrogated me.

These constant interrogations, conducted mostly by Fidoli, came to be a game between us. He would repeatedly ask the same questions, and I would give him the same answers—the truth. Then he would pause, smile, and begin his thoughtful rephrasing tactics as if the reversal or insertion of new words in his inquisitions would somehow bring the truth out of me. It was a game indeed, but I resolved that I wasn't going to break or confess to something I hadn't done. I smiled back and answered the same way I always had. This went on for some time, without much variation, this game of cat and mouse.

The unwritten but well-known mission statement of the interrogators was "Don't talk—that's okay. We'll exhaust you, and then you'll talk!" Strangely enough, during this particular time of interrogations, the inquisitors were never rough with me. They never resorted to physical abuse or torture, and they never used obscene language in my presence, not once. Instead, my interrogators were arrogantly aloof, sometimes seeming stupid, but that was all intentional.

I sometimes heard other interrogations being conducted in the office next to ours, accompanied by violent words and moans of pain. I knew what was happening, but I didn't want to give in to that ugly truth about people, power, and opportunity. Men and women were beaten and raped all around me. Terrible things are done when opportunity sees no immediate confrontation, and there is no accountability to law or justice. Perhaps I was just lucky. Or was I being protected somehow? Was it because Mama always prayed, saying, "Don't worry. God will get us through this"?

I must admit, however, that my favorite interrogator, Fidoli, was a rather nice guy at heart; I actually liked him. Fidoli, as well as others, also seemed to like me. At their request, I began to help some of the interrogators with their English pronunciation and homework, because they all secretly wanted to perfect their grasp of the English language. I was a political prisoner, and I was a victim, but I was also a favorite of most of these officials and interrogators, though I never knew why. That doesn't mean my interrogations ceased. I was just able sometimes to see us all as very human, following the steps laid out for us by the Soviet choreographers.

The interrogations went on and on. This routine proved exhausting, especially when I was ruthlessly interrogated by a different officer, a raving madman. I would return to my cold, dark cell to find that supper had been served hours earlier and my plate of *today's special mystery treat* was sitting on the floor. I could hardly ever bring myself to eat it. The food was barely tolerable when it was warm, but cold—that was unbearable.

Sleep was difficult here too. I never got used to the annoying light constantly shining in my eyes from the dim bare bulb overhead. It was a miserable light, made more distressing because we were not permitted to cover our eyes.

At five o'clock the day started again, with the infamous bell, the bathroom routine, the bread-sugar-and-hot-water breakfast. We were always so bitterly cold that we quickly drank the entire pitcher of water, just to feel warm again for a few moments. Swollen from all that water, our fingers, toes, and faces made us look like puffed-up balloon caricatures. Then at nine, like clockwork, it was back to the interrogation room.

At least the cold in our cell kept the smell down. When the

nauseating parasha was full, Anastasia and I were led naked to the bathroom carrying the nearly overflowing bucket between us. As we emptied and rinsed it out with lye water, a guard stayed feverishly glued to the spy hole. It was painfully humiliating, though my inherent modesty was quickly eroding under these intrusive circumstances. What else could one do? I was a prisoner, after all.

Once every ten days we were allowed to go to the bathhouse. Actually, it was a requirement, but only Anastasia saw it that way. The prisoners were marched naked to the bathhouse in ranks at assigned intervals. Unfortunately, this formal requirement was not strictly enforced. The prison was so filthy that I would have gladly gone to the bathhouse twice a day—even naked! When the ten days came around again, there was nothing any of us needed more urgently than a wash. Anastasia always refused to go; she simply refused to bathe herself. She was the talk of the prison, and she smelled terrible, even in our stinking environment. Everyone knew her ways, and most avoided her like the plague. Except me. I was her cellmate.

Word had it that many years ago Anastasia had been a nun. But something terrible had happened to her, and now her faith was shattered, turning her into a very angry, embittered woman. She spent most of her time on her knees praying, but as if she was in utter misery, rocking back and forth, always chanting, though I could never understand her words.

Feeling isolated and overwhelmed, I tried hard to be her friend in the early days of my imprisonment. I told her about my family and my work and tried to find common ground with her. Though I talked to her, Anastasia seldom replied, and I never learned anything significant about her past. I wanted to be encouraging and positive, but she would not be consoled or comforted. She seemed to have no motivation for living; her eyes were two dead black holes in space. Everyone knew she wasn't all there; something was wrong with her mentally. When the moon was full or when she was aggravated, she had a purely devilish glint. Hoping I could get through to her, I told Anastasia far too much too soon. I didn't tell her everything, but what I did tell her, she carefully remembered.

Eleven

BETRAYED

After I had been in the cell with Anastasia for a few weeks, matters came to a head between us. I had worked to befriend other women and became fairly well liked throughout the prison. Anastasia was feared and hated. We were like oil and water; we absolutely didn't mix. Our spirits smashed together like an inevitable midair collision.

I never saw her change or wash her clothes, and she only had one set. It didn't take me long to discover I had lice due to Anastasia's filth. I was tired of being nice to her. I'd tried respecting her as my elder, despite her stench, but now I'd had enough. Lice had to be dealt with—today.

Knowing no other alternative, the next time I was taken for interrogation, I told Fidoli about the lice, about Anastasia's refusal to bathe. She was promptly removed from our cell and forcibly led to the bathhouse for disinfecting. I was elated! All her clothes and mine were sent through a disinfecting procedure twice, along with our bedding, which consisted of a cotton pad, a thin cotton blanket, and a pillow without a pillowcase.

Lice called for a major cleanup. Everyone in our block of cells got to wash that day. When we returned from the bathhouse, it was time for bed and, for me, not a moment too soon! No filthy Anastasia, no lice. I was ready to crawl under anything that would cover me, and I hoped I wouldn't wake up for several years, hopefully back in Detroit. In the miserable cold of the room, I crawled under my blanket, still wearing my clothes, my coat, and my shoes. I had just drifted off to sleep when the door abruptly opened, and there stood Anastasia with her interrogator, Roslov.

He stood there, leaning his elbow on the door panel, and under his watchful guard, Anastasia walked defiantly toward me. I didn't budge an inch as she squinted her black eyes at me and, with her familiar wicked grin, slurred the words, "You'll get what's coming to you now, Jew!"

"Really?" I asked. "And what is that?" I feigned a lunge toward her face—a ploy, daring her to retaliate and attack me so I would have good reason to make the next move. She didn't answer but carefully backed away from me, as a fearful cat, with its hair rising, takes its natural defensive posture. This woman was pure evil, and I couldn't wait for them to separate us again. Yes, spirit knows spirit, and the wicked spirit inside the shell of Anastasia hated my spirit with a passion. I had no doubt that she, or it, wanted to see me dead.

Roslov barked a command, and she left the cell. I don't know what happened to Anastasia that night, but she didn't stay with me. Surprisingly, I slept like a baby for once; my night was peaceful and sound.

In the morning I was taken away to the same interrogation room and asked the same questions, and I gave Fidoli the same answers in the same hard chair in the corner. It was a torture tool disguised as a chair, which became acutely painful when you sat there for hours. But this time I was kept there all day and half the night. And the questions began to change. Fidoli knew things about my life he had never mentioned before.

I was returned to my cell around three in the morning, and by then I was so tired and overwrought that I couldn't sleep. Anastasia was back in my room, though she wouldn't look at me. At five the next morning, the interrogation began again. I was thoroughly badgered by Fidoli to confess that I had agreed to spy for England's Secret Service. That was my official charge. In essence, that's why I was in prison. A spy for Britain! That was the underhanded spin they put on things, the lie that had landed me in prison. They would not believe that my friendship with the British officers, Leslie and Mac, was innocent, despite my sincerest efforts to convince them.

Anastasia had reported to her interrogator every incriminating word I had ever said to her during our time together: my thoughts, feelings, intentions, past affiliations, relationships. Much of what she reported was merely her lies, fabricated nonsense, which I think the interrogators knew. But, to an unknown degree, I was still exposed. Only time would tell how much.

What a fool I had been for opening my mouth to her in the first place! And to think that all I intended was to help her, encourage her, and be a friend to her when she had none. Anastasia had gathered quite an earful from me over the course of our days together. And it was my own fault; I should have known better. I was much too trusting and entirely too open with this loose cannon of a woman. She never forgave me for turning her in, and for the rest of my life, I have struggled to forgive her for the way she retaliated. What she did to repay me for making her clean up was not an eye for an eye. It was much worse.

My interrogations continued almost around the clock. Exhausted from lack of sleep, I began to hallucinate and couldn't focus my eyes. The severe swelling of my feet and ankles made me barely able to walk. I had tried exercising to regain the use of my muscles, but I was sharply told that exercise was prohibited. The only uninterrupted sleep I got was on Saturdays and Sundays. About a month passed like this, and then I was allowed my first food package from my mother. I cried out loud when I saw the delicious cookies she had baked for me! Those were the first tears I had cried since my arrest—and the best cookies I have ever eaten.

In the interrogation room, I asserted my innocence over and over. Sometimes all the interrogators and prison officials, including Fidoli, would stare at me with an overtly theatrical look of skepticism. I think they were trying to perfect their dramatic acting, believing I would eventually crack and confess to *their* idea of my crimes under the pressure of their continuous expert scrutiny. I found it ridiculous. They would walk toward me with their heads cocked sideways, looking threatening, and say, "Now, come on and tell us the truth or else!" Or else what?

My answers were always the same. "I am telling you the truth! What else would you like me to say?"

When these interrogatory methods failed, and I did not confess, I found out what "or else" meant. They resorted to other tactics. One officer stared me down for several moments, then slowly turned aside and calmly said, "Citizen Werner, how would it be if we went to pick up your mother also, and then you could both be here together? We can go get her right now if you don't immediately cooperate!" I knew this threat was no mere scare tactic. They would arrest Mama in a minute if I didn't say something. They had done it many other times with many other families. I knew I couldn't let that happen, not to my mama! Not after my papa and I had both been railroaded like this.

I agonized over this new threat. Their intimidation worked well. These guys were very good at what they did, but at the core, they were still garden-variety mobsters. And they had a distinct advantage over me: they were holding all the cards, and I held none. So, purely by default, they won. It still took them another month of their clever interrogations before I finally broke from sheer exhaustion. They wore me out, and they broke me. They outwaited and outlasted me.

There came a time, during one particularly long session, when I just couldn't keep my eyes open. In a state of exhaustion, I eventually broke down and signed their confession just to get it over with. Then, and only then, was I allowed to sleep. And did I ever sleep, as if I would never wake up.

When I came to my senses, I realized I would have to pay dearly for this confession. But they simply had worn me out. With incredible skill, they had perfected this form of human manipulation, as any consummate artist perfects his craft. I had lost, and they had won, at least for now. Realizing I had no other options, I finally confessed under the continuous pressure of their coercive tactics. "You're right," I said. "I am guilty of spying for Britain's Secret Service."

Twelve

PRISONER

O nce a month the inmates in the political prison were given a single sheet of paper and a pen. This was our chance to officially register any complaint or request we had. Although it was something between an exercise in futility and a psychological con job, this procedure must have been intended to preserve the appearance of justice and order. I decided that on the next go-round for complaints, I would faithfully recite the method by which the NKVD officials had obtained my so-called confession. I did not expect anything significant to come of it, but I wanted to bear witness to their manipulative and coercive tactics.

But something did come of it. Three weeks later, at the end of January 1946, in the midst of another interrogation, Fidoli stood up unexpectedly. Smiling warmly, he said, "Margaret, you may return to your cell to gather your things. I have been instructed to prepare your transfer papers for Lubyanka." I was going to be transferred from the Gorky jail to the notorious and feared political prison in Moscow. It was two hundred miles from Gorky and from Mama. How would I keep in touch with her? What would happen to me in that awful place?

"But, Fidoli," I pleaded, "are you serious? Why Lubyanka?"

He smiled calmly, shrugged his shoulders, and replied, "Don't worry, Margaret. You'll be fine."

I had no idea what would come next, but I hoped there would be something redeeming about finally getting away from Anastasia.

After being transported in a prisoners' van to Moscow's Lubyanka prison, I was again stripped and subjected to a very thorough and humiliating body search. Then I was locked in a windowless cubbyhole with a small, hard bench and some tiny ventilation holes in the door for air. Everything in sight was dark gray. I still didn't understand why I was here, because I knew that political prisoners like me were not typically housed at Lubyanka. Under Stalin, this notorious institution was reserved for the most hardened offenders of Soviet law: gangsters, murderers, violent criminals of the worst variety.

Why was I here?

I spent many hours jammed in this tiny dark cell. Frightened though I was, it was a relief when a guard finally came to let me out. We walked a long way through the enormous prison to another cell. This one was a pleasant shock: a much larger cell, clean, warm, and bright—not gray—with eight regular iron cots spaced evenly throughout. Of course, in the corner stood the well-known parasha, but this one was made of steel and therefore easier to keep free from odor. Unlike my prior cells, this one seemed fairly livable. I had prepared myself for the worst, so my first thought was that this room had to be a setup. I was rapidly becoming an expert in their tactics, sure they had something else up their sleeves. They usually did.

Seven other women shared this cell, each with her own story. Among them were a well-known doctor from Riga, Latvia, and a famous actress from Moscow, whose name I can't recall now. At that time she was a respected and leading Soviet actress, and I deeply admired her and her work. I quickly made friends with everyone there, obliged to give my testimony, tell my story, and more obliged to hear everyone else's. In the many horrendous and unfathomable stories we told each other, we gained a kind of comfort. We heard about each other's pain, hardships, and suffering. Though our stories were different, they were also much the same. Anguish and sorrow seared us all, connecting us by a common thread. And we shared one great common denominator: *injustice!* None of us had committed the crimes we were charged with. Every one of us had been set up and railroaded by this evil regime. I began to wonder whether anyone incarcerated in the Soviet prison system was truly guilty.

Although we shared and discussed many things, everyone also maintained her private, secluded world of suffering and sadness that went beyond words and beyond the partial comfort we found in mutual understanding. Each of us was here for her own reasons, and we respected the uniqueness of each one's losses. I ached for my parents. I still missed my father terribly, but my waking thoughts were now of my mama and how she'd be able to cope. I knew what she was going through, thinking of her daughter and only child, the only flesh and blood she had left in this world. Her maternal instincts were being squeezed in a vise. I knew that she would have traded places with me, but I was glad I was here instead of her. Though I hated the prison routine, I was strong enough to bear it.

I was thoroughly examined by the female Latvian doctor, in the cell, but at least in a far corner of the room, out of the guards' view. She wasn't favorably impressed with my health, including, she said, my brain. She arrived at that diagnosis and general assessment after closely examining my eyes.

When night fell, we all settled down to sleep, and now I had to comply with a whole new set of night rules. Again the lights were left on, but here we were allowed to sleep with blindfolds. The new problem was that our hands and arms had to be fully exposed at all times throughout the night so the guards could see them. This certainly took some getting used to. If someone tucked her hands under the covers, the guard would rap on the door, waking everyone. This happened at least three or four times a night when a newcomer, like me, was being indoctrinated. It was surprisingly difficult to follow this simple rule. It was like being told that from now on you had to sleep standing up. It took me three nights to learn how to sleep like this; I had to work at it, and that didn't make me too popular with the other women.

We prisoners at Lubyanka did share some lighter moments. The doctor, who was also a professor of criminal medicine, told us many interesting stories from her experiences in homicide and forensics. And the actress, who had a beautiful monkey fur coat with her, was adept at telling ethnic stories and jokes in dialect. She made us all laugh. She also taught me a few German songs, which I still remember.

Every now and then, the door to our cell would slowly creak open, and a guard would whisper a single initial: the first letter of someone's last name. That person was being called for interrogation, and the guard would lead her away. When the guards were leading a prisoner down the hall, they made a strange clucking sound with their tongues to warn any approaching guards. This, I learned, was their formal line of communication. Again, it was important that no prisoner was ever recognized by another prisoner in the halls, even accidentally.

My name wasn't called for about a month. When the guard whispered *W,* I was led a long way through dreary corridors to another nondescript room. There I had to go through the whole procedure all over again: the interrogations, the same mindless questions, my same answers. My prisoner file, which they consulted quite often, was always prominently situated in the same place on the same desk. I was frequently interrogated by a group of officers, but I stuck to my original story, because it was not only the truth but also the only story I had, and the only one I had ever told them. Someone once said, "The nice thing about telling the truth is that it's the only story you ever have to remember."

The interrogators were always pressuring me to change my account to fit their charges, but the truth was the truth, and I was determined to stick to it. I was pleasantly surprised that they did not resort to the underhanded and barbaric tactics of their Gorky counterparts. Instead, I was able to get plenty of sleep at any time of the day or night. When we asked, they would even turn off the cell lights during the day, which brought much relief to our constantly tired eyes.

Lubyanka's food was also significantly better than Gorky's. The doctor was diabetic, so she received a different diet, which included white bread. She generously shared this with me because we were the only ones from Gorky, and for some reason we were not permitted to receive food packages from relatives. Because the doctor was legally blind and unable to wear her glasses in the shower room, I helped her bathe during our designated times.

The actress received numerous packages from her relatives in Moscow and often treated us to candy, cheese, sausage, and cigarettes. She usually saved all of her leftover pieces of face soap for me, as well. By carefully molding these pieces of soap together in my palms with some water, I could make a fairly large piece of soap. Although it was a rather peculiar color, who cared? We did the best we could with what was available.

In the corner of our room, a large grate of fine grillwork covered the heat register. We used the grate for stringing out our bread to dry, in order to make it edible. We pulled coarse strings out of our towels, plaited and greased them, and used them to cut the bread when it was dry. Improvisation was the order of every day. No laundry facilities were available for the prisoners, so we carried our bedsheets to the bathroom one at a time, and with a little bit of soap and a lot of elbow grease, we laundered them in the cell's tiny washbasin—a lengthy ordeal. We then dried the sheets by swinging them in the air. We did the same maneuvers with our clothes.

Once a week we were given a needle and about a foot of thread for necessary clothing repairs. We were also allowed to use a pair of blunt scissors for our fingernails, which seemed to grow more rapidly than normal. A nurse gave us small amounts of cotton every month for our personal times. And aspirin, whenever it was available, was dispensed for our aches and pains. Our diabetic doctor also received her insulin shots on schedule.

We had a surprisingly good selection of books, which helped to pass the time and take our minds off our troubles. The books were politically filtered, however, and never of a subversive or controversial nature or contradictory to good Soviet ideology. There were no Bibles; they were strictly forbidden, as were any references to God. Once a day we were allowed to exercise or go for a walk in the jail yard for about twenty minutes. Our circumstances were difficult but not altogether cruel. Practically everything I had heard about this prison—the dreaded Lubyanka—I personally found to be untrue. I had a lot of time to think, probably more time for that than anything else. And if they said, "There is no God," well, I was beginning to see it much differently.

But as suddenly as I was sent to Moscow, I was returned to Gorky's Vorobyo'vka. I never learned the reason for either transfer. I suspected it had something to do with my complaint, but even this was inconclusive. This time I was assigned to a solitary cell. It was perhaps five by seven feet, with a low ceiling, dingy, smelly, and slimy. And, yes, it was gray. Once again I was sent to my old interrogator, Fidoli, who began his customary protocol. He wanted to make me confess to things I absolutely had not done, things I was entirely unaware of. I wondered whether these people would ever tire of these tactics.

During one typical interrogation session with Fidoli, I refused to put my hands behind my back. Instead, I continuously paced the small room, taking two mockingly rebellious full steps at a time, until I was tired. I figured a little demonstration would make me feel better. It was a momentary one-woman revolt, a harmless spur-of-the-moment uprising. I either had to let out my inner tension or break down completely in front of him. I wanted to change the rules to the game a little, especially since it was only Fidoli, whom I believed to be entirely safe.

"Now, Margaret," he softly chuckled. "What do you hope to accomplish by that?"

Another day, during another routine interrogation, the room

was deadly quiet while he was immersed in writing his endless report. I decided I would break the prolonged silence and a serious Russian taboo at the same time. I suddenly blurted out, "So, Fidoli, tell me what you think about God."

An eternity of deafening silence passed. His eyes remained glued to the paper he was writing, and although he didn't look up at me, he did put down his pen. I could see that he was thinking, but what he thought, I had no idea. I could also tell that he was affected, maybe even shaken just a bit. He sniffled and then cleared his throat to speak.

"Margaret, please listen carefully," he said. "I have purposely tolerated many things from you—things I would never have ordinarily allowed of another person in your shoes. But now I am going to do you a huge favor; I'm going to choose to forget the question you just asked me—as if it didn't happen—and you are going to be happy with that, okay?"

Our roles were now reversed. Fidoli shocked me by what he said and the way he said it, flatly and without smiling. I also had to face what he chose not to say, about the consequences if I repeated my question. Maybe he was taken aback by my question, embarrassed, or angry.

Talk of God, faith, or religion was banned throughout Russia. Stalin, in fact, had issued his ridiculous decree: "God must be out of Russia in five years." I assumed that such a conversation must be very dangerous for a high-ranking interrogating officer like Fidoli. He could not reveal his true feelings on the matter. Perhaps he was wrestling with his own sensitivities. Or maybe he was protecting me. For an American "political," discussing the subject of God was even more dangerous. But, whatever his motives, Fidoli knew how much was at stake, and he instantly drew the line.

And I understood that I was to press him and my luck no further.

Despite my fear and reluctance, words came out of my mouth from somewhere deep within. "Fidoli, I was a ten-year-old American girl when I was forced to come to Russia—not of my choosing. My life was ripped apart, and my dreams were killed by Russia and in Russia! They killed my father. My mother and I have suffered anguish that words cannot express. I have been falsely accused of something I have not done. I am entirely innocent, and yet I am locked up here and speaking with you. Let me tell you something: The only thing I have left to believe in is God. He is real. He exists. One day he will get me out of this insane asylum, I promise you! And I only hope that you too will come to know him. Fidoli, in the end, that is all we will have left to take into eternity—our faith in God."

I stopped, out of breath and surprised by what I'd declared. In some ways I hadn't known what I believed until I spoke it to my interrogator. Fidoli kept his head down and said nothing to me. After a few moments, he got up and walked quietly out of the room without saying a word. Never before had he left during an interrogation, so his leaving seemed out of place. I don't know where he went. I sat there alone for about fifteen minutes, thinking about the words I'd just said. Fidoli finally returned, accompanied by a guard, who waited by the door. He said nothing more to me than, "You may go now," and the guard promptly escorted me back to my cell. I wasn't called for interrogation by Fidoli or any other interrogator for more than a month after that. And prior to that day, I had been drilled at least three or four times a week by one interrogator or another.

Subtle rebellion and silent antagonism grew within me, changing my demeanor and character. I no longer saw myself as another ordinary victim but as a victim with an edge, determined not to let these people triumph over me. Although I could see that resistance could land me in hot water, I resolved that I would not let them beat me down, destroy my spirit, or wipe out the dreams and visions that allowed me to hope for a better day ahead. I would not give up the things I knew to be good and virtuous and desirable. They were not taking these away from me. They couldn't. I would not let them! The things I had learned from my mama and papa, things of the heart, these were the things I needed to keep alive inside of me. Deep down inside I was still that little girl from Detroit, lying in the grass, dreaming of my future as an athlete, a leader, a dancer, a doctor.

One day I suddenly became very ill. I couldn't get out of bed; I had a severe headache and a fever of about 104°. I was taken to the prison doctor, who gave me a halfhearted examination and prescribed some medicine and bed rest. I don't think he knew or cared what my specific problem was. When I was returned to my cell, I collapsed onto my cot and fell into a delirious sleep filled with hallucinations. I was floating into a dark void. My body was out of control. I was filled with unspeakable despair, swept into an endless black abyss.

I heard voices—dark, cold, evil voices—calling to me, "Why go through all of this? Why not just go ahead and take the easy way out?" They were luring me toward death. I believed I was actually dying, and it was not like dying in a dream. I was definitely awake, and still I felt the grip of death, like hands around my neck.

Was I going to perish in this place, like so many others before me? What would happen to Mama if I died here? They told me I had pleurisy, a rare lung condition that could be fatal if not properly treated. Apparently, this medical condition was endemic to Eastern Europe and Central Asia prior to the 1940s. My death loomed over me; I was cold with fear. But I also knew that Mama was praying for me, and I hoped nothing else was as powerful as that.

The devilish infirmity lasted for three physically, emotionally, and spiritually miserable days. I didn't eat a thing the whole time; I couldn't hold anything down. I felt exhausted. I lost nearly fifteen pounds, which I really couldn't spare, during this ghastly three-day episode.

When my fever finally broke, I longed for some strong tea with a bit of lemon, and I was much too weak to go to the door to receive my daily ration of bread, sugar, and hot water. I was lying immobile when one of the guards took it upon himself to look in on me. He walked in and asked, with genuine concern, how I was feeling. He poured tea for me and broke my sugar into smaller lumps that could be dissolved so I could drink. I was too weak to manage even that for myself. I was so grateful for his kindness that I cried. I could see that he was equally touched, pity softening his rugged face. I knew he held back tears only because of his sense of duty and his fear of being seen.

As I began to regain my strength, I had a clear sense of my situation. My goal was to eventually get my life back and to believe, despite the opposition, that it would again be good and worth living. I knew that the only way this would happen would be for me, *right then*, to become stronger, more determined, and more faithful than I had ever been in my life. But I also knew I needed help; I was all out of personal options.

I was confronted with my physical weakness. If it is true that only the strong survive, I knew I didn't stand much of a chance. Deep within, I knew that my ultimate survival would depend largely upon factors that I could not control. I desperately needed outside intervention, from wherever it came, human or divine, and I needed it now. I had very nearly collapsed from the strain of it all, had nearly given in, given up, and succumbed to the spirits, those voices, talking to me. It was clear to me that my individual strength and determination would soon crumble under the pressure of isolation and deprivation, and I looked intently for the helping hand of Mama's God in my life.

In desperation I reached out for Mama's God, and I realized

that his hand was actually there the whole time. The guard who helped me was named Rolf. Now I always looked forward to his shift; he was the captain. He would turn off the lights for me during the day so I could sleep. Seemingly small favors such as these, among the endless waves of human injustice surging around me, somehow made life tolerable again. In Rolf's kindness, I saw hope that when I was at the end of my resources, there would be other resources to help me say no to death and yes to life. I wanted to pay attention to the hand of a greater source rather than listen to the voices of darkness and despair.

Thirteen

SENTENCED

The dreary days in the Gorky prison were suddenly interrupted one spring day. Fidoli gave me a sheet of paper notifying me that on April 24, 1946, I would stand trial in Moscow. I was charged under Article #58-1a for treason, Article #58-10 for anti-Soviet propaganda, and Article #58-6 for espionage. Treason, because I had made the mistake of mentioning to the British officers, Leslie and Mac, that I would love to leave the country and had requested their help to do so. Anti-Soviet propaganda, because I had once described the quality of our former life in the United States and its stark contrast to Soviet life to someone who reported it. Espionage, for conspiring with the Brits.

Very early on the morning of April 24, I appeared at the Moscow general courthouse. There was no audience, and the entire proceedings lasted only about forty-five minutes. Only one witness testified against me, a very close friend of mine, whose name I shall not reveal. I didn't resent her testimony, because I knew how the NKVD went about obtaining its goods on people: coercion, deception, manipulation, and lies. They did not need any real evidence; there usually was none anyway. If they wanted to arrest you, they did; no reason was necessary. Any cooperation my friend may have offered them was motivated by self-preservation, and under the circumstances, she didn't have many options. I was not angry with her, for I understood all too well the factors that went into her false confession. Her testimony against me was very careless but not malicious. However, I don't believe she carefully chose her words or exercised good judgment in her coerced claim against me.

Still, Russia was an unimaginably brutal place, impossible to make sense of. Perhaps I, too, would have frozen under similar conditions and said what I was told to say. Later in the day I smuggled a small note to her, intended for my mother. It was hastily scribbled on a matchbox cover with a burnt match while the courthouse guard wasn't looking. She carried it for me; she meant me no ill, though she was the instrument of my sentence. Just a few years later, ironically, she was convicted of similar indiscretions and sentenced to ten years hard labor.

I was found guilty as charged and officially sentenced by the Military Tribunal of the MVD of the Gorky Region to *ten years hard labor*, coupled with five years loss of civil rights: the right to vote, to travel, to hold public office, or to teach. These people took my father from me; they separated me from my mother; and Nikolai, the love of my life, was killed in the war. But that wasn't enough. Now they were taking another ten years of my life! Where was God in all of this? And where was justice? What is justice anyway? Is it for this lifetime? I would have many days to consider these questions.

For the next fifteen years I would be completely isolated from everyone I loved and everyone who loved me. I could hardly imagine it. But at least I was not denied the right to communicate with my mother, and for that I was sincerely grateful. I also felt a mild relief that my current life in jail, with its restrictions and lack of productivity, was finally over. It was a peculiar comfort. How could it be that I had learned my fate for the next fifteen years, and yet I was comforted? *This has to be God,* I thought. *What—or who—else could it be?*

I was returned to Vorobyo'vka to collect my few personal belongings, then transferred to the large city prison where my father had been. This time I was transported in the infamous *Chornyi Voron* (Black Crow) prisoner van. This windowless vehicle contained eight to ten individual cells, each just large enough for someone to squeeze through the door with their knees smashed against the opposite wall. Sitting in that windowless van on a narrow bench, I was in total darkness. I couldn't see out; others couldn't see in—perhaps an all-too-appropriate symbol for this brutal system that sent so many innocent people on a one-way ride to death and destruction.

At the city prison I was put into a large holding cell with about twenty other women. I was the only political prisoner. Many of the others were so-called *Blatnoi,* Russian slang for prisoners convicted of petty crimes, serious burglaries, and even murder. These women were hard and tough; their language was abominable. I saw how alien I was to their world, and I calculated what I'd have to do to survive in these hostile new surroundings.

I decided to speak as they did to establish common ground and mutual rapport. I would adopt their aggressiveness and severity. I had to become one of them—a Blatnoi. I had to change my attitude, my habits, the way I walked, my very thought patterns. I needed a whole new mind-set. This was strictly on-the-job training. I had to reinvent myself for the survival of the fittest in a mental as well as a physical tough-woman competition. And my new stance of power and clout proved to be an invaluable tactic, because not one of the other women in the cell dared to assault, rob, or otherwise harm me. My act was a suit of armor.

Tough or not, however, I had a miserable night there. The bedbugs were so vicious that we had to lie on the cold concrete floor, covered with wet towels and sheets, just to keep them from biting. To my dismay, even that method didn't work very well; those insidious bedbugs, as if with a predetermined strategy, dropped down from the ceiling in unison. They were absolutely unrelenting! Maybe they could smell fresh flesh. It was a horrible experience, much worse than it sounds. The following morning my body was covered with bites and welts from head to toe and was swollen and itching.

After breakfast I was led to my new cell. As we climbed a steep, worn metal staircase, I had a strong sense that these were the same steps my father had first climbed when he was arrested in 1938. This was certainly a possibility, but my sensation went beyond that. I *knew* he had already been here, right where I was now walking. I don't know *why* I knew or *how* I knew, but I *knew.*

I could see the precipitous drop-offs from the different floors, all the way to the concrete basement slab. The sides of the stairwells were covered with a thick steel mesh, installed to prevent suicide attempts. Many prison stories later confirmed that prisoners had thrown themselves down to their deaths. I sensed a powerful, spiritual presence of desperation, hopelessness, and despair—voices from days gone by.

Gradually I grew accustomed to a new prison routine. The food seemed to be a bit better than before, and we were given more of it. "Enough to live on" would be my description of the usual portion, depending on just how much of the sickening stuff you were willing to stomach. Women prisoners did a lot of embroidery and sewing, not as a recreational activity, but as a necessity. Many of us had only the clothes we wore, a single garment. While walking in the prison yard one day, one of us found a piece of perfectly shaped glass, which we used to cut out and modify garments for the others. All of us soon became masterful improvisers. In this prison we could sleep whenever we wanted; there were no restrictions.

Much of the time we just sat around telling detailed stories, holding nothing back. We knew everything there was to know about one another's nightmares and personal tragedies. We were sisters here, sharing the common denominator of pain. Most of the women were Russian, from Estonia, Latvia, and the Ukraine. There was also a Polish woman, an Italian woman, and a couple of Czechs, but no other Americans. The girls liked me to tell about the few American movies I had seen as a child, so I gladly did. Our group was on the guards' so-called honor list, because we were relatively well behaved and didn't have nearly the fights or arguments of most other group cells. So for a while I guess we received an A in conduct.

Most of the women had not yet had their day in court, so when the day of someone's hearing arrived, we all used the contact with outsiders to smuggle notes to our families. That's the way I was able to inform Mama of my location, circumstances, and needs. Not long afterward, she was allowed to bring me food and some embroidery thread, an unexpected treat. I had surrounded myself with five or six fairly pleasant girls, with whom I shared my goodies from home.

One day in May, without any notice, a prison guard entered our cell and ordered, "Citizen Werner, please stand to your feet." I stood up and looked around, confused. He continued, "We are transferring you to a Siberian labor camp in the morning. Have your personal items ready."

Though unprepared, I had known it was only a matter of time before they sent me to Siberia. I was an embarrassment to them; there was no way I could stay indefinitely in the city prison, which was reserved for common criminals, not subversive foreigners. And the Soviet officials were particularly careful about the disposition and handling of Americans (more so than other foreigners). I believed there was a pervasive fear when it came to the issue of detaining American citizens. People like me, who embarrassed the state, were disposed of in the northern slave labor camps, located primarily in Siberia. Also known as death camps, these labor camps had few survivors. By design, they intended to kill the inmates, be it quickly or slowly. Only the strong and determined few completed their sentences and made it out, but none escaped—ever!

Several women stood there with me, also awaiting transfer. We had to wait for the guards to return our personal items and clothing, which had been in storage. The following morning, carrying our baggage and belongings, we were marched on foot to the railway station, about ten kilometers away. Only essential items were allowed; there was no room for keepsakes. I hauled a large blue canvas bag that my mother had sewn for me, so heavy that I could barely strap it onto my back and tote it. Dressed in my winter coat, hat, and rubber boots, bent over and struggling greatly under this heavy load, I drudged along with the rest.

About four hundred men and women were led through the city streets of Gorky in a ragged, shuffling column in full view of the public. People lined the streets as we passed, as though they were accustomed to this routine. They were kind and sympathetic, discreetly passing us food and cigarettes, trying hard to smile at us through their own despair. Their worn and melancholy faces spoke of a hope that once was, but now was no more. Many of them, I thought, had already been in my shoes; their eyes seemed to say that. My thighs tensed and burned from the weight I had to drag, and I thought I would never make it to the railroad station.

I was nearing the point of collapse when we finally arrived about four o'clock. Like animals, we were herded into railroad cattle cars. These were enclosed, with double-decked platforms at each end, and the parasha, of course, right in the middle. For three days and nights we were locked inside our car, in the heat, and not allowed to leave this oxygen-deprived container for any reason, while the train stood on the siding. The nights were cold, and the days were extremely hot. With practically no ventilation, the stench was unbearable. We were stuck there with nothing to do but sit and stew and—at night—freeze. No one had any idea why we were sitting here, going nowhere.

During our second day in the cattle car, I heard two women talking as they passed by outside. Quickly scribbling them a small note, I maneuvered it through the tiny ventilation slats in the car. I was hoping that the women would see it, pick it up, and either take it themselves or have it delivered to Elisabeth Werner in Gorky. I had no other way to let Mama know the news of my transfer. I needed a providential act of God to make it happen. I didn't really believe in luck. If I had been someone who could be called lucky, then what was I doing here? I did not know it then, but these women saw my note and picked it up, risking their freedom and perhaps their lives.

The note eventually found its way to Mama. I never got to

meet these women or see or thank them, but I was eternally grateful to these faceless, nameless, unknown messengers of kindness. To those women, I was an anonymous human being, a complete stranger. Their benevolence was a small thing, an unselfish human gesture, the infrequent kind. But this small act altered the course of my life.

The following morning we received a small serving of hot millet. Our car finally began to move, but it would be several more hours before our train was on the main track. During our journey, we stopped at all the minor train depots along the way to take on more people, more prisoners. They were people like me, robbed of their youth, their entire futures contingent on this whim or that one, hanging by a thread. We were at the mercy of irrational government and political idiocy of the highest order, but their lives were not like mine for one important reason. They were not Americans. They did not know that life could be different. They had only experienced ongoing, lifelong despair, but I had hope. One day, I told myself, regardless of anything else that could happen to me, I would escape all this nonsense and return to the wonderful United States of America—land of the free and home of the brave!

Deep inside I knew that one day my life would be given back to me. I don't know why, but I just knew. My hope was for and in that coming day. I hoped to live to tell this story to my children and maybe even to their children, when this time and pain would be nothing more to me than a very long and excruciatingly bad dream. *God willing,* that is what I wanted to live to tell.

But the other prisoners piling into our cattle car, these Russians, had no such hope. Their only hope was in their basic day-to-day ability to endure the crazy anguish of life here in their own country. They had no prospect of going elsewhere—like back to America some day. These simple Russians, good people at the core, were subject to endless oppression under these totalitarian conditions from which they were powerless to escape. The personal choices I took for granted while growing up in America—choices about health, happiness, and growth—these dear Russian people had never had. They never knew of such options, not even the simplest ones.

They could not turn to religion for hope; atheism was the Soviet religion. Hopelessness was deeply and permanently etched into their faces. It penetrated below the surface, into their souls. I can still see their faces clearly in my mind's eye today: men and women, young and old, with a look of total resignation, no hope whatsoever. A country without God is a terrible place. A horribly cold, harsh spirit hovered over this country, like a cloud that would not lift. It thickened the air and filled your nostrils everywhere you went. You could feel it crawl into your skin, into your pores. *That* was the condition of their lives and the very look upon their faces, as best I can describe it.

As I hated the terribly oppressive life and conditions the Russians were forced to undergo, I came to love the people more and more. Every time our train stopped at a station, local people came to push things through the ventilation slats in the cars: candy, bread, fruit, sausage, and cigarettes. All were rare luxuries, precious to them. They never stopped trying to help us, to care for the invisible people who were even more oppressed than they were. The locals were used to this routine; they watched for the trains hauling new death-camp inmates to the north and eagerly awaited the next opportunity to provide help. There was a good chance that most of them had a family member jailed, killed, or wrongfully imprisoned as well. In any case, these dear Russian people wanted to apply whatever healing medicine they could to this dreadful cancer called Stalinism.

After another day and night, we finally unloaded, stiff and filthy from our journey. We were in densely forested terrain, somewhere several hundred miles north and east of Gorky, on the southern edge of Siberia. Exhausted and weakened, we had to walk almost four miles to a transitional camp, just outside the feared Burepolom, a lumber camp about which we had heard frightening stories. Prisoners in the log-felling brigades—the so-called *lesso-povalka*—routinely suffered severe injuries. They were also known to intentionally cut off an arm or a leg, a hand or a foot, in hopes of receiving a transfer out. Anyone caught in such an act would again stand trial and receive an additional sentence. Suicides were also a common and steady occurrence here. Pain and human suffering went deep, deeper than one could imagine, and then deeper still.

Fourteen

BUREPOLOM

Our introduction to this transitional camp was rough indeed. We were put to work immediately and left to fend for ourselves among the camp's most violent members. Because so many of the prisoners were criminals, the camp was informally ruled by a powerful organization of robbers, petty thieves, and pickpockets. All too soon, the hardened leader of these Blatnoi men, a tough, gangsterlike fellow named Mikal, started paying attention to me. In short, *he wanted me,* but I was not available for him. One day he made what I perceived to be a backward attempt at a come-on. Trying to be sexy, he nudged me gently with his finger on my thigh and said, "Don't worry. You don't have to be afraid of me. I could really take care of you here. This is a place where you need friends. Do you know what I mean?"

"*Nyet!*" I angrily snapped back, pulling away from him. "I'm not afraid of you. Get away from me!" I'm sure he hadn't anticipated my brazen reply, but if he had wondered about the possibilities, he was clear about them now. He looked shocked, as if he couldn't believe my defiance. It must have touched his machismo. A short while later another girl and I were at work, carrying some twelve-foot logs. Without a word, Mikal walked up to me and punched me so hard in my right arm that I nearly fell down. I spent the next few hours soaking my arm with a wet compress, trying to hold back the tears and the excruciating pain. Nevertheless, I still had to help carry logs to our camp for a building project.

I was struggling along, trying to hold up my end of a rough-cut log, and as we approached the camp gate, I couldn't believe what I saw. Maybe I was hallucinating from the pain...or maybe not? *It was my mother, standing at the gate!* She saw me approaching. Our eyes locked, and she started walking toward me, trying to smile through her tears. But the guard cruelly pushed her back, saying, "Back off. You are not permitted."

That evening I was allowed to spend ten very short minutes with her in the guardhouse, under the watchful eye of a guard. That didn't matter to me in the slightest. I hadn't seen Mama since the day of my arrest. It was incredible that she had traveled all this way and that we had found each other among the hundreds of prisoners in the camp. We hugged tightly, crying, and I buried my head in her shoulder. I felt her heart beating and the firm, loving grip of her arms around my back. I sobbed, "I love you, Mama" through the tears.

She closed her eyes and gently nodded her head in sad

agreement, whispering, "I had to know you were all right, my Maidie. I had to let you know that I'm okay too and that I love you more than anything. I'll wait for you. You can make it, Maidie; never forget that. You are strong. Trust in God and always look to him."

After ten minutes the guard made her leave. She'd come all the way from Gorky just to see I was alive, and now she had to go back.

I returned to my bunk and collapsed. My emotions were nearly overwhelming. So much pain, so much joy, so much sadness, all in one day. My mind was too tired to think, and my body was sore. As I sat on the edge of my bunk with my head in my hands, weeping, I suddenly noticed someone sitting next to me. To my shock, it was the Blatnoi brute who just hours earlier had pulverized me with his punch. I thought, *Oh no, this is all I need. Not him again!* I was afraid he really wanted to hurt me this time. But to my surprise, he was contrite, sincerely apologizing for his earlier behavior.

"I'm very sorry, miss, for the way I acted earlier. I'm sorry for hurting you. It won't happen again. Please forgive me," he said. His tone and look seemed genuine and sincere. I really didn't know what to think. Was he just conning me, or did he mean it?

His new behavior and unexpected demeanor puzzled me. I never understood it, but from that day on I had no trouble of any kind with Mikal. To the contrary, this Blatnoi, the guy I thought might kill me, became my friend and personal bodyguard. He became my protector against other potential rapists, and there were many in the camp. Something inside him changed, and Mikal was suddenly an entirely new man. He even looked different. His whole appearance took on an inner vibrancy and a life of some kind. His eyes changed, literally, noticeably, becoming clearer and brighter somehow.

Mikal was not unlike a starving man, so I trusted him and decided to help him. I actually began teaching him to read and write. He made tremendous progress, and for my willingness to help him, he was very grateful. Whether it was simply a case of his conscience or guilt, I don't know, but something certainly transformed him, and it wasn't me. What else or *who else* but God would have made Mikal feel such shame and then conviction for what he had done to me? All I know is that this man's instant transformation was astonishing—miraculous. I had no doubt it was supernatural.

Soon I was ordered to move into the base camp in Burepolom. We were all assigned to various work brigades and then shown to our barracks. There we found wooden double-deck bunks with no blankets, pillows, or mattresses of any kind. We were each issued one small and one large cloth sack and a blanket. We were supposed to fill the sacks with wood shavings from the nearby sawmill and use them as the pillow and the mattress for our bunks. They were definitely not soft, but they were considerably better than the bare boards.

We slept in all our clothes, whatever we'd carried with us. In the mornings we were awakened at five o'clock and marched to the dining room, where we normally ate two meals a day. Each prisoner had a wooden bowl, a wooden spoon, and an aluminum cup. Breakfast consisted of about fourteen ounces of old and hard black bread—the entire day's allotment—and a bowl of unshucked oatmeal, which we dubbed "chew and spit." In the evenings, for weeks at a stretch, we would have only oatmeal, and then it would be peas—*forever peas*—morning and night. We never saw the slightest trace of meat or other vegetables.

My first task here was hauling large boxes of sawdust from the mill with the aid of a partner. Our normal routine was to work five hours, then take an hour off to eat whatever bread we had saved from breakfast and to nap on top of the huge warm pipes that lined the basement area of the sawmill. It was nearly impossible to rid ourselves of the thick sawdust in ours eyes, ears, mouths, and hair. This dust penetrated my pores, clothes, and every exposed and unexposed part of my body; there was no avoiding it. Then came another four hours of hauling those boxes, which seemed to grow heavier and heavier with each additional trip.

Eventually we'd return to the barracks, attempt to de-sawdust ourselves, and then wait impatiently until our brigade was called to the dining room. The worst thing about the dining room was watching the men. They received the same meager amount of food as the women, though most of them were taller and heavier. As the women ate, men would line up behind them, eagerly waiting to snatch their empty bowls so they could lick them. They would stand there like dogs panting through a fence, riveted on what they couldn't get to. This inhuman treatment cut me to the heart. I thought, *Why is this so? How can this be? It doesn't have to be like this. What did any of these people do to deserve this kind of treatment? What if my papa had to live like this?* I thought about my poor papa, and I cried.

I thought I had already seen the depths of human depravity. But one day I realized I had not. In that same dining room, I witnessed a man beating another prisoner; he was allowed to pulverize another inmate to *death.* They were fighting over some scraps of food, equivalent to perhaps ten soggy cornflakes, left in a bowl. Seeing their desperation, watching the assault, looking at the bloody body on the floor, I screamed inside myself, *What kind of depravity, deprivation, and disregard for human life would make men act this way?* I was left numb from disbelief. I thought that surely more had to be going on than just a fight over food, but by the next day it was already *just another incident,* one of many. Human life held no value in Stalinist Russia. So life in the camp just went on, one backbreaking, mindless day at a time.

I grew to consider Burepolom "home," if not in my heart, then at least in my head. Like it or not, this was where I lived, and I had to see it that way in order to make it through the next day and stay sane.

On rare occasions we inmates had a treat when the camp

commander allowed us to watch a movie at the camp's seldom-used, makeshift outdoor theater. This happened perhaps six or seven times a year, with absolutely no regularity, when and only when the commander was in an exceptionally good mood. We could never predict when we would be blessed like this, but it was always an extraordinary night, a minute and temporary sliver of escape from the harsh everyday realities of life in a labor camp. It usually didn't matter what film or films they permitted us to see. The movies offered us a wonderful momentary means of departure from this ugly place, and our film nights, though random and unexpected, were the only times I actually looked forward to, especially during the earlier years of my sentence.

I'd been infatuated with film and dramatic acting ever since my early childhood in Detroit. Papa and Mama would take me to an old-fashioned theater near our home to see whatever was showing. My eyes would fix on the screen, and it was impossible to divert my attention from the picture. Except for sports and books, there was nothing I enjoyed more than the movies.

One particular evening at the camp's outdoor movie, I noticed a young man sitting nearby. He looked strangely familiar, although I couldn't place him. I couldn't recall why or from where I might have known him. It turned out that I looked more familiar to him than he did to me. He soon came over and sat next to me.

"Don't you remember me?" he asked.

"No," I said, "I don't think so. Should I?" I pondered for moment, then said, "I think maybe I've seen you before, but I'm not sure where, or maybe you just look like someone else I used to know."

Then he smiled and replied, "You should remember me. You know, from the streetcar that day." Suddenly it hit me. I did remember him, and my heart froze and sank to my stomach.

Several years earlier, in Gorky, before my arrest, I had been riding in a streetcar on the way home after work. I was standing in the crowded aisle, crushed by the surrounding crowd, when I happened to glance across the car. I saw a pickpocket reach into the purse of a woman standing near him. I waved and warned her, so she shifted the purse to her other side. In the nick of time, I'd kept her from being victimized by this thief. The crook jumped off the streetcar at that precise moment, but just as he turned, his eyes met mine, and I caught a good look at his face. Now I clearly remembered him from that day. And he realized that I remembered him; my frightened eyes gave me away.

I continued speaking with him, though I grew increasingly worried. This was a criminal with a grudge against me. I wondered what he was thinking. He was contained and relaxed, but I knew my face was flushed, and I was in a state of near panic. I tried to reevaluate the occurrence in the streetcar that day, to try to figure out what he wanted, but I could not. My mind was racing, while his eyes looked calculating. He appeared to be deliberately taking his time, carefully considering what he wanted to say next and how he wanted to say it. Finally he spoke.

"You were very lucky that day we met in the streetcar, and I don't know why. I don't know what stopped me, but something I can't explain stopped my hand from slicing off your nose. You see, I always carried a razor hidden between my fingers, which I used to quickly open purses or suitcases or whatever I wanted. I also used it to punish whoever might see me so that they would remember. And I was ready to cut your face that day when suddenly my arm could not move, and I did not know why. No one was holding me or saw what I was going to do, but I couldn't move my arm. And I was not afraid to cut you, either. I had done it to others, many times." Then he paused, reflecting. "I just thought I'd tell you that."

I could hardly believe my ears. But the sincerity of this fellow's words and the intensity of the look on his face confirmed every word he had just said. It was astonishing. *Why didn't he cut my face that day? And what prevented him from doing so?* As I mulled over what he was saying, I felt an unexpected warmth throughout my entire body, like simple reassurance, I suppose, or even love, coming from somewhere else.

I don't know what the pickpocket intended to do next, but I was staring at him, fascinated, when I suddenly heard a familiar voice behind me. "Is everything all right, Margaret? Are you okay? Is he bothering you?"

I was surprised and relieved to see that it was my Blatnoi friend, Mikal. What perfect timing! "No, Mikal, everything is just fine here," I answered. "This is an old acquaintance of mine from Gorky. We were just talking."

As if on cue, the man sitting next to me calmly stood up, nodded once to me, then to Mikal, and quietly strolled away. I never saw him again. But where had Mikal come from? The last thing I knew, he was far away at the transitional camp.

It was a powerful and perplexing moment.

My second job in Burepolom entailed working on a log-loading brigade. This was by far the most difficult labor I had ever done. Within the confines of the camp, a long train of Pullman cars stood on a loading track. These were the largest cars on the railway, and we had to load them by hand, only two girls per car. The logs were eight feet long, mostly birch and aspen, green timber, and very heavy. That was work! It took me an entire week to learn— the hard way—exactly how to do it. My shoulders were bloody sores, and I would awaken in the morning with my back and all of my muscles screaming from the pain of the previous day's agonizing toil.

In time, I learned to improvise a bit, creating some pads for my shoulders from bits and pieces of discarded leather I had found. Soon the weather changed to constant rain, sleet, and snow, but the work continued regardless. There were weeks when we didn't see the sun, only constant rain, gloom, and gray sky. None of us were properly dressed for the job or for the brutal weather we faced. We were not issued any special winter clothing. At times it was nearly unbearable, as the wretched cold and wetness—feeling like ice blades—seared my clothes and cut my skin like glass.

Our camp was part of the Gulag, the network of slave labor camps located mainly in remote regions of Siberia and the Far North. Under Stalin, the unpaid labor of Gulag prisoners made significant contributions to the Soviet economy: the construction of the White Sea–Baltic Canal, the Moscow-Volga Canal, the Baikal-Amur main railroad line, numerous hydroelectric stations, and strategic roads and industrial enterprises in these inaccessible northern regions. Labor camp manpower—prisoners like me—also did much of the country's lumbering and the mining of coal, copper, and gold.

I had heard that in the camps of the Far North, political prisoners were segregated from the others and were supposedly issued better clothing and better rations. During one especially dismal, wet, cold morning, I decided to go to the head official of the loading department and ask him for a transfer. This official was himself a former political who had remained at the camp after his release, earning his way into a privileged position. I went to see him the next morning at six o'clock sharp.

He asked me what type of work I had done in my civilian life. When he heard that I had experience in tracing blueprints, he immediately sent me to a friend of his who was the head of the Construction Bureau and also a former political prisoner. When I presented myself to this man, he seemed impressed. He instructed me to print a general job application. I did this in minutes, with very little effort, and was hired on the spot. Just four men and I were now working indoors, in a little building with three rooms. I quickly learned that I was far better suited for administrative office work than for hauling logs! These new arrangements were like heaven to me, and silently I thanked God for his grace and the secret divine opening of little doors.

My big problem now was the barracks where I had to live.

One day at work I was standing on the edge of the stove, placing my wet boots on the top shelf to dry. My boss, Yuri, entered the room and spoke to me sternly: "What on earth are you doing up there?"

I told him I was drying my boots. Because we'd had so much theft in the barracks lately, I had to sleep in my clothes with my wet boots under my pillow. Yuri stormed into the other room, went to the phone, called the commander, and arranged for my immediate transfer to the office workers' barracks.

I could hear him talking from the next room. "Hello, my friend. Yuri here. Tell me, why is my new prize worker still living with the animals?" That's all he said. Later that night I slept in a whole new world—entirely new quarters, which felt like a luxury hotel.

The contrast was extreme. Now we had a kind, elderly woman who took care of the routine maintenance and chores in the barracks. She always kept everything spotless and well sanitized. This was the camp's *select* barracks for women, housing twenty-five to thirty of us at any one time. One girl would leave upon completion of her sentence, and a new one would eventually come in. All of us tried to outdo one another in decorating our bunk areas, where we spent what free time we had when our work duties in the camp were finished. It was an undeclared, friendly sort of competition, trying to make something out of nothing. But this was still a forced-labor camp, and despite our tolerable barracks, many women died from natural and not-so-natural causes. A couple of girls mysteriously disappeared, and then others took their place. You couldn't ask what had happened. Like the seasons, life in the barracks continued in this manner. Considering the likely alternative, I was truly grateful to be here. Sometimes it struck me again that, among the thousands of women prisoners, *I was the only American* in the entire camp.

My work group was assigned to one very big project: the initial design for a new city prison for Gorky. We worked diligently on the drawings for some time. Suddenly one day the officials in charge announced that our work had to be completed one month sooner than scheduled. We had already slaved over this project, and the new deadline seemed impossible to meet. But we were forced to continue, working day and night, not even going to our barracks to sleep and taking barely enough time to eat. We didn't have much choice in the matter. Stalin constantly increased the number of projects assigned to the NKVD, leading to an increasing reliance on its forced labor. The Gulag camps also served as a source of workers for economic projects independent of the NKVD, which contracted its prisoners to various economic enterprises, as was the case in this instance.

We stayed at our drafting tables around the clock, catching fragments of sleep whenever we could. I woke up one morning about three and looked out the window to see Yuri, our boss, checking to make sure we were hard at work. If one of us had been caught sleeping, the consequences would have been entirely up to him. The guilty one could have been dismissed from her job and sent back to the hard-labor brigade or severely disciplined before she was sent back. Or, if Yuri had been in a good mood, maybe nothing would have happened. I saw all these things happen to others, but thank God, I never was caught sleeping. Yuri held a position of great power, and some of the girls took immoral advantage of that whenever they could. However, we completed the project on time, and the new prison was constructed using my design for much of its interior. It was a truly perverse system, using prisoners to plan new prisons.

The single most difficult factor I had to overcome in the camp was the twenty-four-hour-a-day invasion of personal privacy. Everything else—the grossly inadequate food rations, the poor housing conditions, the difficult and overly demanding work—I adapted to, but my privacy was a different matter. I missed it and longed for it. I had to be constantly alert, on the lookout for thieves and potential rapists. My friend Mikal was no longer around for protection. I wasn't sure what happened to him; he just suddenly disappeared. Perhaps he was transferred to another camp. But I learned that the tougher you acted, or the tougher you actually were, the easier it was for you. To ward off unwelcome predators or potential offenders, I had to fake a kind of female machismo, and it wasn't easy.

Before I finally gave up smoking, I actually punched a young man in the nose for attempting to steal my cigarettes. I had to do this, not only to defend myself, but also to set an important personal precedent. I had to mark my territory and set a boundary for the rest of my life in this camp, what I would tolerate and what I wouldn't. If I hadn't hit him, who knows what would have come next or what liberties he or any others might have taken. I had to become a good actor. I'd never struck anyone like that before, but I knew I had to, and I hit him really hard.

He promptly hit me back, squarely in my left eye, and I carried around a severe black eye, but he was walking around with two black eyes himself from my boldness and my direct hit to the bridge of his nose. I was actually quite proud of that. One thing of major consequence was established that day: he never approached me again, and, maybe even more important, in the eyes of other spectators, I now had a reputation.

Any woman intending to survive in this labor camp or any other had to display strength, whether real or contrived. There was no other protection from physical abuse, unwanted sexual harassment, and privation. The truth is that only the tough survived, and if you weren't, you didn't.

Another day, as I was enjoying the sunshine during a lunch break, I overheard some women talking about a big robbery that had just taken place in the camp. Some juveniles, who lived segregated from the rest of the contingent in a nearby compound, had broken into the *koptyorka*. This was a supposedly well-guarded warehouse in which all the prisoners' personal belongings were routinely stored. Evidently the intruders were able to topple part of the koptyorka's fence and overcome the guards so they could heist most of the suitcases and belongings stored there. As it turned out, they got mine as well. I was heartbroken and deeply despondent for some time. I had just lost all my winter clothing, important for survival, including some American sweaters. And they had taken a very pretty dress that meant a lot to me, the one I had worn during my reunion dance with Nikolai.

Several weeks later I was climbing the steps to the dining room, walking behind a camp nurse in her white smock. Under her uniform, I caught a glimpse of the skirt of my missing dress. I didn't say anything to the woman; instead, I immediately reported it to the guard in charge, describing the dress and drawing him a sketch as he instructed. He then promptly went into the clinic and moments later returned with my dress. It had been abused by careless handling, but I was elated, nonetheless, just to have it back. I never recovered any of my other possessions stolen that day, though—the things I'd carried on my back all the way from Gorky.

After a few days, I settled down from my sorrow over losing my priceless few keepsakes. I still had my memories, and memories, good and bad, are all we really have to take with us anyway. But it was hard for me to get over that someone had robbed me of precious reminders of the good things in my life. In the harshness and struggle of prison life, those little things had linked me to cherished times.

Another reminder of what I had lost arrived at the beginning of summer in 1948. I was watching a column of newly arrived prisoners, and among them I recognized a stooped, sinister figure dressed in dirty black. It was the old woman, Anastasia, the informer from the Gorky jail. A cold sense of bitterness and resentment gripped me, approaching pure hatred, as I stared at her. Her betrayal had sent me here; the sight of her absolutely jolted me and conjured up ugly feelings and dormant anxieties. I now had more than two years of my sentence behind me, and there was no way I was going to deal with her again. My life had changed; I had changed; I wasn't innocent or helpless anymore. I didn't need any of Anastasia's nonsense. I wasn't going to walk around looking over my shoulder for her, either!

Anastasia recognized me too, and I know she didn't like what she saw: my angry eyes trying to burn a hole into her skull. As I continued to stare, she quickly turned away, avoiding a confrontation. I knew I had to take matters into my own hands to prevent her intrusions into my life and well-being. I would never allow her to injure me again. She had burned me once, and that was enough.

In keeping with standard camp policy, the unwritten moral code of integrity among us all, I spilled my guts about Anastasia. To all who would listen, I told about her long and tainted history at the Gorky prison, her personal infidelity and dishonor, her lies and betrayal. I let them know exactly what to expect from our new guest. And I didn't speak anything about her that wasn't true. I was well connected in camp by now; I had many friends in various places, and I made sure that this traitor was permanently blemished. Stool pigeons were not tolerated among us. Never. In fact, people sometimes mysteriously died in the camp for failing to keep their business *their business.*

I did not physically hurt her, nor did I have anyone else harm her, which I could have easily arranged. I just wanted to make sure that Anastasia regretted her past actions against me more than she regretted anything else in her life. No matter what reward Anastasia had received for informing on me, it was trivial compared to the damage she had caused an innocent person. We said nothing to each other. I wanted it that way. I wanted her to stew in shame and condemnation for what she did to me, if she was able to feel such things. And I tried my best to make sure she did.

Later I learned about the freedom that comes through forgiveness—or maybe more appropriately, the conquering of unforgiveness. But not then. I didn't want to learn it then. I hated Anastasia for what she had done to me, and I wanted to make sure she was marred for life because of it. I wanted her to remember Margaret Werner forever and then some. God alone, and only *if* he saw fit, might forgive her for what she had done, but at this time I simply could not. And I did not. I would not. She had cost me too much, maybe everything.

She had sent me to Burepolom.

Fifteen

THE FAR NORTH

I thought I had figured out how to survive in Russia's severe lumber camp, Burepolom, but nothing in the life of a Gulag prisoner was ever permanent. In midsummer 1948, in the middle of the night, I was awakened from a dead sleep.

"Get your things now. We haven't got much time," was the stern command of the officer in charge. I was getting used to the perpetual shuffling and relocation of individual people in the camps; it was just the luck of the draw, nothing personal. With every subsequent move, I became less and less surprised, less attached, and consequently less confused and upset. There was no sense in becoming an emotional wreck over something as impersonal as a camp transfer. Still, I had become a bit attached to my relatively privileged life here. I minded being even farther away from my mother, who was hanging on in Gorky, and being separated from my many newfound friends. How would I ever contact them? But there were no advocates here, and there was no place to complain. It was another move, and that was that. God only knew to where.

Again we were loaded like cargo into cattle cars. There were only fifteen women among us, all political prisoners. The men were also politicals. No one knew precisely where we were going, but we had a hunch they were shipping us farther north, especially when, after the third horrendous day of travel, we woke to find our drinking water frozen solid and no heat in the car. My guess is that from the time I had fallen asleep to the time I woke up, the temperature had dropped at least forty degrees, from the teeth-chattering-but-somehow-bearable cold to now, the unbearable, loss-of-all-sensation, soul-shivering cold. The word *cold* does no justice in defining this condition. It had to be the equal and opposing contrast to hell's fire. None of us had blankets, so all night we ached with the cold, covering ourselves with everything we owned or could find, trying to become as *small* as possible, then huddling together as tightly as we could. But our train kept moving, going still father north, into more cold.

One of the men, an older and slightly built Italian, was sick and spent nearly the whole night coughing. I couldn't sleep anyway, so it didn't matter. No one slept. The cold was agonizing. If I could shut my eyes and clear my mind for a few minutes at a time, that was "sleep."

The Italian man died during the night. The extreme temperature must have been too much for him. There was no doctor to determine a specific cause of death, but he was no longer covered with the meager blanket he had earlier. Someone had taken it. Two days later a Polish woman died from severe dehydration and pneumonia. No adequate clothing, no water. That's the way it went. They were only people.

We finally arrived in the city of Inta, Komi, ASSR (Autonomous Soviet Socialist Republic—as it was then known), in Far North of Siberia, only about three hours, by train, south of the Arctic Circle. We had traveled more than a thousand miles in the cattle cars to a region absolutely cut off from the rest of Russia. The city's primary inhabitants were a native Eskimo-like nomadic people whose mainstay and means of survival were reindeer husbandry and hunting. Reindeer was the common food, the meat in Siberia, as well as the popular mode of transportation for these nomads. The people rode and also ate the reindeer. They had learned how to live in that killing cold.

Some of Siberia's most notorious labor camps surrounded Inta. The NKVD provided free slave labor to work the numerous coal mines in the area. Coal mining and logging were by far the most difficult and dangerous of all the forced labor in the camps. Only the men worked in the mines. The women were exempt, not because the NKVD believed that the male is the stronger sex, but because the camp officials feared the repercussions of sexual ten-

sion created by men and women working together in the dangerous close quarters of the mine. Any possibility of work disruption
due to gender distraction could easily lead to mechanical failure,
tunnel collapse, or explosion. The mine operators wanted to avoid
fatalities in the work force, but even more, they feared having to
shut down a mine and lose production time.

I stayed for a few weeks at the medical camp in Inta, a treatment center for prisoners needing extensive care. I was then transferred to a series of camps. For the balance of the year, until 1949,
I was assigned to a camp where the women did not have the same
work requirements as the men. Instead, they sewed, knitted, cro-
cheted, and embroidered. This was not a recreational pastime but
the constant work of repairing old or creating new clothing and
bedding for the camp. It was hard and steady toil, with inadequate
materials and little time to rest.

Working in this unit, I met Lina Ivanovna Prokofiev, the Spanish wife of the famous Russian musical composer Sergei Prokofiev.
The two of us spent many hours together, and we shared many
things. I truly admired the integrity of Lina's heart, her openness,
and her lack of pretentiousness. She was refreshing to me, and I
believe the feeling was reciprocated. We enjoyed each other's company immensely. Lina was a true friend.

I listened with interest and sympathy as she shared many
details of her fascinating life when she was a singer on the road
with her husband. Lina had met Sergei many years ago, while she
was in New York on a temporary visa from Spain and singing in

the clubs for a living. She told me she had been about to apply for U.S. citizenship at that time, but then "Sergei came along and changed my mind."

The two were married and traveled extensively as Sergei performed on concert tours throughout the United States, Europe, and other countries. Together, they had lived the lives of the privileged and fortunate few, although she confided that she never felt truly and completely fulfilled inside. Lina often spoke of the strange loneliness she had experienced, the emptiness she felt within, even in the middle of the crowds, the fame, and the tremendous accolades. Their success passed the time, but it failed to fill her heart.

"Margie," she said to me, "there was always something missing, but I never knew what it was. We had all the money we could spend. Life was glamorous. We had more attention than any two people deserve. They took our pictures everywhere we went. And Sergei was not happy either. We hardly even slept together. We were two different people, and nobody ever knew it. People looked at us and thought our life was grand."

She had been down a long road since then and told a tragic story of how the sick Soviet system had wrecked the lives of her husband and children as well as her own. Lina too had been officially labeled an enemy of the state—a vrag naroda, a traitor of the worst degree. She too was a political prisoner, banished from her home. And even worse, because of her political and banished status, neither her Russian husband nor her sons would have anything further to do with her. This sensitive and caring woman was completely abandoned by them, entirely cut off from her family's love. They never visited, and she never received any food or clothing from them.

Lina said that her sons actually had very little to do with it. "What could they do, Margie? Sergei said they had no choice, but I knew that he would never leave Russia—even if he could."

Under Stalin's rule, the official reasons for the deportation and imprisonment of all non-Russian peoples included their resistance to Soviet rule, separatism, and widespread collaboration with German occupation forces during the war. In essence, it was a political crime to be non-Russian, as Lina was. Moreover, for true Russians to associate with such people, whether family or not, meant personal, social, and political suicide. The remaining family members of an arrested vrag naroda always had a choice. It was simple, but agonizing. If you continued to support your arrested vrag naroda, you became one yourself. The other choice was to publicly condemn or denounce your loved one, salute Comrade Stalin and the state, and keep your life as before. Self-preservation is a deeply rooted human instinct. Many people took the path of Lina's family: "Since you're already there, I'll just stay here, okay? After all, better you than me, right?"

How could people treat one another like that? I knew my mama would never abandon me, but why had Lina's family turned on her? Aren't humans supposed to be created in the likeness and image of God? I asked myself a lot of questions as I witnessed these unspeakable cruelties. But in the inhuman jungle of Russia at that time, no one in power believed for an instant that "we" or "they" were "created" in any such likeness. Godlessness lay behind it all.

Lina was soon transferred to another camp, Vorkuta, which was above the Arctic Circle, a place of the most appalling conditions imaginable. I never saw or heard from her again. I missed her terribly, for we had become the best of friends, like sisters.

Our difficult and repetitious life in camp went on drearily until a woman named Tamara was assigned to us. Things were never the same again! Tamara came to play a major role in my life and in the lives of many others in our camp. She was a ballerina who had graduated from the highly reputed Kirov Ballet School in Leningrad. Until her imprisonment, she had lived in Kiev, where she was soloist for the renowned Kiev City Ballet. During the war she had been captured by the Germans when they occupied the Ukraine. They had sent her to Germany and given her the job of organizing concerts for the returning German soldiers. At the end of the war, she was returned to the Soviet Union. Tamara and many others were falsely led to believe that they were being repatriated, but to their horror, when they arrived in Russia, they were all arrested. All were tried for war crimes, including treason, for "allowing" themselves to be caught by the Germans and for working for them. I could hardly fathom the twisted thinking and injustice of this. And all these "repatriated" Russians were swiftly tried and convicted.

Accordingly, Tamara was shipped out to the Far North with a sentence just like mine: ten years hard labor and five years loss of civil rights. This was a pretty standard sentence until later in the 1950s, when the sentences became harsher still for the same so-called crimes. It was not unheard of for the new convicts to receive a twenty- to twenty-five-year sentence for the same trumped-up charges that had inflicted *only a ten-year sentence* during the prior decades.

Tamara was the most stunningly beautiful girl I had seen in all of Russia, even as a prisoner in a labor camp. From the way she walked into a room to the way she smiled into your eyes, she was irresistible. The cameras were always rolling, Tamara was always acting, and she was always an absolute natural. In a mildly seductive and alluring way, she received whatever she requested from the camp officials. She was not accustomed to denial.

Tamara received permission from the authorities to hold dance auditions for the purpose of creating a theatrical troupe. She had identified several women with artistic talents and experience in theater, song, and dance, and she persuaded the camp bureaucrats to let them stage shows and theatrical performances to entertain the camp contingent and, of course, these same camp officials and their families.

As word went around the camp that something new was happening, I asked myself why I shouldn't audition for the entertainment group. After all, I was once a gymnast, an acrobat to some degree, an athlete and competitor, and I had always wanted to dance. So I contacted the group's leaders and officially auditioned. I put some time and effort into a Caucasian dance number from the 1920s, something I remembered from my childhood in Detroit. They seemed to like it. I then did a few acrobatic routines for them as well, and they were more impressed. I was readily accepted into their group.

My camp life changed dramatically. We began extensive daily rehearsals, and for a few hours every evening we were actually able to forget our surroundings. At times it almost seemed like *real life*.

Our first performances of a variety program for the camp inmates and the officials turned out to be an overwhelming success. There was enough talent among us to pull it off. Some of the women imprisoned in this camp had been professional musicians, dancers, singers, and actresses, and they inspired the rest of us, even though we had very little in the way of props, wardrobe, and musical instruments. We had no ballet slippers and no orchestra, but we had several capable guitarists and mandolin players. They were excellent and imaginative. We sewed our own ballet slippers out of scraps and adapted our own clothes for the costumes.

Among us was a brilliant seamstress named Eleonora, who became one of my dearest friends. She sewed many of our costumes for the stage and, with her staff, created the most wonderful stage pieces, intuitively making the most and best out of their scant resources. Eleonora had been transferred here with me from Burepolom. Of Polish descent, she had grown up in Byelorussia, also known as White Russia, in Minsk. Early in the war she was taken prisoner by the Germans, transported to the interior of Germany, and forced to work in a factory until they discovered her talents as a seamstress. That ended her factory work, because she was truly fantastic at dressmaking.

At the war's end, she was arrested, tried for treason, and shipped to Burepolom. There she had a brief (but apparently not too brief) encounter with a young man from her log-felling crew, and when we met in the cattle car on the way to Inta, she informed me that she thought she was about five months pregnant. At the new camp she was placed on a special diet, more suitable for an expectant mother (but only by the harsh, meager standard of the camps). I could not have had a better friend. She shared everything with me, and I always shared my packages with her. I felt particularly sad for her at times, because she had no living relatives.

In camp, she had a way of drawing others toward her, and she always went out of her way to be comforting and kind. She was able to earn a bit of money, food, and tobacco by sewing and altering clothes for the women. The tobacco was a special joy to her; she loved cigarettes. After a while Eleonora was appointed head seamstress within the camp and assigned a staff of ten other women, who produced many beautiful garments for the officials and their families. The camp bureaucrats gladly supplied her with the fabric and thread she needed to weave her magic. Of course this was all *volunteer* work, done in her spare time, after completion of her regular grueling brigade work demands.

Eleonora was a tremendous asset to our theatrical group, and I believe she and her assistants would rival or beat any top costume or wardrobe designer today. She continued working the two jobs far into her pregnancy. One evening after rehearsal we were all standing outside, looking up at a blazing display of aurora borealis, the northern lights, which showed an unusually large band of brilliant red that night. We stared with wonder at God's dazzling natural spectacle. It was breathtaking and for a moment almost made us forget where we were. As we stood there together, like sisters, Eleonora suddenly clutched her stomach and gasped, "It's time to go now!"

We were just a few barracks away from the medical clinic and fortunately made it there just in time for her delivery. About five minutes later, she gave birth to a pretty little girl, whom she named Aleesa. Eleonora was ecstatic, but the doctor came out and asked me what she had eaten during her pregnancy, because the baby had many little white spots on her face and body. I recalled that due to the severe heartburn Eleonora experienced throughout her pregnancy, she had eaten enormous amounts of tooth powder—consisting mostly of chalk—believing it to be a remedy. The baby was taken from her mother and placed in a separate room of the clinic, where a nurse took care of her, allowing Eleonora to nurse Aleesa every four hours. Within a few weeks Aleesa's white spots vanished. I felt very close to this little girl, as if I were her god-mother, though I seldom got to see her.

All of us were soon transferred to a much larger camp, de-signed to house about four thousand women. Aleesa was placed in a special children's facility there, and Eleonora was allowed regular visits with her. This was a rare humane feature in a new life that was far more brutal than what I had known in other camps. Here women did all the daily hard labor details, the same as the men: constructing roads, hauling containers, and loading train cars—in the most dreadfully harsh conditions imaginable. We worked out-side the camp all day long, from morning until night, under the constant supervision of guards and dogs. We dug ditches, freed swamps of tree stumps, and did whatever was necessary to clear the areas for the building of roads. It was extremely difficult, long, and exhausting work in deathly frigid conditions.

Working this far north, we found that the air, coupled with tremendous amounts of snow, was so intensely cold that it some-times took us nearly the entire night to thaw out. Then, long before dawn, the following day brought more of the same. During these brutal winters, we moved immense, waist-high snowdrifts with shovels jury-rigged of wood veneer. And we had to carry on this depleting physical work under life-threatening conditions with very little food and of the poorest quality.

Many workers collapsed from the nearly unbearable physical demands and the devastating emotional strain of camp life. Some chose death as the better alternative, through either intentional starvation or assisted suicide. The ways of killing oneself were creative and many.

All persons in our camp had to wear ID numbers sewn onto our exterior clothes and also onto the dresses we were issued. My number was C-219. This was our means of identification, and it became our very identity; it was who we were. Long before any friendships were established or anyone here truly knew us by name, we were commonly known and called by the numbers we were issued. This is a well-known military tactic, used in the interest of rapid dehumanization; it is a way of leveling the playing field and preventing individual action. I knew the number 219 better than my own name.

We were only allowed to write two letters per year, each consisting of no more than one side of a standard sheet of paper, but we could receive unlimited letters and packages. I never understood the reasoning behind this. Perhaps there was none. But this strange protocol did allow me to stay in contact with Mama. She was still in our tiny one-room apartment in Gorky, just barely making ends meet, doing any work she could find—odd jobs, physical labor, or work pools—for just a few rubles a month. By extraordinary effort, she was able to send me food packages from time to time, and these sometimes included wonderful things she had received from friends and relatives in America. (After the war, this was again allowed.) Her own needs were great, but my mother, in the purest form of unconditional love, always gladly sacrificed everything she could for me. Had it not been for her staunch dedication and self-denial—along with her letters and packages—I never would have survived this nightmare.

Those food packages helped keep me from starving. Conditions were awful; we were actually happy when the camp increased our daily food allotment to about twenty-eight ounces of bread. Rarely did we eat anything else. Occasionally we would get a bit of smoked venison among the frozen cabbage and turnips, and sometimes a few drops of vegetable oil in our cereal, which was made from cornmeal or millet. We never had fresh potatoes or fresh vegetables, and we never saw eggs or milk. Those would have been highly coveted items, luxuries. Some might have even killed for them. Our ration of about two pounds of sugar per month was traded like a commodity. Most of the kitchen workers were corrupt, so a major portion of the products designated for the prisoners' meals was always diverted for their trade in money and/or cigarettes.

We lived in large barracks that accommodated about four hundred women in two large halls. Each hall had two coal-burning stoves topped with iron plates, on which we could boil water for tea or coffee. We were not permitted to cook on them, however. Each barracks was also equipped with a separate drying room, where we left our wet work clothes at night and then retrieved them the following morning. The workday was twelve hours long, six days a week.

The camps were surprisingly clean, as the grounds were stringently policed by a designated sanitary crew every month. The worst offenders and intruders, other than the overly aggressive guards with overly adventurous hands, were the bedbugs. Their bites stung, swelled, and stayed painful for many days. In an attempt to destroy these miserable insects, every month we had to remove all of our belongings from the barracks to properly disinfect the place. The customary process of dipping the slats of our bunks into boiling disinfectant got rid of them for a while, but then we'd have to do it all over again. They were our constant enemies, relentless intruders working full time on a year-round basis.

We were kept warm enough in our barracks, mainly because our camp was centrally located in the dead center of the coal-mining region. The mines were worked by the male prisoners, who were housed in the many camps around us. We were the only women prisoners in the Inta region. Our camp was composed of approximately 60 percent Ukrainians, mainly relatives of the army members formerly led by Stepan Bandera. He was a Ukrainian nationalist who, with his entire army, had defected to the Germans early in the war. These family members were still paying the price. The rest of the prisoners were Latvians, Lithuanians, Estonians, and Russians, in roughly equal numbers. And once again, among these thousands of women and the tens of thousands of men in the camps around us, it became evident that I was the only American.

Sixteen

THE CULTURAL BRIGADE

I n the face of these grim realities, we still had our remarkable leader, Tamara, who never ceased to amaze us with her unpredictable exploits in and around the camp. Under these stunningly harsh conditions, she actually convinced the authorities that we *needed* a *permanent* theatrical group to entertain the women. Tamara could get anything she wanted. She was unbelievable. We constructed a fairly large stage in the dining room, which eventually became a second home to us. In whatever *free* time we could muster, we rehearsed endlessly for our performances.

It made no sense, materially. While we still had to work our punishing jobs during the day and had barely enough energy left to fall into our bunks at night, we cared more about our group rehearsals than anything else. We practiced relentlessly, into the wee hours of the morning, just to ensure that our upcoming performances would be as close to perfect as possible. We sacrificed necessary sleep every night in order to make these shows flawless, because that was exactly what we needed. Spiritually, it kept us human. None of us were forced or coerced; it was the only outlet we had that allowed us to feel normal. It dared us to hope again and allowed us to dream, and that was priceless.

Using her gifts of persuasion, Tamara was amazingly successful in getting anything and everything she wanted, even in this Siberian wasteland. We could hardly wait to hear the news of what she had managed to procure next. Not only was she granted special authority to organize a *select* theatrical group, but she also spread the real news: members of this new group would be exempt from all former work assignments! It was incredible, but she did it. In the bizarre world of our Gulag prison, Tamara still did whatever she wanted.

Now our everyday work routine consisted solely of perfecting our craft on stage with endless rehearsals. We worked mainly to satisfy the camp authorities, and if the inmates were also entertained, well, that was a plus. It was a responsibility that we all took quite seriously, and work we did. In fact, all of us probably worked harder at this new opportunity than at anything we had done before. I was now getting much less sleep than ever before and always went to bed exhausted, mentally and emotionally spent, and physically sore. But dreams, regardless of the toil, remain priceless.

With this new opportunity came a new problem. Our relatively privileged arrangement created intense jealousy and rivalry among the other camp women. Some appreciated the temporary entertainment we created for them, but many others deeply resented the advantages we received in stark contrast to them. And who could blame them? It was easy to understand their natural reactions and bitter feelings toward these changes; circumstances were clearly unfair and biased very much in our favor.

We generally rehearsed in the dining room from about eight in the morning until about ten at night, virtually nonstop, seven days a week, receiving small additional considerations such as relaxed curfew rules. Before an upcoming show, it was not unusual for us to work later into the night and even into the early morning hours. We built our own sets, furniture, decorations, special effects, and anything else that would positively impact our shows. We made our own costumes at first and even had a hair stylist, who made wigs and false eyelashes for us. Our newly formed group included a former theatrical set designer from Paris, a musical director from Lithuania, a former actress—who was our drama coach—from the Malyi Theater in Moscow, and a wonderful pianist named Olga, our oldest member. We loved her dearly, and she became a sort of grandmother to everyone. We took our jobs as seriously as would the most highly esteemed performer on a Broadway stage. And we became very good at what we did, and we knew it.

Our group now lived a separate life, segregated from the other women prisoners. Nevertheless, we still had to tolerate the normal indignities imposed on all prisoners. We were not allowed to forget, even temporarily, that we were still political prisoners in a

Siberian labor camp. Outside of our performances, the camp officials deeply despised us as traitors, spies, and outcasts. And I always sensed that their feelings and their true sentiments went even deeper against me. They were definitely more hostile to me than the others. I was the only American among them, and the NKVD officials, along with the camp authorities, truly despised me more profoundly than all the others for that reason.

In spite of everything, we managed to have some good times giving our fellow inmates stirring and memorable evenings at the theater. We were very proud of the wonderful reviews and comments we heard from the many who enjoyed our work. We were deeply humbled as well, if we provided them even a short-lived escape from the grim life in camp. There were no performers among us who falsely held their heads high or arrogantly thought themselves special, rightfully privileged, or in any way "chosen" over the other women. We were all prisoners in a Siberian death camp; no one ever forgot that reality. And our lives were as humble as could be. Our dramatic performances were only brief diversions, momentary breaks from the madness that engulfed our lives. Most of us, inside as well as outside of our group, truly and sincerely loved one another, and humility was the common thread that joined us.

Members of the theatrical group never neglected to celebrate individual birthdays by giving presents. Maybe it was a few hairpins, a pair of socks, or a small piece of fragrant face soap. I received a lovely present for one of my birthdays before I eventually left this camp. My friends made me a beautiful, intricately knitted, sleeveless sweater.

We always presented something resembling a homemade cake to the birthday girl. To make the cakes, each of us saved our bread and various other food items for about a week. Then we passed the hat, freely donating the items we had saved. We would dry the bread and crush it repeatedly with a bottle, making fine crumbs, then wet the crumbs with a solution of vitamin C syrup (or jam) and water. We would then place a ring of cardboard (the size of the cake desired) on a flat board covered with fancy paper, designed and cut out by our artist, a young Lithuanian girl named Aldona.

The damp crumbs were then pressed down within the cardboard ring and covered with a creamy filling, produced by laboriously hand whipping sugar, butter, and chocolate (all donated items). Alternate layers of crumbs and filling were added until the cake reached the desired height. We frosted it again with the same delicious cream and let it stand for about five hours, until the ring could be removed. Although the crumbs were made from a very hard, black rye bread (the only kind available), our cakes generally turned out to be quite delectable. They were always a pure blessing of enjoyment to receive!

As a member of the brigade, I now received my serious indoctrination into top-level ballet education. One day at rehearsal Sonya let me try her ballet pointes. She was an exceptional German ballerina and a wonderful member of our group. It was the first time I had ever worn real pointes. They were great; they made me feel like a real ballerina. But afterward, my toes were a bloody mess for weeks! I loved it so much that I persisted. And then finally, partly through rest but mostly by continuous practicing and toughing it out, my toes became hardened enough to perform. And they stayed that way for the rest of my life, from those long-ago days of endless ballet practices and performances in the labor camp at Inta.

Leksi was another member of our group and a good friend to me. One day he gave me my very own pair of pointes as a present. "Here, Margaret," he said, handing them to me. "I got these just for you!" I was thrilled. I didn't know what to say. I had no idea where I could get my own pointes nor where Leksi could have gotten them or even why. I didn't ask him; it didn't matter to me. I knew Leksi. I knew his heart. His motives were pure, and I trusted him completely. Leksi was an extremely talented performer himself, but after my routines, he was always the first to offer congratulations, a welcoming hand, or a pat on the back. He was a cheerleader for others, a very special man, kind and gentle. In the middle of this spiritually and literally parched and frozen wasteland, my friend Leksi was truly a refresher of others.

We spent countless hours daily just mending and darning our pointes to keep them properly conditioned and fully supportive for our work. They were the only ones we had, so we had to take good care of them. My strength was acrobatic and character dancing, which called for greater athletic skill and overall creativity than did other parts. That's precisely where my early training came in; I now felt very fortunate to have spent all those years as a competitive athlete. I was also grateful to my parents for allowing and motivating me to devote so much time to sports and dance. Those formative years created the basis for my acceptance into these dance groups, providing me the background and foundation to excel and advance in my new work. At times I could actually feel a sense of purpose in what I did.

Initially, I was the only acrobatic dancer in the entertainment group. So they reserved most of the lesser-used, more physical dance parts for me. I ended up doing virtually all the vigorous female parts, those requiring strong athleticism in addition to dance skills. Being quite thin and agile, I was also able to dance many of the male parts. Basically, I just loved performing on the stage, even in a labor camp, even in Russia. There was nothing quite like it. I loved having a highly appreciative audience watching and enjoying my performance. That's what made it worthwhile. That's why I did it. Why else? If my life had somehow turned out differently, maybe in another time and place I could have been a professional ballerina.

What always inspired me most about the craft was the degree of personal flexibility and innovation allowed the dancer within the actual movement; it was all uniquely *you*, the inherent soul that the routine pleaded for. But the thrill of it all, the athleticism involved, the feedback, was all so exhilarating, so mesmerizing! Looking into the eyes and the hearts of an audience that has been moved by your dance, your performance, is the very reason a dancer dances. There was nothing in the world I loved as much. *This is it!* I thought. *Only not here.*

I was also a member of the stage carpenter crew and the producer of many special effects and accessories used in our shows. We always needed nails and boards, for which we had to scrounge constantly. Occasionally we received packages of food in wooden boxes from friends and relatives. We could barely wait to open them when they came, not only because of the goodies inside, but so we could immediately use the boxes. We spent hours pulling and straightening nails. They could be used again and again on various projects, so we took utmost care in preserving their future usefulness. We used our civilian clothes for stage and performance costumes since we weren't allowed to wear them for routine dress anyway. For our required work details, we were issued padded jackets, pants, and felt boots for the severe cold of winter, along with flimsy leather-and-canvas work shoes.

In the meantime, our little orchestra was expanding and flourishing. Quite surprisingly, we were blessed one day with the acquisition of an old grand piano brought in from another camp. We had no idea how it arrived at our camp. That was very strange in an environment where everything had to be accounted for. Yesterday we had no grand piano; today we do. But no one, including several of the more trusted guards, could tell us where it came from. The mystery piano was quite weathered and neglected and in desperate need of tuning, but we loved it. Our dear Olga had it wonderfully tuned in no time, and she also restored the wood to its former luster. When she was through, the sound coming from this grand prize was the sound of which dreams are made! Oh, how music could so generously take me back to another place and time, a time of peace and tranquillity, a time in my past with Papa and Mama, a time nearly forgotten, a time of pure joy...before life's unforeseen detours. I will never forget the sound emanating from this grand treasure or how much we loved it!

One of our members owned an accordion, and our orchestra leader taught herself to play it. Stefanie, who came from Vilnius, Lithuania, actually mastered the instrument, performing some very complicated musical compositions, all by ear. Equally talented was a woman named Tatiana, from Odessa, who sang popular songs and accompanied herself on the accordion or piano. Tatiana also played for our morning ballet practices. She claimed to have been married to, and divorced from, the mayor of Bucharest. Since she was tall and athletic, she played many of our supporting male roles. A close friend of hers, Regina from Moscow, was one of our better actresses; but she was very stubborn and opinionated and hard to get along with.

Something about this place, this camp, these people, seemed to bring out either the worst or the best a person had to offer. Sharing this burdensome time, one's true colors were fully exposed, because there was no hiding. It was a time of personal pressure, a time of constant testing to see what you were made of. You could fall or climb; it was up to you. Circumstances didn't really change: the difference was in whether or not you could adapt. The choice was always yours.

A memorable part of our group was a very beautiful actress named Larissa, who had been with the Gorky City Theater. She very much resembled Vivien Leigh in *Gone with the Wind*, and whether she was on stage performing or not, she always played the famed Scarlett O'Hara to a *T*, wearing her hair in a low-slung net and tossing her head. She was something to see!

Rita Maas was another important member of our entertainment group. She came from a community of German-speaking people called Volga-Deutsche, who originated in Prussia. These people lived on the Volga River in a tightly knit community, with their own customs and principles, abiding by and within the Soviet regime and system. During World War II, however, the Russians uprooted the Volga-Deutsche, which numbered in the thousands, imprisoning or exiling them to remote areas, scattering them all over the country.

Yet another member of the entertainment group, with a fine contralto voice, was Valentina, who became a good friend of mine. She was one of the few who had survived the devastating bombardment of Dresden, Germany, during the war. Valentina was an engineer by trade, the head of the camp's building group, and she supervised the construction of several new barracks. Her duties also included the general maintenance and upkeep of the entire camp.

Other entertainers in the group came from Latvia, Lithuania, and Estonia. My favorite Latvian was a very tall girl, also named Tamara, who was a natural comedian, a pure delight, and played mainly humorous roles and also did comical dancing. She was probably the all-around crowd favorite during our performances, with the winning lightness of her personality. At times it was hard to tell that she was actually a political prisoner sentenced to a Siberian labor camp. Unlike anyone else in the camp, Tamara had a gentle and pleasant type of indifference, as if sometimes she was here and sometimes she wasn't; as if she could just turn the nonsense off whenever she wanted to. I found it impossible to do that. One day I asked her how she did it.

She said, "We won't be here forever, Margaret. We must remember that. I don't turn it on and off. It's always on. I just decided that I won't let this place make me so bitter that I have no life to live when it's over."

I thought long and hard about her wise words. She had a definite edge, which I couldn't quite figure out but admired. In a way she was like a younger version of my mother. *Could she possibly forget where she was? Or did she possess something I too should have had? Did she know God in such a profound way that it could strip fear of its stronghold and power over her life in this place, or was it something else?*

Tamara was also my favorite partner in the game of Aggravation, which we called Ritch-Ratch. Sometimes we'd play for hours and well into the nights. I manufactured the first game board from a piece of veneer that I found in our stage wood supply. I laid it out with my drafting tools and colored all the moves. Then some girls from the crew working in the city garbage dumps managed to bring me back various colored toothpaste caps, which we used as our game pieces.

One day the camp commander strolled into our barracks while Tamara and I were playing Ritch-Ratch. He was so impressed with the game and the board I had made that he asked me to make twenty more just like it for the other barracks. Of course I didn't have a choice, but I didn't mind. I thought it was an unusually kind gesture to think that the other prisoners might enjoy it as well. So, in time and with some help, I supplied the other barracks with boards. They were an overwhelming success. Soon the entire camp was playing Ritch-Ratch on my game boards. So, in addition to my athletic and dramatic stage roles, I also became the official camp game maker. I produced some checkerboards and domino pieces too, hundreds of them, precisely cut from wood by Valentina's crew, with dots carefully burned on by a soldering iron.

I also used the toothpaste tubes themselves. I sliced them open lengthwise, thoroughly washed and dried them, and straightened out all the wrinkles. This produced very shiny pieces of gold foil, which I used to make sequins, stage jewelry, and ornaments for our hair. Toothpaste tubes also formed a candelabra and chandeliers for the stage. For Tamara, our teacher and now my best friend, we cut out more than two thousand foil discs to cover her costume for a solo she danced in our production of *Faust*.

We always collected old toothbrushes as well. By shaving off the remaining bristles and sharpening the handles with an emery wheel in the tool shop, we made some very effective knives for everyone in the group, not for weapons, but for practical, non-threatening purposes. These knives would not cut wood but were fine for spreading butter or lard on bread, when we were fortunate enough to have it, and for other little tasks. I also made some very fine mascara from coal soot and laundry soap. It's truly amazing what can be improvised when necessity meets motivation.

Improvisation, expression, camaraderie, joy: we all gave much and received much as members of the Cultural Brigade, the official name given to our group. Some of the women assigned to the work brigades believed that we had a softer life, but when they witnessed our sweating during our ballet practices and rehearsals, they gained a whole new perspective. In fact, after watching us, they almost unanimously confessed that they would rather dig ditches! The truth was that rehearsing was *work*, hard, exhausting work. We never goofed around. We worked and worked and then worked some more, extremely hard, day in and day out. Maybe it did not feel like work to me because of my love for ballet.

After rehearsing for hours and days on end, we would stage our official performances late in the evening. Our audience consisted mainly of the officials and the prison guards, but occasionally some of the other prisoners were allowed to watch. Once in a while we would travel to the nearby men's camps to perform for their officials as well.

Then, one day, one of those unforeseen detours caught us all off guard. There was an abrupt change in our camp leadership; a new commander arrived. He took a dim view of what he called our "nonworking brigade." I had secretly wondered just how long our troupe would last, but now our brigade was ordered to join the others and "carry our workload" within the camp. To quote this new commander's cynical view of our theatrical work, we could "no longer take it easy and dance our life away." Any future dramatic preparation would have to be done strictly on our own time, after our mandatory work was finished. "If you want to quit [your drama], you can do that too," was the loud and clear message we received from him.

I had formerly been assigned to a construction brigade, which generally did more physically demanding work than other brigades. Now, in addition to those requirements, I was given the job of hauling water to the kitchen in a horse-drawn cart. Beyond that, I was to clear all the snow and ice from the boardwalks. That alone was steady work; winter lasted forever in northern Siberia—at least nine months of the year. Our former Cultural Brigade now had to keep all the barracks freshly whitewashed, which was a never-ending job. These new work demands drained us and left us with absolutely nothing except maybe time to sleep. We had neither the strength nor the time for ballet practices, much less the energy to perform. Theatrics? Who cared about dancing now? At night we just fell into our bunks.

Soon the other prisoners rose up in protest—a small revolt—that our stage performances had been discontinued. Our dramatic work had brought momentary joy and entertainment to many others in the camp. Theater provided a mental and emotional escape when physical escape was out of the question. The protesters made such noise and resistance that they actually persuaded the new camp hierarchy to let us dance again! For the nearly seven years I spent in the camp at Inta, the Cultural Brigade continued to create a breath of air and hope in the Gulag.

Seventeen

ACTRESSES

O ur theatrical group lived and worked in very close quarters. We came to know one another very well and shared many stressful and disturbing experiences, in addition to our performances and celebrations. I will never forget two of our members who asserted themselves most forcefully.

Natasha was a young Ukrainian woman who stood out as distinct from everyone else in the group. She was always very tense, which we ascribed to her unhappy, tormented childhood. She had no family to speak of. During her time in the camp, she had no contact with anyone from her past, and she didn't receive any material help from anyone else. It was therefore extremely difficult for her to cope with camp life; we all thought she was hungry most of the time. Her situation demonstrated the vital role families played in the prisoners' survival in the camps. But we could not have asked for a more devoted and loyal member of our group. Natasha was talented in both song and dance, and because of her height and build, she often played some of the male characters in our presentations.

When it came to rehearsals, she was one of our most staunchly dedicated and disciplined members. Unless forcibly restrained elsewhere, she would always be found working at her craft. The rewards of her practicing were evident when Natasha and I danced a lovely duet from the ballet *Stone Flower* and also one of the Polovetsian dances from *Prince Igor*.

But Natasha was also highly volatile, with an unpredictable temper and a short fuse. Quite suddenly, out of nowhere, she could become violent. One summer she became especially upset with the producers of our upcoming show because they could not find her a suitable role. At the time she was assigned to one of worst jobs in the camp—driving a horse and wagon to haul the refuse from the latrines to a designated dumping spot. One particular day, enraged with the leaders of our group, she tore onto the stage during full rehearsals at high noon. She threw a bucket of *the stuff* all over the producers, then stormed off. It was shocking, disgusting—and really funny. Despite the dreadful reality around us, I don't think I had ever laughed so hard in my life! I hope Natasha enjoyed it too, because she was immediately incarcerated, then transferred to another camp, and we never saw her again. Years later we heard that she was in a central Asian camp in the Kazakh ASSR, leading an entertainment group there. But no one in our camp ever forgot the day that a prisoner seized the initiative and made her own drama right in front of us.

A very pretty English girl named Betty also worked her way into our entertainment group. She had marvelous blond hair and a very nice voice, and she was a wonderful dancer, but most of us thought she was too fragile to handle our demanding rehearsal and performance schedules. One day she showed us what a false impression we had.

I don't know how or where she became pregnant. Women prisoners fraternized with the male guards, but Betty just didn't seem the type. However it had happened, she did not want to be pregnant, mainly for fear of losing her position in the Cultural Brigade. She felt that if she had to leave the group, she would never survive the hard labor of a work brigade. Evidently that was her only reason for not wanting to have the baby. She was right about one thing: if the prison officials had discovered that she was pregnant, she would have been expelled from the group.

Among our dancers was a girl named Valya, who offered to help Betty. She said she'd had some experience in performing abortions. As a teenager, she had often accompanied her mother, a doctor, in doing abortions to supplement their income. Valya convinced Betty that she knew exactly how to go about it.

It was a very hot summer day. I was lying on my bunk, resting an ankle I had recently sprained during a show. Other members were also lying about the barracks, reading, sewing, talking, or just napping. Since the guards habitually entered our barracks several times a day, without notice and during our most private times, Valya put two girls at the door as lookout.

Betty's bunk was just two away from mine. I knew what was about to happen.

"Betty," I said, "do you know what you're doing? Have you thought this through?" Betty said nothing; she simply ignored me.

Then Tamara, who seemed more upset than anyone else, quickly spoke up. "It's a life, Betty! It's a baby. It's yours. There are other kinds of work you can do, you know? The brigade isn't everything."

Betty coldly snapped, "Shut up, Tammy. It's none of your business! Who asked you anyway?"

Tamara got up in a rage and stormed out of the barracks, knocking the door nearly off its hinges. I didn't know what to do. I was terrified and speechless, and most of the other girls looked either disdainful or sad. A few were noticeably angry but did nothing to interfere as the situation unfolded.

Apparently, the day before, Valya had concocted a potion for Betty to take, and she was now starting to feel its effects. She was beginning to experience severe pain and contractions, and this went on for several hours. Her contractions became more painful and frequent, but Betty never made a single sound. At the end of our barracks lived another small working brigade of women, and Betty didn't want them to know what was happening. She didn't want to run the risk of getting caught or being turned in. I was in awful distress about what was happening, but there wasn't anything I could do about it. I put my head under my pillow.

Valya was trying to comfort Betty, giving her a rag to chew on when her pains became unbearable. Then one of the lookouts suddenly came in and whispered, "Shhhh... The guards are next door!" They were in the barracks beside ours, which meant we would be their next stop. Instantly, everyone in our brigade made a great show of singing and talking loudly to drown out sounds that might come from Betty's corner bunk.

We were extremely tense, but surprisingly, the guards did not stop this time or harass us as they usually did. *Why was that?* I didn't understand. But they soon left, and there were no more interruptions. Maybe there should have been. Nevertheless, Betty and Valya went ahead and did what they did.

The baby appeared. It was a girl and looked well formed, at least five months along. Betty had worn a tight-fitting garment the entire time, effectively concealing her condition, not only from the camp authorities and our group leaders, but also from Valya, who said that she had been misled into believing that Betty was only two months along.

As we watched, horrified, Valya smothered the baby before it could make a sound. Everyone in the room helplessly looked on in shock at the murder happening before our eyes.

Sonya, another German dancer in our group, helped Valya conceal the dead baby and bury her in a construction site next door. Several years later, quite by accident, the little skeleton was discovered, but no one ever reported Betty or Valya. I was scared out of my wits that day, and I don't know why I didn't do anything about it. *Dear God, please have mercy on us all!*

Things were never quite the same in our brigade after that. We never discussed it, but everyone knew something terrible had taken place, and people were now very different. Everybody had an opinion, but I think our hearts were just broken. Even at that time, before I had a developed consciousness of the divine sanctity of that baby's life and when I generally believed in the woman's right to choose, Betty's decision and actions horrified me. I knew it was wrong, but we were not able to talk her out of it. It was her choice, but I had a strong sense that it wasn't what God wanted.

Betty recovered remarkably well and continued with her normal activities in our group almost as if nothing had happened. But I sensed something different about her, although she never said anything else about the abortion. I saw that it was hard for her to pretend that everything was all right. I knew she was faking it, that she was now very different inside, though not in an outwardly remorseful or shameful way. She just seemed more lifeless than she used to be. Her actions seemed the same as always, but her spirit was not. The life in her eyes had vanished. Something else inside of Betty had died…along with her baby.

I guess I should have shown compassion and forgiven Betty for what she had done. But the truth is, I never liked her after that. I avoided her. Her situation had made me intensely aware of my own wasted femininity, these years of deprivation. I had never wanted any man but Nikolai, but I was forcefully reminded that I'd never even had a chance to meet someone else. Now I knew how much I longed to be a mother, to have a husband, to be part of a family again. But I was helpless. I don't recall having ever said another word to Betty, or she to me.

Eighteen

SIBERIA: DESPAIR AND HOPE

The unrelenting harshness of labor-camp life wore down the human spirit in ways unimaginable. One day a Ukrainian girl (who was not a member of our troupe) was notified by the authorities that she was being sent to another camp. She was ordered to gather her belongings immediately, but she resisted leaving her friends, who were deeply dedicated to one another. The group helped her burrow into a very deep snowdrift on the camp premises. Her accomplices supplied her with warm food and drink for three days, but then the inevitable occurred.

The authorities made all of the inmates leave their barracks and stand outdoors at attention in the fierce cold until finally one of the girl's friends could bear up no longer. She broke down and disclosed her friend's whereabouts. When the guards found the missing girl, she was flogged in front of the entire camp. They marched her through the premises to demonstrate the results of her bad decision. She and her friends, including the informant, were then sentenced to an additional five years of imprisonment and shipped out to different camps the next morning. They paid a great price for the human relationships they valued so highly, but it was one of the few aspects of life in the Gulag that actually gave prisoners hope.

Friends and food were some of our most important resources. By bribing the guards, we were able to cook in the drying room every now and then. One time my mother sent me a package containing fresh potatoes and onions. We immediately cleaned and sliced all of the onions, at least three pounds of them, and fried them in a large pan. They were the most delicious food we had eaten in months! Every time we were blessed with potatoes, I prepared a gigantic pot of potato salad, a dish we traditionally ate on my birthday. Other women donated ingredients such as eggs, mayonnaise, and bacon. Such luxuries were bartered for, received as favors from the camp authorities or from friends, or exchanged with neighboring camps for rarities acquired through a particular camp or specific work assignment. Potato salad was the food I desired most of all. Or perhaps it tied for first place with a special Hungarian pastry dish of my mother's—*kipfeln,* an apricot-jam-filled pastry. All my friends eagerly anticipated the next package of Mama's kipfeln. They came very seldom, but each package was enjoyed more than the one before.

Mama's financial resources were very limited, and it was expensive to make and ship these cookies, so she could only send them on rare occasions. She denied herself in order to give me hope. I always knew that someone who loved me was outside the camp, waiting for me to come back. Nothing could ever substitute for that inherent knowledge. My mama's love for me was a constant reminder, a driving force, and all the motivation I needed to one day live again.

I remember another time when a friend gave me food for hope. One day a Russian girl called me over to her barracks, telling me she had a surprise for me. Marina Minkova knew I was an American, and she shocked me when she pulled her hands from behind her back and handed me a genuine peanut-butter sandwich made with American peanut butter! "What do you think of that?" Marina said with pride, her eyes smiling as she handed me the sandwich.

"Wow," is all I could say as my eyes nearly popped out. "How did you get this, Marina?"

Marina said her father had a great job in the Russian army's supply department and was therefore able to send her many gifts and food items, including Spam, powdered eggs, milk, and other such rare treats. I was so grateful to Marina for her thoughtfulness that it made me cry. Peanut butter may be one of life's simple pleasures, but on this day it was much more for me. What an incredible delight, this taste and texture and smell. I had not eaten peanut butter in years. In fact, I had almost forgotten there was such a thing. That peanut-butter sandwich tasted like America! And someday I was going to be there again.

One winter I became dreadfully ill with strep throat and spent an entire week recovering in the hospital. That following summer I contracted a severe bladder infection and was again hospitalized for a week. No sooner did I recover from that infirmity than I came down with a serious infection in my back from a contaminated needle used to inoculate me against cholera. The acute pain put me in the hospital once again, for two weeks this time. By the time I recovered from all these afflictions, I had lost a great deal of weight, which I didn't have to spare, along with most of my strength.

To my amazement, the camp doctor prescribed a diet of milk, white bread, butter, ground beef, and mashed potatoes—foods I hadn't seen in many years. I thought I was dreaming and asked myself, *Is this all I had to do to get this real food again? Did I just have to become deathly ill?* It seemed almost worth the suffering. I remember how good that meal tasted. I enjoyed it as much as any meal I can remember.

Medical care in the camp was minimal but humane. In spite of the intensive surveillance by the guards at the work details and guard posts, some women managed to get pregnant, and it was possible to have a somewhat ordinary pregnancy and a healthy delivery. Considering our surroundings, facilities for mothers nursing their children were modest, certainly strained, but decent. These were, after all, prisoners—political or otherwise—having babies out of wedlock while imprisoned in Siberian labor camps.

These children were, nonetheless, well taken care of in a separate building at the camp: the children's home. The nursing mothers were allowed to care for their babies every four hours, and they received special authorizations to work only within the confines of the camp.

Though a certain amount of medical care was provided, I saw more death during the years I spent in the various Siberian camps than one person should have to witness. The overall camp conditions were unbearably harsh and unforgiving. Prisoners received grossly inadequate food rations and insufficient clothing, which made it hard to endure the severe weather and long working hours. Camp inmates often were physically abused by the guards and officials. The death rate in the camps was extremely high due to exhaustion and disease. Tuberculosis and dysentery were the most common "natural" killers.

Those who could tolerate the cold and the lack of food often succumbed to heart sickness—the emotional and spiritual symptoms of an irreparably broken heart, for which there was no cure. The entire Russian system was cancerous, claiming innocent victims by the millions: prisoners and their families, nationals or otherwise. The best anyone could do was to endure. The challenge was to maintain a semblance of personal peace and to override bitterness and anger of the soul. More prisoners weakened from this not-so-physical disease of the heart than from anything else.

Suicide took on epidemic proportions throughout the Siberian Gulag, affecting some areas and some camps more than others. In

Siberia it was easy to give in to hopelessness and despair, to become consumed with the thought of ending it all. That all-too-real tragedy hit close one day. I had a good friend, Sasha, from southern Latvia. I didn't know her entire background or the story of how she had arrived here, but she had been falsely arrested and then separated from her small child and family in her Latvian home. She was having great difficulty coping with camp life, becoming increasingly despondent. Then, at a time when she appeared to be getting better, she hanged herself from the doorknob of a small shed behind our barracks.

In those terrible times there was much time to think—perhaps more time for that than anything else. I could not easily escape the dark and desolate notions of my mind or those voices always whispering in my ear, "This is too impossible, too insane." But I had reason to continue; I had made plans. So I did not entertain the option of suicide—for longer than the split second of a fleeting thought.

I refused to consider killing myself. Instead, I gained a new motivation that defiantly refused to give up, no matter what the conditions. Or was it the grace of God that gave me a reason to continue? I did believe that *he* had a purpose for me and for my life, although it was hard to see. I knew I was going to live, but I had no idea when I would get out of this wretched place.

During one of my earlier stays in the hospital, I had noticed a particular ward that contained about twenty women who were diagnosed with severe mental illness. There was a higher percentage of such patients in the men's camps. I'm not sure of the reasons for this, but I strongly believe that women survived the Gulag's brutal conditions better than the men did. I saw several possible factors. First, the women were more instinctively able to keep themselves occupied with chores, such as laundry, sewing, and knitting, and by attending to their appearance.

We often organized clandestine religious ceremonies on Easter and Christmas and were able to conduct modest religious services on Sunday—another way to keep a hopeful perspective. The men were certainly under more physical demands and pressures than the women, but both sexes experienced unfathomable emotional and mental pressures, such as had to be experienced to be believed. Still, in general, I observed that the women were more successful than the men in combating their depression and controlling their inner demons. I saw it time and again in the cruel and stark reality of life in the labor camps.

After I had finally recovered from this round of illnesses and was regaining some strength, I was more than a bit chagrined when I fractured my left ankle. While rehearsing a wild Greek folk dance for an upcoming performance, I fell off the stage and landed in the orchestra area. No more dancing for a while. This not-too-comical exploit put me out of action for about six months, but the real pain stemming from this mishap was not in my ankle. The ultimate pain was not being able to dance and perform!

I was still limping quite badly from my injury when a girlfriend from one of the work brigades handed me a note. It read, "My little Maidie, I am here to see you. I miss you so badly. Try to meet me tomorrow if you can. But don't do it if you don't think it will work, okay? I do not want you to be in jeopardy. I love you so very much! Your loving Mama."

I was flabbergasted! How could Mama be here? I was beside myself with joy and could barely control my elation as I frantically quizzed the girls for more information. Mama had arrived in Inta the day before and had secretly solicited the help of my friends in arranging to meet me. There was nothing I wanted to do more than to see my precious mother right now! At that moment I would have traded another five years of imprisonment for just a few minutes with her—to see her face, to hear her voice, and to touch her again!

There was only one way we could possibly meet, and it would be very dangerous and difficult, a radical gamble at best. I needed help, accomplices—several willing accomplices—and the support of true friends. Fortunately, throughout this labor camp at Inta, my reluctant home, I had many of them. The leader of the girls' brigade said she could dress me up as one of them and sneak me out of camp with them on their next work assignment. That sounded like a good plan to me, if some surprise or unforeseen detour didn't derail us. I wasn't forecasting doom, but I knew how strange things would come up when you least expected them. A standard camp policy, a habit or a routine, would be done the same way every day for a thousand years, and then, out of nowhere, a sudden diversion would thwart your plan.

The next morning it was raining, which I hoped would provide a natural distraction. I wrapped a borrowed shawl around my face and shoulders, leaving only my eyes visible, and marched out of my barracks with the brigade. With my heart pounding wildly, I managed to pass inspection at the camp gate undetected. To conceal my obvious limp, my dear friends and accomplices formed a moving shield, like a barrier around me, so I wouldn't be noticed as the group tramped slowly, in close formation, through the mud. I feared that limp might give me away and seal my fate.

We walked over a mile to our destination, and my ankle was threatening to collapse as we arrived. But I couldn't stop now! The brigade's assigned task was to shovel a huge pile of garbage into wheelbarrows, then haul the loads into a waiting dump truck, which was manned by two camp guards. It wouldn't be easy to meet anyone here; at first glance, it appeared impossible. But when the truck was finally filled with the trash, the guards would leave, so that was step one.

In full view of the guards stood a wretched outhouse, which hadn't been cleaned for months. It was filthy, rank, and foul smelling. Only the most desperate prisoners would use it. The guards, we already knew, would not go near it. Even in an extreme emergency, going inside would be a challenge. I nearly fainted when one of the girls told me that my mother was waiting for me inside the outhouse.

My knees buckled. Then someone emphatically whispered, "Margaret, keep your head. You must keep your wits about you. This is no time for foolish mistakes!"

Trying not to breathe, I acted as though I needed to go to the outhouse, and I managed to squeeze inside the door and into my mother's loving arms. The very instant my eyes met Mama's, the disgusting stench seemed to flee, or at least it could be forgotten, dismissed by the power of the moment. She held me tightly, fervently kissing my face, my forehead, my cheeks, and I was doing the same. "Oh, Mama, I love you so much. You don't know how much I've missed you!"

We had to be cautious, quiet, and quick, making the most of these brief and precious moments together. There was so much to say but so little time in which to say it. I couldn't stay in there for more than three minutes, because it would raise suspicions. Any carelessness or stupidity at this moment would have spelled disaster for both of us. But this was a moment of the heart, and words were strictly optional. So we just stood there inside the nauseating outhouse—oblivious to the smell—hugging each other for dear life, while Mama repeated, "How are you? Are you okay? Are you all right?"

Although I was silently standing with Mama in a vile Siberian toilet, it could have been Solomon's palace. Being with Mama was all that mattered—looking deeply into her eyes, deep into the past, both of us wondering our many what-ifs. We spared no tears. They seemed to say it all. Oh, Mama's eyes—how I missed them! Hers looked into mine, through mine, and deep into my heart.

"Have you any word about Papa?" I asked her.

"No word, Maidie," was all she replied. And no other words were necessary, because I got to touch her, if only for a moment.

There wasn't much time left, and Mama sensed it. She placed her cold hands on my cheeks, kissed me sweetly again, and said, "Maidie, do you see the goodness of God? We will make it. We will be all right. Now go!"

I knew it was impossible for me to stay another instant. Someone diverted the guards' attention momentarily, so I bolted out the door and back to the group. *We made it!* My poor mama had to stand in that foul place the rest of the day, until the assignment was finished and the truck left. But she was undetected. I was grateful to the rain for washing away the ocean of tears I spilled that day and even more grateful that God had allowed this most joyous and blessed reunion to take place.

The following day my mother made her way to the camp's main guardhouse. She tried to see me again, to give me some food and clothes she had brought from Gorky. Her request was flatly denied; I was not allowed to see her, nor was she allowed to leave me the package. But I was still exceedingly happy for our brief moments together the day before. Mama had traveled nearly sixteen hundred miles, from Gorky to Inta, just to see me for three minutes in a rank-smelling outhouse. But I was eternally thankful to God that we were able to pull it off. Her love and persistence strengthened my own courage and hope.

The kind and selfless help of my many friends had made our

meeting possible. I knew the attempt could easily have ended in disaster. Had only one of them changed her mind or changed her heart, had she decided to cash in by selling us out, that would have sealed our fate. Soviet camp officials were not people to mess with; they took such offenses seriously and sometimes eliminated such problems permanently.

Later on I was shocked to hear that my mother nearly lost her life that day while boarding the return train to Gorky. A crowd stampeded, trying to get on the train at the very last minute. Mama had to run after the train, which had already started to pull away from the platform. She was just barely able to grab the railings, with nowhere to place her feet, as the train began picking up speed. Just in the nick of time, a very strong man grabbed her by the forearms and pulled her to the safety of the car's platform. Mama told me that if he had not pulled her up precisely when he did, she would have fallen under the train. As it was, the crowd was so large that she had to travel outside on the platform for several miles before she could make her way into the car.

Eventually Mama pushed her way in, where it was terribly crowded and uncomfortable, but everyone was grateful for the warmth. Immediately she tried to find the man who had saved her so she could thank him. But he was nowhere to be found. She wanted him to know how grateful she was for his saving her life. She thoroughly searched that train, up and down, looking everywhere possible, and still she could not find him. Mama said it was just about the strangest thing she had ever experienced. Where was the man? Was he a man? Or did something else happen? The train had not made any other stops since that station where she boarded.

I remember my mama saying to me, "Maidie, I knew I was done for. I felt myself slipping and falling. And where those hands came from, I'll never know." She said, "Maidie, just moments later, when I tried to find him and thank him, he was nowhere to be seen."

Nineteen

GOOD-BYE JOE

On March 5, 1953, Russians everywhere heard the news that Joseph Stalin had died. There was no great sorrow when we prisoners learned he was dead. Instead, throughout the land, mass jubilation and joyous and drunken celebration were the order of the day, even among his own supporters. Stalin had ruled as absolute dictator of the Soviet Union throughout World War II and right up to his death. It is said that twenty-seven million Russians perished during this period of unrivaled inhumanity. Joseph Stalin, whose name I had hated and feared more than any other, was finally no more.

Things soon began to change for the better. We could feel it in the air and all around us, a noticeable season of change. Most refreshing indeed! It felt as if the master of the house had suddenly died, and all of his grateful servants were beginning to celebrate their new lives. Stalin's death marked the end of an era of unparalleled wickedness.

The Soviet system of ruthless oppression, however, had not suddenly ended, but a new hopefulness began to emerge. Perhaps it marked the beginning of a somewhat kinder and gentler Russia. We all wondered how this monumental event would affect our lives in the camps. We waited, wishing and praying for a better day on the horizon, with more hope than any of us had experienced in a great many years. At the pronouncement of Stalin's death, our entire camp enjoyed a three-day respite from work. We used those three days to recuperate, to wash and mend our clothes, and to relax and read. We were not allowed to celebrate outwardly; instead, we did so quietly within.

After Stalin's death the Gulag population was reduced significantly, and conditions for inmates improved somewhat. Forced-labor camps continued to exist, although on a considerably smaller scale, into the Mikhail Gorbachev period, and the government even opened some camps to scrutiny by journalists and human-rights activists. With the advance of democratization, political prisoners and prisoners of conscience eventually all but disappeared from the Russian camps, but such was not the case for me—not yet. I was still an American political prisoner, held against my will in a Siberian labor camp that was still very much open.

A few improvements to our lifestyle were most welcome. We were now allowed to write unlimited letters, which everyone quickly took full advantage of. And a true miracle occurred when we began to be paid for our work. Moreover, a store was established within the camp confines where we could buy fabrics, canned goods, white bread, sunflower seeds, cheese, candy, and cigarettes. None of these items had been available to us before. The identification numbers we were previously forced to wear were removed. No more C-219.

We were astonished to find radishes, peeled onions, and garlic on the tables for the first time in many years. Also sliced bread in lovely, unlimited quantities. We felt like a God-given food bank had just opened for us, and we began to gain weight, which was a good thing. As a rule, any change in the camps was positive. I had always tried to see the cup as half-full, but now I felt as if I was slowly beginning to see the end of my pain, the light at the end of this perpetually dark tunnel.

Our daily menu suddenly became varied, an exciting alternative to the dull sameness. We began to see bits of meat and fat in our daily servings, a wonderful new thing. A small restaurant even opened, where we could purchase tasty meals if we saved enough money. Of course, our pay never lasted the full month, but at least now we had plenty of bread. I considered bread to be the essential and most-desired food item of all.

Another blessed new freedom was the creation of a communal kitchen, converted from a small wooden shack. We could now cook meals from the food we received from home or purchased in our store. What a pleasure that was. So many people applied for cooking time that a sign-up schedule was strictly enforced. We were also happy when a young woman from Moscow with an education in nutrition made a suggestion to the camp authorities. We had forever been served a kind of little salted fish, one large bowl per table. They weren't very appetizing and were frequently discarded. We knew there were several large barrels of these fish in the kitchen, and we would have to face them every day. This woman proposed that the fish should first be smoked, promising they would be ten times better. She constructed a makeshift outdoor smoker from wooden boards and rocks, and she was right. Smoked, those fish became downright tasty.

Eventually, we smoked all these thousands of fish, and we didn't want to run out of them. Though the fish was delicious, I was glad I wasn't the one who had to sit there day after day stringing them on wires to be cooked. This same woman was subsequently appointed to manage our kitchen, and the camp was treated to some nice diversions from our regular menu. She basically used the same ingredients as before but in many new and exciting ways. These new creations became the spice of our lives.

Another important new privilege afforded our brigade was the opportunity to travel, under guard of course, to the men's camps to perform our repertoire. Our visits were received with overwhelming appreciation. Our shows included several operas, such as *The Queen of Spades, Carmen, Faust,* and *La Traviata.* We also did many Russian-authored comedies and dramas and full-length ballets, such as *The Stone Flower* and *The Red Poppy,* and some ballet excerpts such as the Polovetsian dances from *Prince Igor* and *Swan Lake.*

We staged many wonderful variety programs as well, featuring musical, dancing, dramatic, and comic performances. We received many presents, including money, from the men in the audience. We rarely had a day off, because when we were not performing, we were rehearsing, building sets, and sewing costumes. All in all, things seemed to be truly improving.

Most of the guards were tolerable, especially the men, but their leader stood out as a wicked little man, whom we loved to hate. In fact, we detested Lieutenant Igor in a multitude of ways. And our feelings were reciprocated by this weasel on a daily basis. Igor held us in great disdain, with a loathing he never tried to hide. He was one of the most sadistic men I had ever met, constantly abusing his position of power. This was his camp. We were inferior; he was far superior. Every time this little grunt of a man was on duty, we knew that he would concoct some new plan to hassle or humiliate us. I believe that's what he enjoyed the most—thinking of new and better methods to ruin our lives.

One of Igor's favorite routines was to get us out of bed in the middle of the night and make us stand outside in the torturous cold. He and his crew would then examine all of our things, ostensibly seeking forbidden items such as knives, razors, scissors, notes to men in other camps, and the like. This process normally lasted at least two hours. He and his guards would wait inside, where it was warm, while we all stood outside in the icy cold, waiting for them to finish. When they finally let us back in, it would take us the remainder of the night to put things back in order. Igor made sure the guards scattered everything we had from one end of the barracks to the other. In such predictable ways, he declared his ultimate control over us, reminding us of his power.

We couldn't wait until the so-called movie nights came around. Anything good that would break the routine, the monotony, was a treat. There were never enough seats, so we just sat on the floor. Whenever we could get away with it, we would sit through several showings at a time. I remember seeing *The Hunchback of Notre Dame* and a few other American movies—those judged suitable for our viewing—but the vast majority were the typical, safe Russian propaganda movies. Never were we shown a film offering even a hint of a non-Soviet point of view nor one dealing with such forbidden topics as religion, freedom, or democracy.

One nasty, cold, damp evening, about two thousand of us were anxiously awaiting to enter the building to see the current film. Then the hated Lieutenant Igor came forth, saying that he wanted to see us lined up in parade formation. Underneath his carefully maintained military facade beat the heart of a common Blatnoi, a street thug. No one was surprised or alarmed by his actions; his cruelty had become expected. So we gathered in parade formation as ordered and then just stood there—for two hours. When Igor finally returned, he said, "You can all go back to your barracks now; it is well past curfew." We couldn't see the movie the next day either, because he had already ordered it to be returned.

About this time, we once again lost our camp commandant, this one a fairly pleasant man, who was transferred to another camp in Siberia. Taking his place was a very strict young colonel, a disciplinarian, who, like a few before him, decided to clamp down on the so-called freedoms we enjoyed. He too was determined that our Cultural Brigade be usefully employed for the benefit of the entire camp. And he also professed to be a patron of the arts and regularly sat through many of our rehearsals, which he seemed to thoroughly enjoy. Later it became clear that his motivation was more compulsive and lustful than artistic: he had an insatiable desire for one of our dancers—Liza, from somewhere in Austria. She was very young and petite, beautiful, with a dark complexion, dark hair, and dark eyes.

I was suspicious of this new commandant when he called me into his office one day. Evidently my friend Tamara had told him that I had some knowledge of drafting. "Please sit down, comrade," he said in a cynical voice. "I hear you have some drafting experience, and I hear you used to work for Yuri. Is that correct?"

"Yes," I said, "I worked with him on the Gorky prison designs."

"That is fantastic," he responded. "Then you should be able to do this for me with no problem."

I questioned his motives, but I followed his lead; I had no choice. It was possible he was sincere. He told me to render a drawing for him of an old, discarded lathe, lying outside in the yard. It was a simple task, except that it was the dead of winter, and the temperatures were as low as -50°F. By the end of the week, with my hands and every other part of me frozen to the core, I presented him with a fairly well-executed drawing. He was clearly impressed with my work, and I now had a new job.

I became the draftsman for a small construction group. We worked in a tiny but nicely decorated building in a remote area of the camp. It was generally very quiet there, warm and peaceful, and all things considered, I was relatively happy with these new circumstances. Somehow I was adopted by a stray calico cat, which lived under the building and followed me around wherever I went. One day when I ventured into the building's basement, I was surprised to see that she had given birth to a litter of nine or ten kittens. Soon they too were following me everywhere I went. I grew very fond of these cute little kittens and took care of them until I had to leave the camp.

Pets were officially outlawed in the camp, but we never gave that directive too much consideration. Tamara, our ballet teacher, avidly loved animals. A dog would have been harder to conceal, so she managed to acquire a flea-bitten, disreputable-looking white male cat with only one ear. She adopted him and named him Pirate and always shared her food with him. Tamara hid him in the hothouse, a small private shack near the barracks, while she did her work assignments. She loved that cat.

Some of the other girls and I adopted a stray pup, a hound, whom we nurtured, petted constantly, and loved very much. Whenever he saw us coming, he wagged his tail wildly and jumped up in the air with all four feet, charming us until we had no choice but to feed him. What did we name him? I can't remember. But one day he was missing. The puppy was generally right where we expected him to be, but not today. I had an uneasy feeling in my stomach about this. I suspected something was wrong but didn't want to admit it. We thought he might have wandered into another barracks looking for scraps and handouts, as he regularly did. We looked everywhere, throughout the entire camp, but he was nowhere to be found. We were puzzled. There wasn't anywhere else he could have gone, and he had never disappeared like this before.

Then Talia came running into the barracks, weeping and terribly distraught. "What's wrong, Talia?" we asked.

"Come," she said.

She led us to a field on the outskirts of camp, where we learned the sickening truth of the matter. Someone had strung our dog up a tree by his front paws with some rope, left him hanging there, and used him for target practice. We were heartbroken and outraged about the suffering of this poor little puppy that loved us so much. We had strong suspicions of who had done this dastardly thing, but we couldn't prove it. I knew it was one of the night guards who patrolled our barracks, but I didn't dare confront him. Without saying a word, he made sure we all knew he did it. In the deepest desires of our hearts, we all wanted to tie him to the same tree and do the same to him. *Oh, what evil lies in the hearts of men!*

Not long after that incident, one of the kind women guards brought us a big, fluffy white cat, which we called Bella, after a friend of mine. This cat spent practically all of its time on our stage, next to the oven, which was at the rear of the platform. She was well behaved and, as if instinctively knowing the protocol, never strayed onto the stage during a performance; she always waited until the show was over. She'd mingle with us during rehearsals but, oddly enough, never during an actual show. We could never quite figure out how that cat was so smart. When Bella delivered a huge litter of kittens, we found willing and welcoming homes for them all in the other barracks.

Perhaps the gradual softening of Russia's hard line in the days after Stalin was allowing us to soften a bit too, to take into our hearts the little creatures we could not afford to notice when all our energies were devoted to day-to-day survival.

Twenty

NOT QUITE FREEDOM

Nineteen fifty-three. I had been in Siberia since 1946. One beautiful summer day a uniformed stranger summoned me from my work outside the barracks. He ordered me to pack my things because I was "going on a trip." There was a chance I would be back, but it wasn't certain. "The van will be leaving in thirty minutes. Do not be late! You have been requested in Gorky."

What? I thought. *Why Gorky? Why now?* But I didn't argue. Mama was in Gorky, so I hurriedly gathered my things.

But how could I possibly leave in just thirty minutes? I had spent many years here; I had made intimate, lifelong friendships in this camp. "At least give me a couple of hours to see everybody, to say good-bye as I should," I pleaded. But it was no use.

The official repeated, "Thirty minutes—that's all. Be ready!" Quickly I gathered my odds and ends and threw them into my bags. Then I sprinted through the camp, trying to find everybody.

Where was Tamara? Eleonora? I had to see her first. And where was Olga and Sonya and...oh, where was everyone?

Some of my friends were on their daily assignments in their work brigades, and I would not be able to find them in time. The van would leave, and I had to be on it. I would not see them one more time, bid them farewell, look into their eyes, hug them tightly, or cry with them just once more. We had formed an indefinable closeness, relationships that would surely endure no matter what else happened to us. I loved these women! Why did I have to leave so abruptly now? I couldn't say the things I needed to say, the things they needed to hear from me, the things you say only in private.

Would I return? There was no way of knowing. If this was a step closer to my mother and my freedom, then I was more than ready to go. But what if this was only a temporary derailment, another detour to another labor camp? That would make no sense. But I had no choice; I would be leaving in minutes.

I said my tearful good-byes to the few friends I was able to find. Tears ran down our faces as I kissed and hugged my closest comrades, and then I was ordered into the back of a dingy, beat-up white van, and we pulled out of camp. I tried my best not to look back, not to cry. Again I was told that we were going to Gorky. Sorrow and anxiety made the trip an emotionally agonizing three days, but it passed without incident. I focused on the possibility of seeing Mama again, though I had no idea how long I'd be in Gorky or even why I was going there.

I was taken back to Gorky's well-known Vorobyo'vka, where I'd been imprisoned when I was first arrested in 1945. I was placed in a solitary cell without explanation. And I was terrified all over again. I had heard the horror stories; I had already lived through some of them. I knew what could be expected and what had happened to countless others in similar circumstances. But why was I being sent back here *now* just as my official sentence and term of imprisonment were approaching their end?

No one knew why these people in the Soviet system did what they did. Trying to figure that out put you in an endless sea of unanswerable questions. Mystification and mayhem, bonded with darkness, operated every day in Russian life. The less time I spent considering why, the more tolerable it was for me. Simple resignation was better than trying to figure out something that made no sense. I no longer wondered *why.* I was only concerned with *how* and more so with *when.*

I was left alone in a dark cell for an entire day. I was given water and nothing else. Late in the day a guard came down the corridor and opened my cell. He didn't cuff me or harass me. He just said, "Up, now! Come with me."

He led me to an interrogation room, the same one I had visited many times before, years earlier. It looked the same as it always had. An official came in and told me to sit down. Someone would be in to see me shortly.

"Okay," I said, "but let me ask you something. Do you happen to know a man named Fidoli?"

The man said, "Yes, I do…I did. Fidoli died just last year. Why do you ask?"

I slumped in my hard chair and said, "Oh, it's nothing. I just wondered if he was still here." Sadness came over me. I remembered my former interrogator quite well. There was something about Fidoli that I always liked, although he was clearly on the other side. I thought about Fidoli often. I recalled that special conversation we once had, and I wondered if his life had changed with the passing of the years. Specifically, I wondered if he had met God before he died.

The man left the room, and I was briefly alone again. I had no idea whom I was waiting for, but I considered the possibility that the purpose for my trip to Gorky was so the MVD could use me to recruit my mother as an informer. That wasn't far-fetched, and I knew this had happened to others. Why else would I be here? For them to contemplate such an unethical plan made me burn with indignation.

Another official led me into another room. In the drab little office stood a table overflowing with assorted food and fruits. It was a bountiful buffet, more than I had seen for years. And sitting by the smorgasbord of delectable food was my own mama! But she did not look comfortable. She was tense and pale, as if someone were holding a gun to her back. Her face was downcast and sullen, almost ashamed; she looked absolutely miserable. I could tell the scene was staged.

And I thought, *Now if this doesn't take all.* It was like honey on a bear trap, nothing but a setup. Did they really think we were going to buy this routine simply because we were hungry? Did they expect to use Mama to sell me this tainted bill of goods? Oh, these people, these schemes! They thought too highly of themselves. But the sordid trap was overshadowed by the fact that Mama was here with me. I felt agony coupled with pure outrage as I saw, even from across the room, the pain on her face. I ran to her as she stood up, and we embraced tightly, as if our lives depended on it. We didn't speak. Nothing needed explanation; we both knew what was happening.

The MVD officer who had led me to this rendezvous left Mama and me alone for a while. We knew their sleazy tactics. I could almost see the wheels turning in their minds. They wanted us to enjoy their food, but we didn't touch it. I thank God for giving us the will to withstand the outlandish temptation. I whispered very faintly to Mama, "We must be very careful to speak quietly. They might have the room bugged. They might be listening."

"Okay, Maidie," she whispered back. I told her why I suspected they had brought her here, but she was way ahead of me. She already knew.

In whispers, my mother told me that she had been approached by the MVD in her home. She had refused to help them, saying her frail health and advanced age would keep her from being of any benefit to them. We continued our quiet conversation, not touching the incredible ocean of food surrounding us, not paying attention to the delicious smells filling our nostrils. I was also able to tell her about some of the improvements in my life in camp, allaying her worries. In just a few minutes, we both became fairly settled. We knew what we had to do.

I thanked her for the packages she had sent to me. The guard returned in a few minutes and motioned for Mama to leave. "Mama," I said hurriedly, "we will be out of this hellhole soon, and we can start all over, okay? We will go back home, and we will build new lives. Everything will be just wonderful, you'll see. I'll be back soon, I promise. I love you so much, Mama!" As I watched her going out the door, I realized that I had once again spoken the very same words that Papa had said. An overwhelming sadness enveloped me. The sorrows and losses of our family had just multiplied.

After she left, I was called to report to the authorities. I repeated what my mother had said: that she was much too fragile for such an assignment and that she did not know the language well enough to be of any real value to them. I wasn't sure they bought that excuse completely, but it seemed to satisfy them for the time being.

They kept me at the Vorobyo'vka for approximately a month and a half under reasonably livable circumstances. I was treated fairly well and wasn't subjected to any particular abuse beyond what I had come to know as customary. I still didn't know precisely why I was here or what they wanted with me.

One day a certain well-spoken, very well-mannered, high-ranking MVD official unlocked my cell door. He entered my room and declared, "Werner, you will return to your camp at Inta in the morning. We have no further need for you here."

I was elated. They had evidently decided not to use my mother in their schemes. Or did they decide? Was this another simple twist of fate, or was this exactly the way God wanted to work this out? I didn't know, and it really didn't matter. The important thing was that Mama was now cleared of all suspicions as I returned to Inta to complete my term.

This was a pivotal time for us, I thought. It was now the fall of 1953, and I actually felt as if I could see daylight ahead. My sentence was approaching its end, and I would soon be released. I felt that the elements against us had retreated somewhat, resigned maybe, or even surrendered. Was it simply an answer to prayer? Whatever it was, it looked as though the authorities weren't going to bother us anymore. The truth was that Mama actually knew quite a bit of sensitive information. If they had known how much, they would not have let her go. But now the matter was nearly over, and so was my sentence. Now I could begin to envision a new life and a fresh start for Mama and me.

The joy I felt leaving Gorky and returning to my camp was indescribable. It was almost as if I had been released from my imprisonment and my political status, as if normal life had been returned to me. Now I had another chance to say the things I didn't get to say to those women I loved so dearly. And now I could clearly see the light ahead. The last ten years of my life had been shrouded in dark despair, but now there appeared to be more light than darkness. God had given me a vision and hope for the future.

The ride back to the Siberian north was ten times more pleasant than my trip south, although I couldn't anticipate seeing my dear mother at this journey's end. When I got out of the van at Inta, I knelt down, kissed the stage floor, and began looking for my friends. Nothing had changed while I was away. The girls and I had a joyous reunion—laughing, recalling, but mainly crying. I could see the love on their faces. I knew they had missed me as much as I had missed them. The camp was not my home, but these women were. We were always *home* for one another.

And back in Gorky, the MVD officials never harassed my mother again.

Thank you, Lord! I prayed.

For the next year or so my life at Inta continued as expected, with no major deviations from the prison norm. During the winter of 1954 we were allowed to flood our parade grounds with water so we could ice-skate. Given the cold Siberian winter, the water didn't take long to freeze. Our camp had only a few pairs of skates, but all the avid skaters gladly shared them. Among us was a former champion ice skater from the Ukraine, who flew like a graceful bird across the ice. My childhood passion for skating had never left me, and my heart lifted every time I went on the ice. During our nonworking hours, we skated with the reckless abandon of youthful freedom and exuberance, forgetting our prison.

We skated like children without a worry in the world. It was a time of mysterious joy, a feeling I cannot describe or forget.

Our ice-skating fun came to a crashing halt one day that winter. I had almost forgotten that I was still an American political prisoner assigned to a labor camp in Siberia. Like a rush of cold water to my face, without warning, all of us were ordered to pack our things. No problem—I was already an expert in packing! We were being transferred to a much smaller camp, and our present camp was going to be occupied by men. We had to walk the entire distance, but this time the authorities took care of our baggage and personal belongings.

Unanimously, we hated the confines and conditions at our new camp. Compared to this, our old camp looked very good. We were seasoned improvisers, but in this new place we would definitely need to readapt. We were cramped for space, and our brigade was assigned the tiniest, dingiest, hole-in-the-wall berthing quarters available.

The miserably small auditorium and stage on which we would perform was the worst part. There was no one we could complain to; I already knew that. But I was now on my way out. I was a short-timer; I just had to hang on a little while longer. We eventually staged a few concerts and dramatic performances, using our older and more perfected routines, but my heart was no longer in it. We muddled through, but the passion we had shared was now gone. Things were not the same. We particularly missed our friend and teacher, Tamara, who had been freed a few months earlier and now lived somewhere in the city of Inta. I thought about Tamara quite often, and I missed my special friend. But I felt so be it, because a new life was on the horizon.

Not long before I was due for release, I was called to an assembly in the dining hall to hear a speech. The camp commandant was announcing the imminent release of some of the inmates and wishing everyone a successful life in the future.

You've got to be kidding, I thought. Then I questioned myself. *Margaret, you're not going to blow it now, are you?*

Nearly one hundred inmates attended the assembly. I looked around at the living and recalled the dead. There should have been at least another thirty of us, according to my calculations, but those women didn't make it. Those were the sad cases, the unfortunate ones who did not finish the race. I knew those women, I knew their stories, and I knew of their lives. What I didn't always know was the singular thing that made them snap and kept them from finishing. I thought about these women, the dead. I remembered them all in great detail.

The commandant spoke in glowing terms of our "prospects," "opportunities awaiting us" in the town, and our "future usefulness to society." He enthused about what we would do when we were out. It was a good speech; I knew he had worked on it. His whole delivery, with proper voice inflection, was impeccable. During this well-aimed and even genuine speech, I was impressed, but I felt a familiar uneasy feeling growing within me. It was the same kind of indignation that rose up one day in 1938 when I sat in an assembly of schoolchildren in Gorky and was told to denounce my father. Those same emotions intensified as the commandant talked.

I boiled over with the need to speak. I stood and shouted out, "Sir, may I ask you…on the subject of prospects, as you say. I hope you will excuse me for saying, but we have no prospects! We have no jobs, we have nowhere to live, and we have no money. So what prospects do you refer to? How are we to deal with these circumstances? And how, exactly, have we been prepared to cope with these very real and immediate problems in order to become—let's see, how did you say it?—'more productive'?"

Before he could respond, I continued, "And what, pray tell, is awaiting us outside these camp gates? Is opportunity awaiting us out there? Of course not! Who is available to help us out there? I, for one, have done nothing wrong, and yet, falsely accused, I stand here—an American citizen in Russia. I have just given up *ten years of my life!* And for what? For nothing, damn it! And who is going to fix that?"

I stood, considering what else to say, on the verge of tears, torn between righteous indignation, rebellion, and unforgiveness. Although deeply distraught, I remained outwardly calm and subdued. I was not stupid; I knew I had crossed a line I should not have crossed. Where did my stubborn and foolish pride come from? Was it the same pride that had gotten Papa arrested, imprisoned, and killed? And why couldn't I control it? I wished I had carefully considered the parameters and the consequences involved. I should have been more aware of my limitations and boundaries.

Gradually I realized that the commander was more than a little embarrassed by my questions, though not aggravated or angry. He seemed a bit shaken and nervous, but he was especially contained, almost apologetic. *Was Mama praying for me?* I wondered. *Was she praying to God for me at this moment?* When I was through, he was virtually speechless. He did not answer my questions but nervously closed the meeting and his speech immediately. The commander had been respectful and unusually kind in his response to my shocking comments. A million thoughts raced through my head. All at once I was happy and yet melancholy, rebellious yet humble, outspoken but somewhat under control. I was faithful yet hopelessly fearful at the same time. *O God, please help me!*

Twenty-One

RELEASED

N early ten years in the making, March 3, 1955, was here at last, *na endlich.* The day of my release had been a tiny white speck on the outer edge of eternity's dark horizon. But now the faint glimmer of hope was realized. My release came approximately nine months earlier than I had expected, because I was given "time off for good behavior." I was simultaneously grateful and humiliated.

This time I could say the honest and tearful good-byes to all my dear friends and prepare myself to walk out the camp gate. Most of my worldly goods were strapped to my back, and I carried a suitcase that had been made for me by some men in another camp. I set off on foot for the great unknown, a person who had aged many more years than the nine-plus I had served. And now, with this citation for good behavior in my pocket, plus a dime, I could probably buy a cup of coffee somewhere in America. My only problem was that America was a long way off, and I was still a long, long way from home.

Not sure which way to go, I felt the whole weight of the world upon me. I was lost, afraid, and nervous. But I was also expectant, anticipating wonderful things ahead. I wanted to be picked up right there and supernaturally transported to a new start. God had already given me faith, even if it sometimes looked like blind optimism: choosing to see things in a positive light despite the darkened situation. And now, when I was overwhelmed with these conflicting emotions, I poured out my heart to God. *Lord, if you're there, if you can hear me, if you care for me—then I need you right now!*

I reached for help from God, and at that moment I felt as though he heard me. I had come to know his essential character during the desperate times. I had seen irrefutable evidence of the divine, and it was clear to me now that he had chosen to save my life on several occasions. God had walked with me in the dark, and I was learning to trust him. Since he had seen me through these last painful nine years, I could trust that he would also see me through the years ahead. Indeed, he would look after my mother and pave a way for our future as well. Although the weight of the world seemed to be upon my shoulders at this moment, it was not as heavy as it might have been. *I believed that he was carrying me through!*

I could hardly wait to see Mama. Since she was still 1,587

miles away in Gorky, and I was officially confined to the Inta region for the next five years, Mama was making plans to take the long trip to visit me in Inta. Oh, how I anticipated that reunion!

I was free, whatever that meant. Not being in prison was good, but what did it mean to be out? What, exactly, would I do next? I was apprehensive about how I would earn a living, something I hadn't thought about for the last nine years. Prison life had a perverse kind of security. Imprisoned and oppressed, I didn't know what it was like to worry about providing my next meal or having a roof over my head. The years spent behind barbed wire did not prepare me for life outside camp confines, in an unfamiliar city, without relatives or resources for help.

Furthermore, I had only the freedom to leave the labor camp, but the conditions of my release mandated that I stay within the region. I could move somewhat freely within the borders of Inta; no one would harass me as long as my intentions were purely local. This was not true freedom, without borders or limitations; it was not even passport freedom. I didn't have the right to leave the city, and certainly not the country. Yes, I was out, but I would have to report once a month to the local police department. I would be a prisoner of the city for another five years. To be allowed to work for pay, I had to obtain an official work permit, identifying me as a newly released political prisoner.

I was headed for the house of my former teacher and wonderful friend, Tamara. She had invited me to share a room with her until I could find a place of my own. I was positively lightheaded as I walked alone through the frosty cold of Inta, with no guard breathing down my neck for the first time in more than nine years!

I finally made it to Tamara's place, where both of us were deeply happy to see each other again. She had already set up a folding cot for me in her room. "The guards come by at about five in the morning," she said, looking at me seriously. I paused in unpacking my bag. Only when Tammy erupted in laughter did I understand it was a joke.

A few weeks earlier Tamara had landed a job in the local theater, teaching ballet. She also possessed strong planning and leadership skills and had big hopes of organizing what she called "enough local talent" to stage a concert in the near future. I was happy to hear that I was included in her plans. She said, "I couldn't wait for you to get here, Margaret! I want you to dance. I have some great parts for you."

I joined Tamara's classes with an energy and joy that had been missing in my life for a long time. I had missed her presence and enthusiasm during my final months in camp. She taught in the back room of an old storage facility, a warehouse in the inner city. It was great to be out of the camp, but the social atmosphere was not welcoming. As former politicals, we were looked down upon by the rest of the class. It didn't matter much, because Tamara was the teacher. Still, it hurt. We tried to ignore the students' stereotypes and false perceptions of us, but it wasn't easy. All the same, we knew we had fulfilled our sentences; we had done our time. We were survivors. Facing prejudice was definitely the easy part.

While we were in the camp's Cultural Brigade, I used to perform a solo snake dance. Now Tamara wanted to make it a duet, featuring me and a young man named Kostya, who had also just been released from prison. We performed well together on stage, and we danced as partners in quite a few different pieces. Kostya was from Czechoslovakia, the homeland of my old friend, Sanya Dubcek. Through the years since I first left Gorky, I wondered and thought about Sanya, and I felt kindly toward Kostya for that reason. And I felt even more kindly toward a friend of Kostya's, whom I met soon after.

Günter Tobien was a young German who had been arrested when he was only fifteen, toward the end of the war, during the Russian occupation of Germany. He was originally sentenced to death, but when his captors discovered his qualifications as an expert mechanic, a decree soon commuted his sentence to ten years hard labor in Russia. They shipped him to the Far North, to Inta, to a men's camp near ours, where he ultimately served his full term in the coal mines, maintaining the machinery. He had been there the entire time I had, just down the road in another camp. Günter had been released to the confines of Inta just prior to my release. He had no hope of returning to Germany or to the free West, where he had parents, a brother, and a sister. The sad truth was that he had not heard from them, nor had they heard from him, in more than twelve years. His family believed that he had been killed during the war, and he had no way to get word to them of his whereabouts.

Günter was like Papa in some ways: knowledgeable, strong,

and hard working. And I delighted in speaking with him in the German language of my childhood.

I soon found new temporary living quarters. One of Tamara's friends allowed me to use her apartment's storage bin in the basement of her building. It was really just a big concrete box with a tiny ventilation hole near the ceiling and a small single bed and mattress. With Tamara's and Günter's help, I furnished my room with sheets, a small table, two stools, and a shelf, which stood on the table with my meager supply of dishes. This was the place I now called home. It was not Detroit, but it wasn't labor-camp imprisonment either. And that was a blessing. A pail containing drinking water stood under the table. I filled it at another cellar apartment and then hauled it back. The only toilet was outdoors, a detestable little outhouse that was cleaned only during warm months.

Tamara made a pretty bedspread and pillowcases for me from some fabric Günter purchased in the city, along with a reindeer-skin throw rug for the floor. I kept warm with a hot plate, on which I also cooked my meals when I could buy enough food. I was thankful I didn't have to pay rent or electricity bills. That would have made it impossible for me to survive.

After several weeks of looking for work, I found a job as a clerk and typist for the supply department of a local fabrication company. It was a modest income, even by current Soviet standards, but I was adjusting to somewhat normal life again and was relatively satisfied with my circumstances. I liked my job and the people I worked with. I was happy, and I was in love.

Günter and I didn't want to lose any more time than we had already lost to our years in prison. We both wanted a family, so we married a short time after we met. By late April 1955 I was pregnant with our first child.

I continued to rehearse diligently, because my mother was planning to visit us from Gorky, and I wanted very much to perform for her. Not yet showing, but feeling the fatigue of my first month of pregnancy, I managed to pull off that performance. What truly made it worthwhile was that Mama was watching me, smiling proudly. And this was a very special night, because I really needed her to be here for this one. As it turned out, Mama got to see me the very last time I ever danced or performed on stage—the very last ballet performance of my life.

Of course, Mama met Günter and learned of her coming grandchild. How wonderful it was to share my life with her again, if only for a short visit. A good friend of mine named Teresa, a former member of our brigade, let Mama stay with her for a few nights until it was once again time to say good-bye. We had become experts in good-byes and were no strangers to long separations, but they all hurt. I believed, however, Lord willing, that there wouldn't be many more farewells in our future. Günter and I hoped we'd be permitted to move to Gorky in order to live near Mama. We believed that the many hurtful departures and all the painful good-byes would soon be things of the past.

I was expected to give birth in February 1956. Apparently nobody informed the new arrival of that fact, however, because on

January 24, I began having an assortment of very strange pains. I tried to block them out of my mind, and Günter and I went out to the movies that evening anyway. After we returned home, these unfamiliar abdominal pains became more concentrated and unbearable, so Günter quickly fetched a doctor. The doctor, my friend Eleonora's husband, examined me and immediately sent me to the hospital. This was not going to be a routine or normal childbirth.

After three days and nights of horrible pain, I was worn out. They finally gave me a pituitrine shot in the early afternoon of January 27, and about thirty minutes later, I gave birth to a beautiful five-pound baby boy. I underwent all this, including the scraping of the afterbirth, without any medical aids or anesthetic. It's not that I refused medication; there were none available. More accurately, there were none for me, a former political prisoner— and an American.

Eventually the pain subsided, and I suddenly realized I was famished. Günter rounded up some food, which I ate heartily. Then I fell blissfully asleep. Some time later a nurse woke me up, presenting my healthy baby boy, Karl. I called him Karlie and received him as a blessing. At nearly thirty-five, I was considered quite old to be having children.

It was a strange time to start a new family. My mother was thousands of miles away. My father, in all likelihood, was dead. I felt it inside my heart. How I mourned that my father, Carl Werner, could not see his beautiful new grandson, Karl. I hoped that such a meeting would take place in the life to come, the one for all eternity, the life in which there will be no more pain.

In the present, however, things were very difficult for Günter and me. Work, food, housing—all were in short supply. We came from different cultures and were cut off from our families. And our years in the labor camps had not prepared either of us for living as man and wife. We struggled with each other over every problem that we faced. And they were many.

For months Günter and I had been trying to secure adequate living quarters through the city officials. Now there were three of us. So Günter formulated a plan: when my expected hospital discharge date came around (usually nine days after giving birth), I would refuse to leave the hospital premises. Günter thought this would force them to find us an apartment. Unfortunately, he was wrong. Though I had no place to go, after my discharge date, the hospital denied me food—for three weeks. Since I was a nursing mother requiring nourishment, I was forced to leave with Karl, who had been deliberately neglected by the hospital's nursing staff. After all, I was a hated American, but their lack of regard for my innocent baby was utterly inhumane. Proper medical care was available for Karl but not given. Much of his little body was chafed raw. Babies born to Russian mothers were never treated like this.

During this awful time, encouragement came out of the blue. Several days before I went into the hospital, I had written an appeal to the Military Tribunal of the Moscow Military Region. Upon the personal recommendation of a friend, I candidly stated the circumstances of my case and respectfully requested a formal review. I didn't seriously expect that the responsible parties would admit to any error, but there were some indications of change in official procedures. Still, I doubted if I would hear back, and if I did, it certainly would not be for months or perhaps years.

While I was still in the hospital's maternity ward, however, I was handed an all-important document. I received an unconditional pardon, because proof of guilt could not be verified, and I was to be considered free of any criminal record. I was incredulous! *I would not be exiled in Inta for the next four years.* I had thought that writing my appeal had been an exercise in futility! Of course, this wasn't justice—what had happened to the last ten years of my life?—but it was indeed good news.

I was stunned and happy on top of my indignation and resentment. However, I was more happy than indignant, more humble than vengeful. I wasn't going to give my oppressors any more of my time. They had already stolen too many years from me. How horrible that any government could wipe out nearly ten years of an innocent person's life.

One of the most important powers of that precious document was the restoration of my civil rights, primarily the freedom to travel, to choose a home in a different area of the country. More than anything I wanted to be reunited with my mother, and now I had the ticket to do so. No more years could be taken from us.

In Gorky, the climate was less harsh, and little Karlie would undoubtedly have a better home and a better life in all respects. Naturally, my choice was to take my baby and return to Gorky and my mother.

Günter and I discussed this possibility in great detail. We really didn't have other choices. Because of our political status, we would probably never get an apartment of our own in Inta. So where would we live? Where would our little Karlie live, and what would his new circumstances be like if we stayed here? As foreigners, we would never be treated well. Now that I was free to move, I couldn't bear the thought of staying in Inta a moment longer than I had to. So I wrote a letter to Mama, informing her that little Karl and I would soon be coming home to her, but according to regulations, she first had to come to Inta to sign the necessary paperwork.

Günter was also allowed to leave Inta, but we agreed that he would remain behind to work and would send us money every month, until better conditions became available. Our considerations were economically motivated: necessity and financial practicality as well as housing conditions and availability. This decision was made in the best interest of my child, who was my primary focus at the time. But I was not thrilled with the idea of leaving Inta without my husband.

Of course, my mother wanted nothing more than to help us. In my mind, I imagined returning with my baby to a wonderful home that included my papa and mama and me with little Karl.

☆

I was sure I would never return to Inta, so before I left, I was determined to find out what I could about my father's fate. In going to the MVD, I knew I had to be very cautious, carefully calculating my approach. Attempting to gather sensitive and guarded information was a serious action on my part. It involved treading on sacred ground. If I said the wrong thing or made the wrong moves, I could quite possibly be imprisoned again or worse. Information was at a premium in Russia, and the sealing up of information was a source of power. The very root of this political system was secrecy. I would have to bridle my tongue better than I had in the past.

When I found the building of the MVD, I stood a long time in different offices to inquire about my father. Eventually an impatient official told me curtly that Carl Werner had died, but the cause of his death, its date and location, were officially listed as unknown. I was furious. In the same degrading tone he used on me, I boldly replied to the officer, "Oh, that's interesting. I see. Then perhaps you can tell me where he's buried so I can put some flowers on his grave, okay? Or would that also be against the rules?"

His eyes snapped up. He looked at me coldly. Then he answered calmly but cynically, "You will never find out where his body is. Now what else can I do for you today, Citizen Werner?" I was stunned and scared too, so I backed off. I saw I was pressing my luck.

☆

According to the legal regulations and provisions of my final release from Inta—with my child—my mother had to sign certain sponsorship documents on my behalf, verifying Gorky residence. This would officially allow us unrestricted travel back to Gorky. So Mama made a return trip to Inta to sign the papers.

After a frantic farewell to Günter, Kostya, Tamara, Eleonora, and her husband at the railway station, Mama and I managed to secure two seats, quite a distance from each other, and then settled down for the night. Baby Karl traveled well, and three uneventful days and nights later, we happily arrived at our destination, our home in Gorky. Though Gorky was not America, it was familiar and felt more secure to me than anything I'd known in a long time. I was flooded with hope for the future. Those years hadn't robbed me of the promise and the expectancy that still flourished within. Not today! I was a person of potential. This was who God made me to be. It felt like a new day, a new beginning, the best new beginning I had ever felt. This day was even more meaningful to me than the day I was released.

My first few days in Gorky were spent reacquainting myself with my former friends and surroundings and the neighborhood I had known so well. It hadn't changed much in eleven years; it just seemed smaller and shabbier. And I was glad to see the Oka River once again, the scene of so many happy memories. That's where I grew up. That's where I would talk for hours with my wonderful friend, Sanya Dubcek. That's where a certain lifeguard taught me certain things, where I first fell in love with my Nikolai. Many memories came swiftly rushing back. Yes, I knew the Oka.

Twenty-Two

APPEAL TO NIKITA

Our new life in Gorky was very simple but deeply pleasing to me. Helping Mama in the household routines and making do with our few resources seemed relaxing after the crushing pressures of Siberia. I took Karl out for many walks, at all hours of the day or night, in his secondhand buggy. I'd set him out to nap in the outer hallway of our building, where the air was fresh. Our neighbors thought that was rather strange, but I had no fear. Things seemed very safe here now, without the perpetual anxiety of life under Stalin. Everything seemed perfectly normal to me. Then one day I moved Karl and his buggy into the hallway for his usual afternoon nap, peeking out the door now and then to check on him. When I looked out the door for about the third time, he was gone. The carriage was still there, but it was empty. I rushed outside, flew down the stairs, and knocked on all the doors like a crazy woman. No Karlie!

I climbed the stairs toward the apartment, thinking I was going to die and absolutely hating myself. *How could I have done this?* I thought. *How could I have been so stupid, so neglectful?* I sat down in the hallway and wept hysterically.

Suddenly I heard a woman coming down the steps from her apartment on the floor above. She was holding my Karlie and saying, "I couldn't resist taking your baby just to show my husband how adorable he is."

Relief and fury poured over me. Relief won out, however, because I didn't beat that woman to death right then and there. I thought, *Lady, don't you know how dangerous I am? Don't you know I could have killed you right now with my bare hands, just for doing something so stupid? Don't you know that I've just spent nine years in a Siberian death camp? Don't you know?* I didn't say these words, and when I cooled off later, I didn't even mean them. But I felt like that, and with murderous looks, I grabbed my baby out of her arms and ran back into my apartment. I held Karl tightly and kissed him feverishly, as though I couldn't get enough, until he began to cry. I was probably more frightened about losing him than about anything else in my life, including my terrifying Gulag years.

Günter sent us enough money to provide a relatively good living, supplying most of our needs. The stores in Gorky were much better stocked than they were in Inta, and for the first time in many years I saw fresh eggs, milk, good meat, and vegetables! I nursed Karl, so he received the full benefit of this much-improved diet. He was a delightful baby, and I adored him. All of our friends and neighbors loved him too and enjoyed holding and playing with him. Of course, Mama was exceedingly proud. I only wished that Papa were here to see him too.

It was very difficult for Günter to remain in Inta without us. Faithful financial support was one thing; a faithful marriage was another. So when the baby was about four months of age, Günter and I decided that I should return to Inta. Some friends of ours were leaving on an extended vacation for two months, and they wanted someone to take care of their small apartment in their absence. It was only a room and a primitive kitchen, but to us it seemed luxurious. It had many windows, and I thought this little place would be perfect for us, if it were ours, if only the elements of a good marriage were also in place. It was still a daily struggle for us to get along, but we lived in the little dwelling as if it were our own, until it began to feel like it was.

Then, quite mysteriously, Karl became ill one night, with a very high temperature. We rushed him to the hospital, where they determined he had a rapidly developing case of pneumonia and dysentery. Since I was a nursing mother, the common Soviet hospital protocol of that day allowed me to remain in the hospital with him, in a bed right beside his crib. He was indeed very ill, and I didn't understand the nature of his sickness. I was puzzled, but I believed that he would soon be well. God had seen me through so much. Surely he would help my son through this infirmity. We stayed there, under decent medical care, until he was transferred to a nearby hospital that specialized in contagious diseases. There we stayed for an entire month. When he was discharged and we were told that he was healed, I was determined to get him out of Inta, where he had contracted these diseases. We promptly left for Gorky.

No sooner had we returned than Karlie's symptoms suddenly reappeared. I spent another month in the hospital with a very sick baby. The sudden severe sicknesses, the shots and the medicine, the constant supervision, all changed him into a very nervous little fellow. When he was released, despite my best motherly intentions and caring, he chronically cried throughout the nights. Mother and I were completely worn out by this persistent new condition, and we could only sleep during the day's rare moments when Karl also slept.

My baby was physically troubled by something, but I didn't know what it was. I didn't know what to do for him, so I just held him, sang to him, and lovingly tried to rock him back to sleep as often as he'd let me. Nothing else seemed to work.

Mama and I continued to seek information about my father's fate. After yet another request to the authorities, on May 29, 1956, we finally received a death certificate. This document stated that dysentery was the official cause of his death. Purportedly, he had died on August 25, 1942, more than three years before my arrest. The notification and the cause of Papa's death did not shock me, because many years earlier, I had already arrived at the certainty that he was gone. It was my heart, more than my head, that already knew the truth of the matter. What was now so harrowing and so difficult for me to believe was the reported time of death. Under other circumstances, I wouldn't have paid such close attention to the time of death. But I had paid dearly, with many years of my own life, simply for inquiring about the fate of my father.

Had Mama and I been notified of Papa's death at the time it occurred—August 1942—or at least shortly thereafter, there's a reasonable chance I would have never been arrested. I felt that the only reason for my arrest was my persistent curiosity about my father's fate. We couldn't find out anything on our own, and no one was rushing to help us—neither the government nor the Ford Motor Company. That's why I unofficially solicited aid from Leslie and Mac, to obtain outside help in determining Papa's whereabouts. Had I known that my father was already dead, my course of action would have been entirely different. My unanswered question would have been answered, leaving me no urgency to inquire further, other than what would be routinely expected for the grieving family of the deceased. It was my not knowing that got me arrested and ultimately convicted.

The date of his death was reported as August 25, 1942. The location where he died was left blank. I was outraged. I determined to try to clear my father's name. As I had done in my own case, I wrote a lengthy appeal to the Moscow Military Tribunal, the MVD. I stated all the known facts of my father's life and respectfully requested a formal review of his case.

Months later I received a document dated December 11, 1956: Carl Werner's arrest and subsequent conviction—by a troika (three judges) of the NKVD (People's Commissariat for Internal Affairs) on November 3, 1938—was now "overturned for lack of evidence." He was posthumously declared pardoned. We finally knew that Papa had been held in jail for five months before being sentenced and that he died four years and five months after his initial arrest. And for what? The state that had destroyed him now declared him innocent.

I accepted bitterly that nothing good could result from additional inquiries. In my own interest and in the interest of my loved ones, I chose from that time forward to be silent.

In 1957 a new step in international diplomacy changed our lives forever. West German chancellor Konrad Adenauer visited Moscow to discuss with Nikita Khrushchev the possibility of establishing a war prisoner exchange agreement. This covenant would repatriate all German and Russian POWs. When the agreement was ratified, thousands of surviving German prisoners in Russia surged with hope. Günter would be directly affected. With urgency and great excitement, we discussed these new possibilities by mail.

We knew that he would be allowed to return to his native Germany. This was wonderful! But how could he get out of Russia with his American family and mother-in-law? I would have to go to Moscow and request permission from the government for our small family to immigrate legally, with my husband, to East Germany. It would be my job to convince them.

I traveled to Moscow, leaving Karl at home with my mother. I arranged to stay with my friend Mara, formerly from the camps at

Inta. She understood my current predicament and wanted to help. At the appointed location in Moscow, in a cold, dreary, gray office building, I spent many nervous hours waiting in many rooms for someone, anyone, to listen to my case. Finally I was called to the central office of the MVD. I stated my request to immigrate to East Germany with my husband, son, and mother.

I can still hear the precise words of the man in uniform: "What, may I ask, has caused you, dear citizen, to believe and work so hard for something you know is impossible for us to grant you?"

When I humbly asked, "Why is this impossible?" he smugly responded, "We do not at this time consider it appropriate to permit you to leave the country."

I had known in my heart they would not approve. I was deeply disappointed and weary of these futile appeals. My father and I were both officially pardoned, but that made no difference. Downcast and weary, I spent the evening discussing my current situation with some other friends, also from Inta, now living in Moscow. They were sympathetic and actually encouraging. In fact, a friend suggested a wonderful new approach to my dilemma.

He simply said, "Why don't you just try to bypass this bureaucracy altogether? Why not write a letter directly to the prime minister? Yeah, why not? It couldn't hurt. Compose a good letter, directly from you to Nikita Khrushchev! Tell him of your troubled background, your false arrest, your many years at the camps, and appeal to his sense of honor and comradeship. Margaret, you never know. Perhaps that would work. Stranger things have happened."

I saw no downside to this advice. At worst, Khrushchev would read and ignore my letter. More likely, it would never get to him at all, a busy man, insulated with go-betweens and buffers at the Kremlin. I doubted he would read a letter from a former political prisoner or be interested in some American's hard-luck story, but I said, "Maybe you're right. What could it hurt?"

I returned to Mara's place and sat up in bed nearly all night long, composing this special letter to Nikita Khrushchev. It read something like this:

Dear Comrade Khrushchev,

Knowing that you are an honorable and compassionate
man, my purpose in writing you today is to respectfully ask
for your help.

My name is Margaret Werner Tobien. I am a (former)
citizen of the United States, now living in Gorky. My family
and I first traveled here from America in 1932. My father
desired to establish a life and build a future for his family
here in our blessed Soviet Union. We lived in the former
"American Village" in Gorky, where my father worked in
the Autostroy automotive factory. In 1938, under Stalin, he
was falsely arrested as a vrag naroda and imprisoned near
Gorky, where he died in 1942. His name was Carl Werner.
He was a good man.

During the German occupation of Gorky, my mother

and I barely survived but did all that we could do to defend our Russian heritage and to help our innocent soldiers during the war. I was also later falsely arrested in 1945, accused of espionage and treason, imprisoned and sentenced to a ten-year term in the Siberian camps, where I faithfully served out my sentence as a model prisoner and was then released just last year.

My husband, Günter Tobien, was a former German war prisoner who was sentenced and exiled to Siberia, where we met and married. We have a beautiful young son, Karl. My husband, my mother, my child, and I would now like permission to immigrate to East Germany, in accordance with your wonderful new War Prisoner Exchange Agreement, a sterling illustration of morality and human rights, for the world to see and admire!

We again request and deeply appreciate your favorable consideration in allowing us to do so. I believe all of my documents and papers are on record with the MVD in Moscow, for your inspection and review.

Comrade Khrushchev, you are a shining example of truth, justice, and democracy in our fair Russian motherland! And in your every word and deed, you most splendidly exemplify what a true world leader should be! You are indeed a man among men! Therefore, I thank you most sincerely, on behalf of my family, for your earnest considera-

tion in this matter, and I firmly pledge my undying gratitude and loyalty to you sir, and to our most sacred land!

With all respect, I remain faithfully yours,
Margaret Werner Tobien

I had to hold back laughter while writing such absurdities, but
I thought the idea was brilliant. Early the following morning I
mailed this bold but contrived personal appeal directly to Nikita
Khrushchev. I only wanted him to buy what my letter was trying
to sell.

I immediately returned to Gorky. Mama was amazed at this
ingenious idea and surprised that I had already mailed the letter.
Of course, she began to pray. I was always happy when she did
that, but I wasn't sure it would do any good. Maybe I thought this
was too much for God to handle.

Just a few days later I was astonished to be summoned to an
office of the presidium of the Supreme Soviet in Moscow. I spoke
to a panel of four or five delegates, who encouraged me to tell my
story at length and in full detail. I had never had this chance to be
heard by someone in a position to effect change. The delegates
seemed to be sensitive to my statements and concerns, and I saw
in them indications that it might be possible for them to grant my
request. I couldn't tell, but I prayed, *God, please.*

If my request was to be seriously considered, it wouldn't be for the genuine humanitarian reasons behind it but for more practical reasons—political posturing or public relations. Everything these bureaucrats said and did, every word and deed, was carefully measured, and every decision was anchored in fear and paranoia. But if it worked, I wouldn't care about the why. At the hearing's conclusion, I was harshly ordered, "Return now to Gorky and await further developments."

I returned home on the very next train, arriving at our apartment at about six in the morning. Very quietly I opened the door to our room, trying hard not to create a disturbance, but Karlie and Mama instantly opened their eyes as I entered. When Karl saw me, he said, "Mama, darling, please come home to Karlie!" I hadn't been gone very long, and I could not believe what he said! My precious mother had taught him to say those words just so he could deliver that line upon my return.

My little son was thriving, and with all our love and attention, his speech was quite advanced for his age. At only eighteen months, he was rapidly acquiring both Russian and German, along with a bit of English. I was glad to be back home in Gorky with my mama and my son. I found I really did love the city and its people. Gorky was the only home I had known after my early life in Detroit. The city, the people, I loved. It was the government we could all do without.

When I first returned from Moscow, I felt a tremendous surge of hope about this endeavor to change our circumstances. I had wonderful premonitions of a successful conclusion to this chapter of our lives, and suddenly time seemed to fly by. I kept noticing special things about the city, about my neighbors, because I would soon be leaving.

But months and more months went by, and I received no word back from Moscow. Gradually I gave in to dejection and resignation—defeated again. For years and years all I had heard was no news.

When Karl was nearly two years old, a letter finally arrived. It was a glorious day, when in December 1957, we were all granted permission to leave the country! We had a specified time to settle our personal affairs, put things in order, and then "promptly leave the country."

Did Nikita Khrushchev, in fact, believe my letter? I wish I knew if that's what triggered the decision. As the Germans say, *es macht nichts*—it doesn't matter! But I immediately wrote to my dear friend in Moscow to tell him the good news. His advice had been priceless.

Our remaining time in Gorky was very hectic. We had few personal possessions, but the necessary paperwork and formalities were time consuming and frustrating. Getting all the documents together convinced me that every official held an advanced degree in general idiocy or the art of stalling. Some of them were so obtuse that we had to explain that GDR meant the German Democratic

Republic. The Russians were experts in red tape and hoop jump-ing, but worst of all was their universal stance of self-righteous hostile authority. One official, a female office worker in Moscow, actually told my mother that if it were up to her, she would never have permitted my mother to leave the country.

This whole process was profoundly exasperating. But now, especially for me, silence was golden! And if I could only keep my mouth shut a little while longer, we might finally get out of this frightful place.

The papers were finally completed and stamped. We emptied Mama's little apartment and packed our few things. Günter arrived from Inta. On February 17, 1958, as if awakening from a long bad dream, we left the Soviet Union behind us. We crossed into East Germany at the city of Fürstenwalde an der Spree. Though we were still firmly behind the iron curtain, we were now out of Rus-sia forever!

Twenty-Three

THE ESCAPE

Crossing into East Germany, we took a taxi to Finsterwalde, Günter's hometown, about a hundred kilometers away. We spent the first two months in one room of an apartment that belonged to Günter's brother, Max. Then we found a modest place of our own, a small but livable unit in a two-hundred-year-old house in the center of town.

Günter found a job in a local factory that produced materials for the Soviet Union, translating work manuals and directions from German into Russian. Though we had a small income, food was still rationed. Potatoes and onions weren't always available, and meat was too expensive for ordinary people. When, rarely, bananas or oranges appeared in the stores, only one piece of fruit was allotted per family.

Our circumstances were still difficult, but the biggest problem that Günter and I now faced was our increasingly troubled marriage.

Our early months in Germany were stormy, as the same problems faced us again. And just four and a half months later, this tense and distressing time grew dramatically worse. I found a letter addressed to Günter from a Russian woman we had known in Inta, a member of my old dance ensemble. My sister-in-law and I read it immediately. It was a passionate love letter, reminding him of the intimate times they had shared and telling him how much she missed him and longed for him to return. I was stunned and horrified at the woman's audacity but more so at my husband's infidelity. And I was angry at my own stupidity: not knowing what should have been obvious to me all along.

This was supposedly a friend of mine, whose name I will not reveal. I had recently gained what I wanted through writing a letter, so I immediately answered her letter with one of my own. I pointed out to her my husband's marital status and his responsibilities to his family. I felt especially threatened because I was now pregnant, and I let loose with my anger and warned her to take me seriously. When I confronted Günter, he showed little or no remorse. This episode caused much bitterness between us and irreparably damaged our marriage. He wanted no forgiveness, and I wasn't offering any.

Now our son Karl became seriously ill with a bladder inflammation, and he was taken to a hospital about fifty kilometers away. He was there for a month, and I became worn out worrying over him. Then I miscarried and was sent to the local hospital myself. I hadn't wanted another child of Günter's at this time, but I would never have done anything to prevent its birth. I remembered Betty's choice all too well. During the week I was in the hospital, powerful and mixed emotions flooded me. I was saddened to the core of my being as I dealt with the child I had suddenly lost. I was heartbroken about the state of my marriage and the rest of my life. Greater freedom had not brought me greater good.

At this embittered time, Günter and I began thinking seriously about leaving East Germany. Watching Günter's brother and sister, we saw that we could never survive in the GDR; it was too much like Russia! We could not be satisfied, knowing that unlimited possibilities lay just across the border in the West. We both believed we could have better lives by defecting to the West by way of West Berlin. The risks seemed well worth it. I felt as if we were in a film, two archrivals or foes linked together by the intent to accomplish one mutual objective: ultimate freedom. After that, *es macht nichts!* We could go our separate ways, but we stood a better chance of getting out of East Germany together.

So together Günter and I weighed all the factors. My main hope was that my mother, my child, and I would eventually make it back to our true home: the United States of America. I could see other benefits, but that was what made the risk worthwhile for me.

West Germany was the strategic place for launching us back to the United States. This was my private plan within the larger plan, because I knew that Günter had no intention of immigrating to America. I wasn't sure if I even wanted him to. He didn't fully understand my true motives, but I didn't know his either. In any case, the plan united us in the determination to make it to the democratic West at any cost.

At this time the infamous wall separating the Germanys had not yet been erected. Instead, heavily armed militia patrolled the strategic points along the border. It was a crime even to plan to leave East Germany, so we were in danger long before we actually attempted a crossing. If we were exposed, we would be arrested. And if we were caught at the border and detained by the Soviet-controlled Volks-polizei (People's Police, or VOPOs, as they were called), we could be killed on the spot for attempted desertion. It was tense and stressful for all of us, including my mother. The success or failure of this escape would dictate our futures in one swift movement!

Our plan was solid, well thought out, and well rehearsed. We envisioned every detail long before we put it into motion. We planned our escape for June 28, 1958. This was the beginning of a long holiday weekend, so the border guards in Berlin would be distracted. We had heard that they didn't pay as much attention at festive times as they normally would. So we chose that date and determined to make it work.

The night before our attempt, we each dressed in two sets of underwear and two sets of outer clothing and a raincoat for the wet, cold weather. It was like a scene in a spy-thriller movie, with one great difference: the personal cost of this production if we blew the scene was death, and we knew we would only get one take, one chance to get it right.

Despite the sufferings of my life, something deep inside me

was still childlike and adventurous. This night I remembered the innocent games I used to play with my friends at night, outside my home in Detroit, while Papa was inside reading and Mama was doing her chores. I now felt the same exhilaration and excitement, tinged with fear. I felt a great freedom, despite the gravity of our risk, because I felt I had nothing more to lose.

We left virtually everything we owned in our apartment. My mother and I each took a purse with our documents and a few valuables, and I carried a small bag with some of Karl's clothes and diapers. We only took one large item, a portable sewing machine: the prop.

It was still dark and very cold at five in the morning. We took a taxi all the way to East Berlin, some sixty-two miles away. We asked the driver to drop us off at the Soviet Embassy, ostensibly to extend our passports, which had to be periodically stamped by the East German and the Soviet authorities. When the taxi departed, we hurried away on foot toward the subway station. Our plan was to board a train for the Zoo Station at the border in Berlin. There a mutual friend was awaiting our arrival.

Before we reached the subway, we stopped to rest and to rehearse the crucial elements of our strategy. We had only one chance at this; we had to be flawless. Günter proposed that he go down to the station first to evaluate the situation. When he returned a short while later, he was pale and shaken. Günter was always very confident, but now he wanted to change his mind. His voice shook with fear and indecision.

He said, "Maidie, there are at least ten VOPOs down there, patrolling the station! They are doing heavy interrogations on everyone. There's just no way, Maidie! I don't think we can make it. Not now. We better go home and maybe try again later, at a better time, okay?"

Would I have to go into the subway station by myself? I still loved Günter, and I knew that, in his heart, he wanted out of the country too. I didn't know how much time together we actually had left. He'd already blown it for us as a couple, and I was fairly certain we were heading for divorce. So whether he would still be my husband didn't matter to me now. I knew what I wanted: to get across the border and back to America. I wasn't going to allow him to disrupt my life or my happiness for one more day. For this operation, he was simply my accomplice. I needed him, and he needed me in order to pull this off.

I believed this was the most advantageous time we would ever have, and we knew people were successfully making it out. And my mother would go with me wherever I went. That sealed it for me. I looked him straight in the face. He could see I was ready to try it alone, if that's the way it had to be.

I was adamant. "Günter, my husband, listen to me. We have no better time than this! Our time together is running out as it is. I know you want this as badly as I do. It's now or never!"

I had swayed him. I could see the life return to his eyes. We were going for it. Now it was raining hard on the cobblestone street. It was cold and it was still dark, and I could feel my knees shaking. Günter had conceived our escape plan, and now we put the drama into action.

Mama and Karl waited upstairs in a public area while Günter and I made our way down the stairs to the commandant's office at the gate. The plan was that I was to pose as a Russian who didn't understand a word of German. I had an imaginary brother named Alexander in the Russian army, stationed in Potsdam. I was taking this sewing machine to him and his wife, and I had to travel across West Berlin to get to Potsdam. Günter had given me a slip of paper with Alexander's ostensible address, but he thought the officials would be convinced by my sense of loyalty to my brother.

Günter started to explain the situation to the woman in charge. But despite the best acting job I had ever seen him do, she was not buying it. She was impatient and indifferent to the story he was spinning. This was not in the script. It was nerve-racking, but it was now my turn. As planned, Günter began a second laborious explanation to the woman, and I became very agitated, repeatedly interrupting her and Günter with angry questions—all in Russian. Günter translated, shrugging apologetically, *"Sie sprecht kein Deutsch."*

The woman was becoming nervous, and as I went on scolding, she was definitely getting upset. I believe she feared making the wrong decision. So I helped her out a bit more. I continued my routine, pointing to the sewing machine, looking very distraught, crying and cursing…only in Russian.

From their nearby posts, three or four guards were watching

this scene, and they started to move in our direction as we continued our act. They stopped directly in front of us. In confusion and
frustration, one of them asked, *"Was machtst du? Was ist los hier?"*
(What are you doing? What's the matter here?) But the woman
official promptly and decisively took charge: *"Es ist kein problem."*
Everything was fine, she said. Evidently she didn't want the guards
to think she couldn't control the situation. "It's all okay," she said.
"No problem." She motioned them away; she would take care of
it. Günter and I could see that our performance was making the
desired impression.

Our fate was now up to this woman. She was the judge. She still
hadn't let us through, but I knew we were close. Günter and I had
to do this together, and together we seemed to have nearly pulled it
off. His acting was absolutely wonderful, deserving of an Oscar! He
said the same about mine. Even in the dismal state of our marriage
and life together, this joint cause felt like a major victory. I thought,
Now if only we could cooperate as well in our marriage.

Though she was our judge, this woman was really just a player
in this drama. I knew there was a higher judge in the case. God,
and not she, would make the final decisions and determine the
outcome of my life. As I stood sniffling and Günter tried to calm
me down, the woman at the gate finally pulled out a form from her
desk drawer. She took down our names and destination, signed
and stamped the paper, and all four of us boarded the next train,
carrying the sewing machine. *We made it out!*

Twenty-Four

GÜNTER

Although we were afraid even to breathe abnormally, once we were on the train, we were virtually home free, because the VOPOs did not board the trains. Only minutes later we arrived at the Zoo Station in West Berlin. We were finally free people. We knew that refugees like us were being housed in camps, and we would have to undergo various political screenings by representatives of the English, French, and American sectors of Berlin. But we felt tremendous joy; these things were a small price to pay for the freedom we had just gained. We didn't worry about these formalities. The major obstacles had already been conquered.

We stayed in various refugee camps in West Berlin, including two months at a camp in Zehlendorf. During our brief stay, we visited the Kaiser Wilhelm Memorial at Die Gedächtniskirche, a bombed-out church on Kurfürstendamm, in the center of the town. The Berliners had preserved the partially destroyed building as a macabre monument to the war and the tremendous destruction of the city. For many blocks in all directions, the war-torn buildings bore witness to the overwhelming devastation of World War II.

Moving freely around the city, I was acutely aware of being in a free country for the first time in more than twenty-five years. It was not the United States, not America, but a democratic society nonetheless. It felt wonderful. I saw it as the second-to-last hurdle before I returned to my true home. Berlin was not home, but it was a very tolerable and a very fortunate place for us. I was grateful for West Germany and grateful also to Günter, whose grand scheme had brought us here.

I made a point of visiting the American Embassy in Berlin to ask about returning to America. The regular employee at that desk was on vacation, and a poorly informed substitute clerk advised me that "no procedures can be initiated regarding your return to the United States unless you are in possession of a Western passport." I learned later that this was a major error on his part, another nearly unforgivable event in this ongoing comedy of errors that made up my life. Therefore, due to this expert advice, I applied for a German passport instead, along with one for my mother. These passports were promptly granted, permitting us to move out of the refugee camp and officially enter West Germany.

The West Berlin Refugee Organization flew us out to a refugee camp called Friedland, where we stayed for a month. In September 1958 we left by train for Hanover, where an old friend of ours from Inta had already helped Günter get a job at the Volkswagen plant. Our railway carriage didn't have seats for all three of us, so I left Karl with my mother in one car, and I found a space in the next. This reasonable alternative turned into a frantic adventure; unbeknownst to us, our adjoining cars were disconnected at one of the stations along the way. When I got off the train in Hanover, Karl and Mama were missing, throwing me into shock and panic. *Where was my little Karlie?* Once again, awful scenes from my past came up, and I vividly imagined all of the horrible possibilities. Fortunately, there were Red Cross staff at the train station, and they went into action at my frenzied appeal. Two hours later we were reunited, to everyone's delight and relief.

For the next three years we subleased a portion of an apartment in Hanover. A wonderful family—a husband, wife, and two young daughters—let us use two of their six rooms. The daughters, older than baby Karl, would play with him for hours. There was no kitchen or running water in our living space; we converted an unheated solarium into a makeshift kitchen, installing a double-burner, propane-gas tabletop stove. In the winters we had to crack the built-up ice and heat water on the stove in order to wash up. These awkward daily arrangements seemed quite tolerable, however, in light of the conditions we had already survived.

Things between Günter and me were relatively peaceful, but much was missing. My child and my mother were being well cared for, but a major part of me was unsatisfied, lonely, and desperately crying out for something more. I didn't know how to fill that void, and neither did Günter. I don't think he really tried, keeping very much to himself. We were growing increasingly distant. Our marriage was like a dam that had sprung a leak. If it couldn't be fixed quickly, it would soon give way entirely; the impending flood would sweep away whatever foundation was left. A part of me still cared, but I didn't have much left. And I don't know whether Günter cared anymore or not. Maybe there was nothing left for him to give me.

Perhaps we were both damaged goods and just didn't know it. Perhaps all the difficult years before we were together had depleted our endurance and undermined our motivation for marriage. Even before we met, our lives had been nearly destroyed, our spirits nearly crushed. We had deep-rooted issues that required attention, but neither of us had the resources to remedy them. It was also possible that, in my haste to start a family, I had married the wrong person. And Günter, well, maybe he shouldn't have married at all; he wasn't a man for such commitment and responsibility. I don't think he really wanted our marriage to continue, and I was beginning to feel the same way. Nevertheless, our life together continued to limp along.

We learned that the West German government was providing special help for returning war prisoners. My husband was entitled to considerable retroactive compensation, a fixed amount of money per diem, counting from the very first day of his captivity until the day he was officially released from the Soviet Union. As a former political prisoner, I too was entitled to a generous compensation and an additional, smaller allotment for my son. We owned only a few worn and tattered clothes and had no furniture, so this new-found wealth was very welcome. Most of it went for warm clothes and necessary home furnishings. Working at the Volkswagen factory in Hanover, Günter was making a reasonable wage and provided us with a relatively decent standard of living. Having our finances on a smoother track helped lessen the tensions between us.

I began to realize that I was missing my good friends in Russia. Those women knew my inner secrets, the longings of my heart, and they had shaped the person I had become. They had always stayed in my mind and in my prayers. Now I felt a serious urge to see them again, but I had to face the fact that this was virtually impossible. I could never correspond with them from the West for fear of jeopardizing their lives and exposing our whereabouts to the Russian authorities.

The Soviets were masters of intrigue and information gathering and still used ironclad methods for handling defectors wherever they found them, in Germany or abroad. They had long arms. They had their ways. It did not matter that I was *and am* an American citizen who had never requested or accepted Soviet citizenship during my long-extended "vacation" in Russia. It would have been foolish for me to reveal my location on paper via letters to friends. We heard terrible stories about individuals and families who had gotten away only to be destroyed by Soviet agents. The Russians never gave up, and I knew they had people looking for us even now. Nothing was worth the risk of exposure. Secrecy was paramount.

I continued to miss my friends until one of them came to visit us from Paris. Mama and I had known this dear woman since our days in the American Village in Gorky. She had lost her husband, sister, and brother-in-law during the purges of 1937–38 and had finally escaped from Russia to Poland. There she managed to raise her infant son and orphaned niece. She had entered France to visit her sister, who had been a member of the French Resistance during the German occupation. She was a true survivor; she had it inside her not to give in but to triumph over all opposition. She made it out, to complete the life they could never take from her. She was too strong for them. Like so many of the women I knew in Russia, her character shone in adversity. She has an eternal place in my heart, and perhaps I have one in hers as well.

The joy of her visit was a painful contrast to my marriage. In the spring of 1959, my husband was granted a one-month vacation in a German resort, fully paid by the government. He departed alone, said his good-byes, and sent me a few postcards. I expected him to return on a certain date, but he did not come. I began to worry and wrote a letter to the director of the resort, asking for information. He wrote back that Günter had left the resort at the official end of his stay, "together with one of the women who had been there with him." I was stunned, but after a while I realized that the signs had been there. There had been other infidelities, but this time I wasn't going to tolerate it. When he finally did return, days later, he gave one of his typical excuses, but I confronted him with the truth. I watched as he adamantly gestured this way and that, still denying what he had done.

This was the man I had sworn a lifelong allegiance to, under God. We had taken an oath that I regarded seriously and he did not. Because he was the father of my child, I returned with him to our day-to-day existence, in two rooms of someone else's apartment, in the middle of Nowhere, West Germany. Though Hanover was, and is, a lovely German city, it didn't really matter to me anymore, because I was lost and miserable. I was in prison again, only this time as a free woman.

Günter returned to work for Volkswagen, and we continued to reside—but certainly not live—together. Every Friday he would pack a suitcase and take it with him to work. He wouldn't return until the following Monday night, bringing his suitcase of soiled clothes for me to wash. This went on for some time, with many ugly scenes between us. Probably because of his own frustrations and guilt, he became increasingly abusive toward Karl and me. Günter made no attempt to restore our marriage; it had become a facade. We could not continue under these conditions. In fact, there were days I believed he might kill me. I knew I needed help, some kind of divine guidance.

Finally one day he didn't come home at all. I didn't miss him terribly and waited three weeks before going to the police to file a missing-persons report. I was still concerned for his safety, at least for the man I used to know. I hoped that man was still inside him, but I had no more time or patience to look for him. Günter had already appeared and disappeared too many times, and now he was long gone.

Another month passed, and still no word from Günter. Now I was convinced that he was gone for good. Something had to be done. There was no money coming in, and there was no one else to provide for my family. I looked to God for help; I had nowhere else to turn.

My neighbor told me about the Telefunken factory's ad in the newspaper. Telefunken was a major German audio communications and telephone enterprise. I applied for a job, took an aptitude test, and was immediately hired as an inspector. Shortly thereafter I was promoted to aligner. It was a good job, and I rapidly advanced to the top in that department, making friends and earning a good wage. I continued to work there from June 15, 1959, until November 15, 1961.

Since I was caring for Karl and Mama, I needed to free myself from my nonexistent marriage. I finally engaged the services of a lawyer. After filing for divorce, I would have to wait another six months before it was final. The date for our hearing was posted in the courthouse to notify the public and, presumably, Günter. He had left no forwarding address, so my lawyer could not send him the court summons.

Little Karl had a history of sore throats, and now he had to have his tonsils removed. When he was released from the hospital in Hanover, he needed to recuperate. Like almost all the children in Hanover, he suffered from a form of bronchial asthma, brought on by the continuous damp climate. He went away to the island of Spiekeroog, in the North Sea. He returned much stronger, and we decided to visit a good friend of ours in Italy. She had traveled with us from Detroit to Russia in 1932, along with her husband and nine-month-old son. They had somehow survived the terrible purges in Russia and were eventually permitted to leave the country and settle in Turin. We visited them in July 1960 for ten days. The time was delightful for me, but Karl seemed uncomfortable and uneasy. The very day we returned from Italy, Karl broke out with the measles.

In August 1960 I was officially granted a divorce. Because my husband was absent, the procedure was brief and to the point. My mother and my landlord testified to Günter's abandonment and his physical violence and brutality, especially toward his son. I requested no child support, because I intended to return to the United States as soon as possible. I was not aware that, by German law, when child abuse is alleged during any court procedure, the state automatically initiates a civil case against the guilty party. If convicted, the abuser could be imprisoned.

The police found Günter in Bremen and notified him of the court's ruling and the consequences he faced for mistreating his son. Like a streak of light, Günter came running to me in Hanover, begging me to drop the charges. I explained to him that I had not initiated any action against him. Together we composed a letter to the court. I stated that I believed Günter to be sincere in his repentance, and I asked the court to discontinue any pending criminal procedures against him. I signed this paper and submitted it to the courthouse. Red tape kept me waiting three more months, and then the divorce was final. I never saw Günter again.

Twenty-Five

COMING HOME

The curtain closed on my failed pas de deux with Günter. My life in Russia, and now in Germany, was also coming to a close. And I was anxiously looking forward to the next act: our return to America. But this was not simple or guaranteed.

The horrible advice I was given at the embassy in Berlin had created an unforeseen problem. In applying for a German passport, I had inadvertently given up my American citizenship. Now I learned that, under American law, I would have continued to be a citizen of the United States during the years I was in Russia, even though I could not afford to extend my passport. By the careless stroke of someone else's pen, I had lost my citizenship rights and could no longer return home as an American. My request to immigrate was now suspect. In a flurry of visits to the American Embassy in Hamburg, I was thoroughly and not so subtly grilled by the vice consul of the embassy. I had to defend the purposes for my desired U.S. immigration. Furthermore, I would have to wait my turn to immigrate to the United States, according to the quota for West Germany. Over and over I protested, "But wait… How can this be? I was…I mean, I *am*, an American citizen!

But I did not just sit back and despair. I did all I could, gathering the documents we would need. I wrote innumerable letters to friends and relatives in the States, primarily to my cousins Lucy and Ernst in New York and to my cousin Theresa in Cincinnati. I also wrote to friends in Detroit, soliciting their official sponsorship. It didn't seem right to need a sponsor to return to my country of origin, but I was determined to get there regardless of the red tape. Theresa and her husband, Chris, soon sent us an official affidavit of sponsorship. Now we could go to Ohio when our turn finally came.

In the winter of 1960, U.S. authorities sent me a letter summoning me to Hameln. This is the city made famous in the fairy tale where the renowned Pied Piper led the rats out of town. I hoped that was a good omen! The authorities photographed my Russian passport and interrogated me for two hours. Particulars of my early life in Detroit were closely scrutinized. The officials also questioned me extensively about the fur coat I was wearing. It was a gift I had received from an anonymous American during my brief stay at the refugee camp in Friedland.

Then I returned to Hanover to await word regarding our request. For nearly a year we heard nothing whatsoever. I went to work every day, and Mama looked after Karl, but we felt as if we were suspended in the air, not really here, and not able to move, either.

Finally, the phone rang one day. A man from the German emigration office in Berlin said, "Miss Tobien, I have some good news for you. Your papers have been approved for your immigration to America. I am sending them to you today…"

In the sheer euphoria of the moment, I must have hung up the phone, because I don't remember saying anything to him in return. I just remember my heart beating wildly, and then I ran to grab Karlie and Mama. This was the news we had been waiting for, the best news in my entire life!

A hectic time followed. There were many final details and preparations, all undertaken with a whole new mind-set, a freshness of energy, and a quickening of my spirit. *We were really going back home!* Because only a certain weight was allowed per ticket, we had to get rid of most of our belongings and find suitable crates to pack the rest. And I had to obtain a formal discharge from the factory. We said our farewells to the dear friends who shared the apartment, whom I continued to correspond with for many years. There were many pressures, but it was one of the most exhilarating phases of my life.

The day of departure came at last. As in the dream that consumed my thoughts for years, we took a taxi to the railroad station, boarded the train at about six in the evening, and only five hours later arrived in Rotterdam, Holland. We spent the night in a hotel. Karl slept like a rock, but Mama and I hardly slept at all. Our emotions and adrenaline were running much too high to allow for something as optional as sleep!

I had spent many oppressive years in prison, in seclusion, mostly helpless and many times hopeless, but now I was going home. I had to pinch myself, wondering, *Can this really be happening?*

The following morning, November 21, 1961, we boarded our beautiful ship and set sail just before noon. It was the SS *Statendam* of the Holland-American Line, a wonderful introduction to our new life. In the dining room, I was thrilled to see stalks of celery again—one of life's simple pleasures and something I had not seen for twenty-nine years! Mama and I sat in our stateroom filled with unspeakable thanks. This day—this one particular day—was the dawning of a new beginning! It was freedom, fresh air, new life, the fulfillment of my vision at last! We were finally on our way *home* to the United States of America.

Our crossing met with an especially rough storm in the Atlantic, lasting two full days, and we all had some mild seasickness. But after that it was smooth sailing all the way. On November 29, 1961, at about six in the morning, in the far distance we saw that beautiful lady, the exquisite Statue of Liberty at the entrance to New York Harbor. Pure joy and delight poured over me and flowed into my soul as I gazed at her sheer magnificence. It was not the tradition of watching for the statue or even her meaning as a powerful patriotic symbol that moved me. It was what she represented to me specifically and personally at that very moment. It was indescribable; words do not do justice.

Memories of all the years behind me—both good and bad— came rushing in, clarifying who I was and who I was created to be. I realized that my life had already been more than remarkable; it had been miraculous. Someday I would have to speak of it. My story was too much to keep bottled inside. My life had been stolen from me, but now it was being returned. The forces of evil had destroyed much of my life, yet, if but for a moment, I almost felt as if I hadn't missed a thing. I knew I could just as easily have died out there, given up and folded my hands. Many others had done that. I knew them. I knew their faces. But God had other plans. God had given me a chance in a million, a chance to start all over again. I was free. Here was my life, waiting for me, as if I had just been born.

There was no way that any of it could have happened without the ever-merciful hand of God: the power that simply cannot be defined, contained, or understood. And there wasn't a thing I could have done to earn it. It just was because *he* is! His ways are beyond comprehension or explanation. He's the one who said, "I will repay you for the years the locusts have eaten."

That was the certainty that rested upon my heart as I peered longingly into the harbor of my country, barely able to contain myself. It was no accident or coincidence that had brought me home again. No, it was part of a divine plan. It was his plan. Thank God, it was his plan for me.

The very first thing I did when we stepped off the ship was kneel down and kiss the boards of the pier. I was really and truly home again. I had come full circle!

EPILOGUE

by Karl Tobien

Don't you want to be there, don't you want to know?
Where the grace and simple truth of childhood go
Don't you want to be there when the trumpets blow
Blow for those born into hunger,
Blow for those lost 'neath the train
Blow for those choking in anger
Blow for those driven insane
And those you have wronged, you know
You need to let them know some way
And those who have wronged you, know
You'll have to let them go someday.
Don't you want to be there?

Don't you want to see where the angels appear
Don't you want to be where there's strength and love
In the place of fear.
 —Jackson Browne, "Don't You Want to Be There"

M argaret Werner Tobien was the only American woman
known to have survived the Siberian slave-labor camps of
twentieth-century Stalinist Russia, to have escaped from exile, and
to have returned to the United States.

I am the child who was born to Margaret and Günter Tobien on
January 27, 1956, in northern Siberia. I am a child of each of
them, and as shadow and light are separate but merge in the twi-
light, I am a child of both of them. I escaped with them through
the iron curtain into freedom on that historic day. And as I think
back upon my life, I recall sorrows and joys and new beginnings,
and I continually think of my mother. As I consider this miraculous legacy of how I came to be, I miss her more and more.

I was there, though I do not remember, on that glorious day in
November 1961 when she knelt down and kissed the pier of her
home in America. Through the years I saw this woman who had
been denied many things live her life to its absolute fullest. I

remember most her joyous expectancy and constant excitement about life, the exuberance of her personality.

I grew up listening to, and sometimes only overhearing, the stories my mother shared with others about her life and trials in Russia. For most of my life, I never took the time to explore this history or to ask her questions. I was a child and then a young man in utter disarray, busy being fearful, resentful, and bitter. As an outsider in many ways, I was unsettled, rebellious, and angry about what I believed I lacked. The reality was that I lacked for nothing except character, maturity—and God. I never imagined that I would want to write this chronicle of my mother's extraordinary survival.

Margaret Werner Tobien experienced horror and sorrow during the course of her life to degrees the human heart would rather not consider. Still, she prevailed when most others did not. Why was that? Was it luck? I don't think so; neither did she. Rather, I think it was because of something very special she had inside, something not easily explained.

Returning to America in 1961 with little more than the clothes on our backs, she began again. She built a new life for us, virtually unassisted and from scratch. She was forty years old, but she never wore her past around her neck like a ribbon, a trophy, or a yoke, never sought sympathy or public acknowledgment. Her life was nothing like that. Meeting her for the first time, no one would have guessed the nature of her past. She never had a hard-luck story to tell. Her presence exuded warmth, energy, and eternal optimism.

While I was growing up, I recall a couple of special men in her life—everyone was attracted to her—but apparently there were no more Nikolais, and she never remarried. She always attempted to fill the place of the father I really never had. In fact, it was my grandmother, Elisabeth Werner, who was more like a mother to me. After all, she was half of the family where Margaret got her "stuff." And that was our small family during my childhood.

During the early years of our return, it became clear to Margaret that her dream of attending medical school and becoming a doctor was no longer possible. Though she often spoke of that heartfelt longing, she had to work to support her family. I consider that her life, like that of Job in the Bible, was not fair to her; she was dealt a bad hand and endured great pain and sadness. Nevertheless, she always made the most of what was available, a trait she had perfected during her formative years in Russia.

She worked for many years as a lab technician and draftsperson for an electronics company in Cincinnati. She was directly responsible, though not credited, for many innovative, technically sophisticated designs and drawings for video circuitry components. These state-of-the-art concepts were widely utilized in the television industry and in many recent media applications.

During her later years, my mother used her artistic aptitude and flair for the creative in the ceramic arts. She entered and won a variety of national ceramics contests. Remember her innovative contributions in the Russian camps? She became well known for her distinctive ideas and amazed people with her inimitable ingenuity and concern for perfection. Her craft always left people with their mouths open in admiration.

Several years after her retirement, she volunteered at Cincinnati's Jewish Community Center as a translator for the many Russian Jews immigrating to the United States through our city. I remember how dearly she loved them and the deep compassion she always had for the Russian people. She had an uncompromising, unconditional love for people that extended far beyond arbitrary surface deeds that others often do for show.

I could write another book about all the wonderful things she did during the thirty-five years of her life after returning to America—the years I knew her. God created a very special one here; there will never be another woman like Margaret Werner Tobien.

As I consider her profound touch on so many lives, before and after the troubled years of this story, and the eternal gifts she left us, I now understand that her life truly was, as she once described it, a "full circle." It didn't end the day she returned to America. Nor did it end when her physical body stopped working. Her life goes on, even today, around and upward—like a rising spiral, extending far beyond us. She was much more than the mere survivor of a certain time in history. She was an American patriot, with a red-white-and-blue heart, a champion through and through.

Even if she had not been my mother, I would still prize her. She was uniquely gifted, multitalented, and articulate (actually brilliant), and these talents were part of the most genuinely thoughtful, kind, compassionate, and naturally loving person I have ever known. All those wonderful things are true, but they barely scratch the surface of her true self. In addition to the spiritual certainties she came to understand, accept as her own, and treasure so deeply, she also believed strongly in the personal power and ability of every human being. Her own life demonstrated this belief.

I suspect she was much like her father, Carl Werner, whom of course I never knew. I do know that she was much like her mother, Elisabeth Werner, whom I did know, and I thank God for that. I know firsthand the qualities that Elisabeth passed on to her daughter.

My grandmother was always the talk of the neighborhood kids. She defied the natural limits of a woman's physical ability well into her eighties, and she defied the normal limits of human kindness toward everyone she encountered. She was deeply loved and cherished, not only by every kid on the block, but by everyone who knew her for miles around. In their hearts, she was everyone's grandma. As a young child, I noticed people always watching her in disbelief: shoveling snow, mowing grass, climbing ladders, painting the house, and every other chore imaginable. She could dig up and replant an entire backyard garden from scratch. And that was all before lunch! And guess who made lunch? I've never seen such physical resiliency or determination in any other person, regardless of age or gender. You just had to see her to believe her.

After a long hard day at play on the local ball fields, all my friends would scramble to come back home with me, if they could. The reason? Elisabeth Werner was also the best cook on the planet. (She now has competition from my dear wife.) We're talking cheeseburgers to die for and, unlike their Russian counterparts, the best potatoes you could eat, in whatever form she prepared them.

I loved Elisabeth Werner more than I can say. And it was through her that I encountered the Creator of all things, the Lord Jesus Christ, in a personal, life-changing way. She was near death, in a comatose state, when I sat with her in a hospital room on April 12, 1984. On that day I witnessed the awesome resurrection power of God: he instantly raised her up before my eyes and gave her more years to live, and he raised my desperately empty and longing spirit along with her. I saw the irrefutable power of God in this absolute miracle. I had no idea that such things were possible, and if I had not been there, I would never have believed it to be true. But I *was* there and with my own eyes beheld the glory of the Lord. Now I am a believer, because now I know.

My grandmother went *home* to heaven in 1987 to be with her beloved husband, Carl. And if I had to guess, I'd say there's a good chance she's in charge of the kitchen!

Cast in the same mold was my mother. Margaret Werner was definitely Elisabeth's daughter. And in her integrity, she showed the trait her father always held in such high regard. It wasn't integrity for the sake of fashion or display; it was a foundational godlike integrity for its own sake. Surely her lifelong experiences and the strength of character she always exemplified had much to do with her ability to influence others. When you met her, you were drawn to whatever she had to say to you.

My mother had many things to say to me over the years. However, of all the wisdom she possessed and passed on, the most simple yet compelling thing she ever said was, "Karl, just be good to people. That's all. It will not be wasted, and it will always come back to you. If there's nothing else you remember from me, then please remember this; it will suit you well."

Though Margaret had been on a personal quest for God nearly all her life, throughout all her trials and troubles in Russia, seeing and realizing the hand of God in her life all along the way, it was in the fall of 1991 that she actually invited Christ into her life, establishing that relationship, making him Lord and Savior, sealing her eternal fate.

On April 7, 1997, I found the lifeless shell of my mother's body slumped across her bathroom floor. She was gone. I couldn't think straight, and I didn't know what to do. I fell to the floor and cried like a baby until I thought my heart would explode. It's tough to put into words the searing pain of that moment. I couldn't breathe, and I struggled to pray. I didn't expect her to die, not yet! She was not supposed to leave this way. Instead, she was supposed to live to see her story realized and shared with the world.

Now I was the only one left to finish this story my mother gave me, to tell the world what happened to her, what she did, and what her life meant. Thirty-six years earlier, three of us had returned to

America, and now there was only me. As I write this, some six years later, I recall that particular day as the most devastating but also the most hopeful day of my life. I realized that her life had reached its earthly fullness. She was tired. She was ready for her promotion.

Before her death, my mother gave me yet another priceless legacy. Working through her friends from her days in the camps, she made it possible for me to be reunited with my father. That is a remarkable story in itself, perhaps for another time. But she acted unselfishly to let me reestablish this significant relationship.

My father, Günter Tobien, had married a German woman named Anna-Marie. They had no children. They resided for my father's whole life in the northern German city of Bremen. In March 1994, some thirty-three years after I left Germany as a child with my mother and grandmother, I finally saw my father again. We were reunited at his home. My father spoke virtually no English, and my command of German was only a remnant of what it had once been. Fortunately, he spoke slowly and deliberately and straight from his heart. He said things I needed to hear. I suspect it went both ways. We connected, but for most of that time together we spoke only the universal unwritten language of tears and smiles, trying to redeem the lost years. All thirty-three of them.

Those years could not be recaptured or relived, but it was a powerful reunion all the same. My father and I formed a bond as if all those years hadn't mattered. He was my father, and I loved him. I also knew that he loved me. A part of me that had been missing for so long had just been found, and I finally felt completed. He was a very thoughtful, sensitive, compassionate, and loving man who had missed and longed for me as much as I had missed him. I could see him being filled inside, in a place that had been empty. And I didn't feel as though I had anything to forgive him for. Instead, I just loved him, and it was easy to do.

The following year, 1995, he and his wife came to our home for a two-week visit. It was their first time in the United States. They both fell in love with my wife, Tina, and our family. Günter met his three beautiful grandchildren—Karla, Matthew, and Kaleb —and clearly his heart was filled with love and joy. (Since that time our sweet Khloe and Karla's precious children, Olivia Margaret and Elijah, have joined us.) I understood that something eternal was being fulfilled, fully satisfied for him during this magical time together. Perhaps it was also sort of a circle coming around for him.

My father died in October 1996. It was natural I suppose, and yet it felt very unnatural to me. It was hard to lose what I had just gained. However, the relationship was not lost. My dad and I had made our peace; we filled each other's voids, said whatever there was to say, and then we loved unconditionally. Günter and Anna-Marie Tobien had become a permanent part of our family. Anna-Marie is still precious to us; we call her Oma.

Those renewed relationships were my mother's parting gift before she heard her heavenly Father calling on that day in April 1997. I believe she left gladly, on her way to another reunion. Though I know she was sorry to leave us behind, she was eager to go and see her papa and mama once again. This time no one could take them away from her. There would be no more good-byes or tears, no more pain.

She left behind much more than the usual remnants of a life. For all of us who knew her and felt that very special love from her, she left a huge deposit. She left us her heart. It is permanently embedded in our lives, shaping who we are today. She completes us, circling us in love, lifting us upward by her life.

TIME LINE

1910—Ford sells its first automobile in Russia.

1918—End of World War I; Lenin founds Russian Communist Party.

1921—Margaret Werner is born to Carl and Elisabeth in Bay City, Michigan.

1922—U.S.S.R. (Soviet Union) officially forms.

1928–29—Stalin implements first Five-Year Plan. United States' stock market crashes; Great Depression begins (October). In the Soviet Union, agricultural collectivization begins.

1930–32—Ford Motor Company sends employees to its Russian manufacturing facility; Russia officially changes the name of the city of Nizhni Novgorod to Gorky.

1932—Werner family leaves Detroit with Ford Motor Company and arrives in Russia.

1933—Stalin's second Five-Year Plan begins along with Russian purges. Walter Reuther arrives in Gorky. The Werners visit relatives in Austria and Czechoslovakia.

1937—The Great Terror, or Yezhovshchina, begins, the most severe of Stalin's great purges throughout the nation.

1938—Stalin's third Five-Year Plan begins. Soviet secret police arrest Carl Werner. Margaret, age 17, refuses to denounce her father at a Soviet youth rally.

1941—Germany invades Russia. Germany occupies Leningrad in the 900-Day Siege. Gorky is bombed. Margaret is mobilized to dig antitank trenches.

1942—Most brutal winter in Russian history. Germans obliterate Gorky by bombing. Carl Werner dies in prison (not known until 1956).

1945—World War II ends. U.S. President Roosevelt, British Prime Minister Churchill, and Soviet Premier Stalin confer at Yalta. Margaret, age 24, is arrested and imprisoned in Gorky's Vorobyo'vka prison.

1946—Margaret is transferred to Lubyanka prison in Moscow, then back to Gorky, then returned to Moscow, where she's sentenced to ten years hard labor and shipped to the brutal lumber camp Burepolom.

1947—Henry Ford dies in April.

1948—Margaret is officially transferred to the labor camp at Inta (Komi, ASSR) in Northern Siberia.

1953—Joseph Stalin dies (March). Margaret returns to Gorky to meet with the secret police for jails and prison camps, who detain Elisabeth under suspicion of complicity in Margaret's charges of espionage.

1955—Margaret is released March 3 and marries former German POW Günter Tobien. Nikita Khrushchev takes control of the Russian Communist Party.

1956—Karl is born in Inta (January 27). Margaret, age 35, returns to Gorky with her baby and reunites with her mother, Elisabeth.

1957—Russia and Germany enter the War Prisoner Exchange Agreement and begin repatriation. Margaret, Elisabeth, and Karl receive permission to go to East Germany (GDR).

1958—Margaret, Elisabeth, and Karl cross into GDR in February, escape to West Berlin on June 28 (twenty years to the day since Carl Werner's arrest), and settle in Hanover, Germany.

1960—Margaret and Karl visit Italy. Margaret divorces Günter and goes to Hameln for an immigration interview.

1961—Margaret, Elisabeth, and Karl sail from Rotterdam, Holland, and arrive November 29 in the United States.

1987—Elisabeth Werner dies on February 24.

1991—The city of Gorky reverts to its original name of Nizhni Novgorod.

1996—Günter dies on October 26.

1997—Margaret dies on April 7, fifty years to the day after the death of Henry Ford.

HISTORICAL NOTES

Victor Herman

After Victor Herman's arrest in July 1938 (less than thirty days after Carl Werner's arrest), he was tried, sentenced, and sent to the Siberia Gulag, where he remained until 1956. After much hardship and suffering, Victor finally returned to the United States in 1976. His Russian wife and two daughters eventually received emigration visas from the Soviet government, permitting them to leave Russia and reunite with Victor in the United States. The account of his experiences was published in *Coming Out of the Ice: An Unexpected Life*.

Upon his return home, Victor Herman sought compensation from the Ford Motor Company for the fate his family suffered (both parents died), but the company informed him: "The former employment of Sam Herman could not be verified or confirmed." They flatly rejected him. They categorically denied that Victor's father, Sam Herman, had ever worked for the Ford Motor Company! In his ultimate frustration and with nowhere else to turn, Victor Herman responded by publicly referring to America as "a stepmother nation." His siblings remained in Russia. Miriam completed medical school and became a doctor, and Leo committed suicide by hanging.

WALTER REUTHER

It was later confirmed that Walter Reuther had been in Russia on assignment, acting as an official delegate to the Gorky factory for Henry Ford. In the years to follow, after his return to America, he became head of the United Auto Workers and of the world's most powerful labor union, the AFL-CIO. His sympathetic views toward Communism and socialism are well known and documented. Walter Reuther eventually became an influential advisor to Franklin and Eleanor Roosevelt and a leading voice for the Democratic Party for nearly four decades. He must have been oblivious to the horrors of the Russian political structure he formerly supported. Walter Reuther died in a plane crash in 1970, under what authorities called "mysterious circumstances."

ALEXANDER DUBCEK

Alexander "Sanya" Dubcek eventually returned to his native Czechoslovakia to become the country's most prominent political figure and chancellor. Though his political persuasion was Communist, it was clear he tried to pursue a milder form of Communist reform: "socialism with a heart." The Soviets questioned his politics and practices in Czechoslovakia, as well as his loyalty to Russia and Communism in general. When he pleaded with them not to invade his country, the Soviets saw his tears as a sign of weakness, and they promptly sent in tanks.

Alexander Dubcek had a chance to set his people free by opposing the Russians, but he missed it. His intentions were noble, but his misguided beliefs doomed many of his countrymen to suffering. Later in life, however, after Czechoslovakia was free from Soviet domination, Dubcek stood in a moment of triumph with the country's first "elected" leader, Vaclav Havel, and was voted leader of the federal assembly.

In subsequent years, Sanya Dubcek's political career floundered. After the Soviet domination of his country, he was forced out of office and had to earn his living as a locksmith, a little known fact about his later life. Margaret Werner recalled, "I knew that we cared for one another quite deeply, but after those innocent days we spent together in Gorky—a time I will truly never forget—we never saw one another again…ever."

LINA PROKOFIEV

In a newspaper article Margaret Werner read many years later, she learned that Lina spent eight years in Vorkuta in confinement.

Sergei Prokofiev officially disowned his wife during World War II to live with a young poet and Communist Party worker, Mira Mendelssohn. When Sergei died in 1953, there was a legal battle over the rights to his estate, particularly as to whether Lina or his supposed new wife, Myra, had full entitlement. Myra had since died, and their marriage was never conclusively documented. The article reported that Lina was finally allowed to leave the Soviet Union in 1974. She moved to Chicago. A book entitled *Sergei Prokofiev: A Soviet Tragedy* was later written by Victor Seroff, detailing the life of this famous Russian composer.

Margaret reflected: "I thought that maybe too many years had passed in the interim for either Lina or me to attempt personal contact. Twenty-five years is a very long time. For some, the war was never over. The Soviet reach went far and deep. And primarily for safety and personal reasons, I intentionally tried to keep my whereabouts out of the spotlight. I suppose it was the easier out and for some—like me—a milder and gentler form of denial. It may be the memories that hurt the most, particularly when you're trying to make sense of it all, maybe even pointing blame, asking 'why me,' and hearing no response."

Henry Ford

Though Ford Motor Company insists its American workers in Gorky returned to the United States in 1932, Carl Werner was still living there in 1938 and working at the plant Ford built to manufacture the trucks essential to Stalin's Five-Year Plans. What did the Ford Motor Company in Detroit know, and what didn't they know about the affairs going on in Gorky? What did they disclose, and what did they conceal? And why? What was their involvement, their level of support for their people? Why had they abandoned their employees? What, if anything, was their liability? Now, long after the fact, I still pose the questions, not that I have the historically definitive answers. But it has been suggested that if the Nazi industrialists brought to trial at Nuremberg were even remotely guilty of so-called crimes against mankind, then so must be their collaborators in the Ford family, Henry and his son, Edsel. Certainly they knew of the horrible atrocities taking place in the Soviet Union and specifically in Gorky. And what was the U.S. government doing about all the Americans who were there in harm's way? Indeed, there are many more questions than answers, and things are not always as they first appear.

There is much documentary evidence that the Ford Motor Company worked for both sides during World War II. While Russia was at war with the Germans, the United States, as an official ally to Russia and Britain, was certainly also at war with Germany. And Henry Ford was doing business simultaneously with the two archrivals—Hitler and Stalin—supplying cars, financing, and political influence, for profit, to each. The Ford story was concealed by Washington, however, like almost everything else of that genre that could touch the name and sustenance of the Wall Street elite.

Further information on Henry Ford's activities in Russia can

be found on these Web sites: http://beagle.u-bordeaux4.fr/ifrede/
Ford/Pdf/Shpotov.pdf and http://reformed-theology.org/html/
books/wall_street/chapter _06.htm.

RELIGION

The Soviet Union was the first nation of the world to have as an
ideological objective the elimination of organized religion. Toward
that end, the Communist regime confiscated church property,
ridiculed anything vaguely resembling religious behavior, harassed
believers, and openly propagated atheism in the schools. Treatment
of particular religions, however, was determined by differing state
interests, and most organized religions were never officially outlawed. But Christianity faced the most oppression and suffered the
worst of all persecutions. The main target of the antireligious cam-
paigns in the 1920s and 1930s was the Russian Orthodox Church,
which had the largest number of faithful. Nearly its entire clergy
and many of its believers were executed or sent to labor camps.
Theological schools were closed, and church publications were
prohibited. By 1939 only about five hundred of more than fifty
thousand churches remained open.

To maintain the party's ideological authority, religion was condemned outright and history periodically revised to match the current party line. Books and magazines viewed as politically incorrect
were removed from libraries. Scientists, artists, poets, and others,
including many who did not think of themselves as dissidents but

whose work appeared critical of Soviet life, were systematically persecuted and even prosecuted. Often they were declared either enemies of the state—and consequently imprisoned—or insane and therefore committed to punitive mental hospitals. Thus the state destroyed both faith and freedom by fear.

CHALLENGE TO THE READER

Today's world is not always big on real truth, as in clear definitions of right and wrong, moral absolutes, and the like. We don't often see, hear, or read about real truth. Instead, we're busy being led astray by false comforts, lies, and pure deception.

I didn't know my grandfather Carl Werner personally, but I sense that he was very concerned about this issue of truth.

In our society we have callously discarded our principles, our moralities, indeed our very integrity, and, instead, we have graciously bowed down to the god of popular opinion and caved in to the law of political correctness as substitutes for plain and simple truth. "Such nonsense!" is what Carl Werner would probably say. But truth, nonetheless, is the patent reality and very foundation upon which this story is based. And sometimes, no matter what the cost, we simply have to tell the truth.

It's almost funny to me how, in the late 1920s, Joseph Stalin heretically and arrogantly proclaimed, "God must be out of Russia in five years." How ridiculous is that? Imagine the nerve of such a statement. But now it's 2006, and I think it's plain to see that same hideous message bombarding us right here in America of all places, a nation built upon the rock of "In God We Trust." What has happened to us?

When will we wake up and realize that, not so unlike Stalinist Russia, our godless (otherwise known as progressive) liberal organizations and faithless media moguls have an agenda. There's actually a purpose and a goal behind the absurdities we hear in the press day after day. Their business is that of shaping our perceptions with tainted information. Whose voices are we hearing, anyway?

Our society can do without aimless excuses—failing to take responsibility for our actions and then creating some new dysfunction in order to alleviate or redirect the blame. Misinformation, useless oratory, and baseless explanations all have to go, along with all of the proposed band-aid cures for the earth's rapidly perishing collective soul.

An unfortunate reality is that this world, in all of its complexities, with its unfathomable banks of information and its depth of knowledge, seems to utilize so little true wisdom. Wisdom is entirely different from knowledge. What truly makes people wise is what they choose to do with all the knowledge they've obtained. The world has many knowledgeable fools, those who have turned their backs on God and who would not understand wisdom if it bit them on the leg! Why is that, you ask?

There is a prevailing element of spiritual death innately residing within the much-flawed human condition of unregenerated man. It must be dealt with. Step one is simple recognition; we must first get our eyes on the ball. The Bible states, "Do you have eyes but fail to see, and ears but fail to hear? And don't you remember?" (Mark 8:18). We are weak, we are terribly flawed, and we certainly need help!

Until personal awakening and a true spiritual makeover have taken place in a person's life, the perpetual path of the same old, same old remains continually hopeless. But there is a remedy. It's called change, transformation. It's available through humility, transparency, and faith. It came to us by way of incredible sacrifice. It was freely offered through amazing grace. Mercy is its foundation. And it is here because of extraordinary love in the person of Jesus Christ.

It doesn't take a genius to see that humanity, within the futility of its own mind and perceived resources, has not found and will not (if not by now) find the answers that have inevitably escaped its grasp for so long.

Answers cannot be found in ordinary education, rehabilitation, legislation, standardization (political correctness), psychology, therapy, counseling, extramarital affairs, psychic hotlines, self-help programs, cosmetic surgeries, workout routines, or cryogenics. All of these, as well as the other assorted magical answers, potions, and cures that are intended to be good things, do not and will not ever solve the problem that we all need to be solved. Nor will they bring the slightest degree of true fulfillment and permanence into the human heart or into our lives.

The world, having forgotten God as its Creator, has no remedy for its inherently iniquitous condition. Nor do we, as individuals, have a solution for ours. We are working from an untenable spiritual deficit, and apart from our acceptance of the grace and mercy of a loving God, there is no resolution. We need something more lasting, more permanent than the empty promises to which we have grown accustomed. We need something much stronger than what our often misplaced and shortsighted intellect leads us to believe.

We need truth—absolute truth—and we absolutely need it now! We need it in our homes. Our children desperately need it in their schools. We need it at the workplace. We need it in our government. We need it to fill our lives, and certainly we need it in our churches!

If we, as a society, continue to blindly endorse and believe the lie that morality and decency are somehow adjustable, contingent, or even optional, then we are also hopelessly lost—lost and without hope. We can no more effectively legislate goodness and human morality than we can accept the twisted premise that somewhere, deep below Stalin's or Hitler's malevolent conduct, there existed good intent. We've heard that particular nonsense before.

The world has not accidentally but purposely substituted God's laws and the clear moral absolutes given us from the beginning—

good things, intended to be our very lifelines—with situational ethics as the acceptable standard of our time. We have blatantly condoned the everyday arrogance of godless and defiant fly-by-the-seat-of-your-pants morality as the order of the day. No, it is impossible to govern the human heart. And if we continue in that same increasingly indignant humanist mind-set, then we will indeed be forever shrouded with hopelessness, eternally lost.

What we need, what the world requires, is simple truth. Our human heart urgently pleads for it. Truth is universal, fundamental, unchanging, and everlasting. It is something we can stand upon, something that will not crumble. We need a sure and firm foundation: the rock of Christ and the Word of God.

Truth is not a concept or a belief. It is not idealism, a theory, an alternative (as some would say), or ever an option. Truth is not open to interpretation, debate, or negotiation; it has no time for that. It matters not in the least degree whether you happen to like it or not, if it's convenient to you or not—truth is still truth. And it doesn't worry about political correctness, stepping on toes, because it will surely do that. Truth will always be offensive to some. It stirs up hearts and minds that would, sadly, rather be left alone to relax in pretentiousness, indifference, and even deception.

The fact is that the world always needed truth and help. More so than ever, we need help today! Surely that's a hard thing for our prideful nature to recognize and to admit. But we have no other workable alternative. Plain and simple: we all need help! And help, if we really want it, is right in our midst. He's been here all along. In fact, help stands at the door and knocks. We only need, with a little bit of faith, to answer the door.

Margaret Werner Tobien's life was miraculously preserved. Author Don Milam so aptly states in his illuminating book *The Ancient Language of Eden* that "Father is always moved to divine action by the sorrow flowing from man's troubles. There is always a divine response to the human predicament." During all of my mother's calamitous times, she was protected, shielded, and cared for by a divinely omnipotent God who loved her. And he loves us all infinitely more than we could ever imagine.

My mother came to know that reality firsthand and then learned to apply it to her life—a life filled with disappointment and heartbreak, a life in desperate need of help. Forsaking the common worldly lie and with total humility, she came to fully understand and appreciate her natural dependence upon God, the Creator of the heavens and the earth. She knew that she needed help. We all do. By faith, she reached out for that help in order to receive back, for herself, God's wonderful grace and eternity's final reward.

And God has said, "Nothing will be impossible for you" (Matthew 17:20).

Just look around you. Our world is hopelessly lost and all but consumed by darkness. But this world, the Lord also admonishes us, is not our own. He said, "Take heart! I have overcome the world" (John 16:33). There is only one answer, none other: the Lord Jesus Christ, whom God gave us as one eternally bright light to dispel and conquer this darkness. The truth is that we all need a Savior. We are powerless to save ourselves. "For there is no other name under heaven given to man by which we must be saved" (Acts 4:12). Our safe eternal passage is marked by these words: "If you confess with your mouth, 'Jesus is Lord,' and believe in your heart that God raised him from the dead, you will be saved" (Romans 10:9). And that, my friends, is the best news of all! For *that* is the true gospel.

In case you don't happen to recognize Margaret Werner in heaven—when you go—she'll be the one conducting the ballet recitals in the Lord's outer courts, dancing and beaming radiantly from ear to ear, thanking God for his incredible love!

On behalf of my mother, whom I've no doubt is dancing still, I bless you and wish you peace eternal.

ACKNOWLEDGMENTS

I wish to express my heartfelt thanks, love, respect, and eternal gratitude to the following people, who in their unique way have contributed to my life—beyond measure—and, in so doing, the ultimate telling of this story.

Karla, Matthew, Kaleb, and Khloe Tate Tobien (along with my *magnetic* son-in-law, Ryan Snow, and my precious grandchildren, Olivia *Margaret* and Elijah Louis), *for bringing me more joy than a father deserves; you are the jewels in my crown!*

Pastor Wilbur Jackson, *my spiritual father; a man among men!*

Pierre Paroz, *mein Bruder; my feeble words would be far too inadequate to express...*

David Remenowsky, *my special friend; with the heart of David.*

Denise Willen, *for "the truth" in 1984.*

Eric Helmick, *ere the Academy Award; I love you, man!*

William C. Keene, *a.k.a. "the Whirl"; we made plans, huh?*

Henry Walker, *for a special season of guardianship during the gauntlet.*

David and Ziva Rutherford, *a passionately divine appointment. Shalom!*

Ron Weinbender, *for being there, brother; with hope...and "connections!"*

Ruth Hoskins, *for a very sweet time of preparation, I thank his special handmaiden.*

Also, for important "plugs" along this sometimes broken road of life, I must thank the following: (*You know who you are, and, of equal importance, why I thank you.*)

Jerry, Danny, Bobby and Billy Harris (*for so many early dreams in the grass. Can we still get back there?*); Bill Shepherd, *a prophet;* Tom Cook; Orther Shell (*for going against the grain. I'll never forget*); Joel Crowe; Ken and Reva Calloway; Marty Celaya; Carol Hughes; Josephine Tringali; Arlene Piersall; Mabel Leach; Pat Fannon; Dave Lovejoy; Todd Cole; Rod Best; Art and Nina; Smiling Bea; Sandy Zimmerman; Leo Rittenhouse; Donna and Nathan Johnson; Char and Gordon Lumley; Fermon Williams; Dora Whitaker and Stephen Gerzeli; Debra Graves; Larry Albaugh; George Denlinger; Larry Lloyd; "Coach Mike" Connaway; Michael Gilliland; Darrell W. Davis; Jerry Kunin; Chuck Burke; the boys at "Friars"; Tony and Susan Faeth; Randall Dunn; Kathy Morris; Mike and Tammy Fisher; Leon and Joyce Barrett; Dan Norris; Tim Lamphier; Dan Petrey; Mark Ertel; Chris Dolle; Max Meyers; Luis Chiappi; Laurin Hiteman; Dr. Daniel Courtade (*for precious "time"*); Jackson Browne, *special thanks…for everyman!*

In addition to their personal support and friendship, I owe a profound debt of gratitude and thanks to these folks for their inspired professional guidance, direction, vision, and creative talents in so many different areas of my project, which have greatly contributed to its completion:

B. J. Parker—*for ignition and takeoff; for painting a great roadmap!*

Tomm Knutson—*thanks…for catching it! (You did not fumble; God had other plans.)*

Don Pape—*thank you, sir! ("That cover will jump off the shelves!")*

Bruce Nygren—*thank you for your gentle ways and your discerning "steel tip shoes."*

Mark Ford—*for the cover that is "jumping off the shelves!"*

Phyllis Gail Klein—*for your tough-love, brilliant, inspired editing, I am most grateful.*

Carol Bartley—*Max was right; you are incredible!*

Joel Kneedler—*for vision…and for not missing a beat.*

Don Milam—*my special friend; I can't thank you enough, brother, for your heart…and for everything else! Don't forget: we have a date.*

Alice Crider—*for your prophetic, visionary ways; your faith; your comforting and encouraging spirit of support; for teaching and for always knowing—and sharing—the right approach; for dealing with my psychotic e-mails; and for those three Dobermans of yours…I thank you, my friend!*

My mother, Margaret Werner, who's surely *dancing* circles around the throne room now, would undoubtedly like to thank her very special friends and loved ones:

Tina Tobien, *her best friend, the daughter she never had;* her loving grandkids: Karla, Matthew, and Kaleb Tobien, *whom she loved more than life itself,* and Khloe: *God just brought you a little too late, sweetheart, to meet your incredible Grandma Margaret, but you will see her later, I promise!;* Marie Nesbitt, *a true and precious friend!;* Harro Hall *(for so very much, then and after, which eternity will not forget);* Marita und Sylvia Kadlec; Nellie Burnet; Mildred Venable; Orther Shell; Bob Lenon; Chris and Teresa Holman *(for such new beginnings; for more than words can express!);* the Sehrs; the Prugels; the Knolls; Margie Cook; Carl Werner... *now you have found integrity!;* Elisabeth Werner, *her precious Mama, whom she loved most and best of all!*

There are, no question, a host of others whom Maidie would need to thank. Some, I'm sure, she has and others now in her prayers, whom the dependable laws of this grand harvest have faithfully logged and have certainly not forgotten...

GLOSSARY

American Village—Housing location for the Americans and all foreign workers under contract with Ford at Gorky's automobile factory

aurora borealis—The northern lights, or "paintings in the sky," best seen in the northwestern hemisphere, which are brilliantly colorful and luminous displays of earth's natural lights

Autostroy—Automobile factory in Gorky under contract with Detroit's Ford Motor Company

Blatnoi—A petty thief or common criminal

Bolsheviks—The radical faction of the Democratic Labor Party that eventually became the Russian Communist Party (in 1918) under Lenin

Bremen—West German city

Brno—Czechoslovakian city

Burepolom—A much-feared Siberian lumber camp

Byelorussia—A landlocked republic in Eastern Europe now known as Belarus; formerly a Soviet republic; sometimes spelled Belorussia or Byeloroosia and often referred to as White Russia

Chornyi Voron—Trucks or vans called "Black Crows"; used to transport prisoners to and from the prisons of the Gulag

collectivization—From 1929 to 1932, the Soviet policy that prohibited landowners and peasants from farming their ground for profit. Instead, their land and agricultural resources were pooled as a collective.

Cultural Brigade—Official name given to the theatrical entertainment troupe in the labor camp

Donauschwaben—German-speaking Hungarians with a unique German dialect

Dresden—German city nearly obliterated during World War II by the incendiary bombings of the Allied forces

Finsterwalde—East German city

Fürstenwalde—East German city

Gedächtniskirche—The Kaiser Wilhelm Memorial Church in Berlin; devastated by Allied bombing in 1943 and preserved in its debilitated state as a reminder of the destruction of war

Great Terror—Sometimes referred to simply as "1937"—a time of acute persecution, injustice, and suffering throughout Russia

Gulag—Political term for the place, the administration, and the operations of all Soviet labor camps. The secret police division that managed the camps was also commonly referred to as the gulag.

Hanover—West German city

Inta—Coal-mining town and site of several slave-labor camps in the far northern Siberian Republic of Komi. The city was built during World War II for the purpose of supplying coal to Leningrad (St. Petersburg) during the German siege.

Kanavino—Suburb and major industrial center of Gorky

Kazakh ASSR—In central Asia; now known as the Republic of Kazakhstan

Kiev—The capital of Ukraine

Kiev City Ballet—World-renowned ballet company in the Ukraine

kipfeln—An apricot-jam-filled pastry of Hungarian origin

Kirov Ballet School—The world's oldest and perhaps most respected performing ballet company, headquartered in Leningrad

kolkhoz—A collective farm

Kolyma—An area in the far northeastern corner of Russia, on the Pacific coast, and home to one of the largest labor-camp networks in the Soviet Union

Komi—The northeastern section of European Russia, west of the Urals; now known as the Komi Republic

koptyorka—A Russian warehouse or storage facility

Krasnoyarsk—Sub-Arctic lumbering region of Siberia well known for its brutal labor camp

kulak—Term used to describe a wealthy peasant and those who opposed Soviet authority or the collectivization policy

Lend-Lease Act—Also known as "lease-lend" in the U.K. This 1941 legislation permitted President Franklin D. Roosevelt to sell, exchange, lend, lease, or otherwise dispense to any Allied government matériel or services that could be repaid after the war.

Leningrad—Seaport city in northwestern Russia (also called St. Petersburg), founded in 1703 by Peter the Great. It was besieged and nearly destroyed by German forces during World War II.

lesso-povalka—Russian term given to the logging brigades of the labor camps

Lubyanka—Notorious Moscow prison

Malyi Theater—Originating in Moscow in 1756, Russia's oldest drama theater

Minsk—Capital city of Belarus (formerly known as Byeloroosia or White Russia)

MVD—Ministry of Internal Affairs (secret police in charge of jails and prison camps)

Nine-hundred day German blockade—The Siege of Leningrad or the Leningrad blockade, September 8, 1941–January 27, 1944, during which several hundred thousand Russians perished, due to starvation, disease, and cold during the German occupation

Nizhni Novgorod—City situated at the confluence of the Oka and Volga rivers; from 1932 to 1991 known as Gorky in honor of Maxim Gorky, Russian novelist, short-story writer, and dramatist, who was born there

NKVD—People's Commissariat for Internal Affairs (secret police during the 1930s and World War II)

Oka River—Approximately six hundred miles long; located in southern and central Siberia

parasha—The common toilet or slop bucket in prison cells and barracks

People's Court—Gorky's pre–World War II court, where Russian nationals were unjustly brought to trial by the NKVD for petty crimes based on trumped-up charges

pleurisy—Medical condition caused by swelling and irritation of the membrane that surrounds the lungs

Presidium of the Supreme Soviet—An executive committee (similar in most Communist countries) headed by the president and having power to act for a larger governing body

Prater—Famous amusement park in Vienna, Austria

Proletarian Party—U.S. political party involved in worker education and industrial labor movements; founded in 1920 by a group of Michigan radicals who were expelled from both the Socialist and Communist parties

Riga—The capital of Latvia

Spiekeroog—A small, remote island in the North Sea

SS *Statendam*—International ocean liner of the Holland-American Line

Telefunken—German audio communications and telephone enterprise

troika—Beginning in 1937, in lieu of traditional courts, a set of three judges who sentenced prisoners during periods of mass arrests

Volga-Deutsche—Now called Volga Germans; a Russian contingent of tight-knit Germans living near the Volga River and the Black Sea who maintained the German culture, language, religion, and traditions

Volga River—Approximately twenty-three hundred miles long, it is Europe's (and Russia's) longest river.

Volkspolizei—Soviet-controlled East German border police; translated "People's Police"; also known as VOPOs

Vorobyo'vka—Gorky's jail for political prisoners

Vorkuta—Coal-mining town and labor camp in northeastern Siberia, just north of the Arctic Circle

vrag naroda—Russian term meaning "enemy of the state"

War Prisoner Exchange Agreement—Reached in 1957 between West German chancellor Konrad Adenauer and Nikita Khrushchev, provisionally allowing for the repatriation of former German and Russian POWs

West Berlin Refugee Organization—A former agency of the United Nations

Yalta Conference—Also known as the Crimea Conference, held in February 1945; detailed agreements reached between Franklin D. Roosevelt, Winston Churchill, and Joseph Stalin with respect to, among other issues, world reorganization, the liberation of Europe, and the dismemberment of Germany

Yezhovshchina—"The Yezhov Affair," describing the time from 1937 to mid-1938 when widespread repression and purges were at their worst in Russia; named for Nikolai Yezhov, Stalin's assistant

Young Pioneers—A national Soviet youth organization designed to prepare the country's youth for future political roles

Zehlendorf—East German city and suburb of Berlin that was the site of a German refugee camp after World War II

Zoo Station—Or Zoo Bahnhof, the train station on the border of West Berlin

ABOUT THE AUTHOR

KARL TOBIEN was born in 1956 just outside a Soviet slave-labor camp in Siberia. He arrived in America in 1961 with his mother and grandmother. Today Karl is a management consultant, speaker, and author. He resides in Cincinnati, Ohio, with his wife, Tina, and their four children.

To learn more about WaterBrook Press and view
our catalog of products, log on to our Web site:
www.waterbrookpress.com

WATERBROOK
PRESS